What reviewers are saying

The BPI Blueprint

Business analysts, Lean Six Sigma practitioners, and other BPI leaders and project team members...

"We have used Shelley Sweet's process improvement methodology and tools in our workplace and found them to be direct, engaging, challenging and always respectful. I am very pleased to see that she has written this book so that larger audiences will benefit from her years of facilitation."

Vera Potapenko, PhD, Chief Human Resources Officer, Lawrence Berkeley National Laboratory

"This book is... a straightforward how-to guide for anyone interested in Continuous Improvement. The tools and techniques outlined encourage team participation and focus attention on improving to meet the goals of the organization."

Stephanie Venimore, BA BPMP, Business Performance Advisor, Canadian Local Municipal Government

"Offering a wealth of practical advice from her 20 years' experience in the field, Shelley Sweet provides a valuable guide on how to launch your new BPI project, how to get the right people and roles involved, and how to avoid some of the common pitfalls in order to ensure that your effort is successful."

Jay Ashford, MBA, PMP, TekSystems

"This book gives you a helpful structure to facilitate a complete BPI-project. For example, how to get everyone on one page and what are the must-do process analyses? You'll find it in The BPI Blueprint. The book breathes years of experience in business process improvement and also years in teaching about it. A must read!"

Marcel Wuytenburg, Business Analyst, Copaco, Netherlands

"A must read for any business process enthusiast and/or practitioner. Shelley's step by step guide takes the guess work away and shows how to extract tangible gains from process improvement projects."

Naveen Adibhatla, Product Manager, Internet online search startup

"Whether you are an old hand or just starting out, Shelley Sweet has provided a step-by-step guide on how to engage in your business process initiative. She explains how to overcome resistance and engage the correct people at all levels to obtain a successful improvement project."

Kevin Browne, Project Manager, The Sharbot Group Ltd

"This book is not only easy to understand, but provides a step-by-step guide to realize dramatic results.... I have attended Shelley's onsite workshops, and I can confidently say that this book is an excellent reflection of how she assists clients in creating real and sustainable results."

Shelly Berlin, Berlin Eaton Management Consultants

BPM Industry thought leaders...

"Shelley Sweet has delivered a terrific book on how to make process improvement successful, providing guidance on everything from process mapping and analysis to organizational dynamics and politics.... I highly recommend this book as a must read for business leaders and others who want a step-by-step manual on real-world best practices for process improvement."

Brian Safron, Worldwide Program Director, Smarter Process, IBM

"With *The BPI Blueprint*, Sweet has delivered the solution to a long-standing need in the process improvement arena — a structured approach that works equally for practitioners and business leaders. This book is recommended for those seeking to lead change and improvement initiatives in their own organizations, as well as those seeking to bring out the best in their customer enterprises."

Nathaniel Palmer, VP and CTO, Business Process Management, Inc.

"Shelley has achieved a unique goal – bringing clarity and simplicity to the discipline of business process improvement, which was further enhanced by her effective tie-in to related roles, including that of the business architect."

William Ulrich, President, TSG, Co-chair, Business Architecture Guild

"This book gives a well-organized and easy to follow approach to improving your business processes... with key insights to navigate around pitfalls that can derail efforts. This book is a treasure map to success in process improvement.""

Keith Swenson, Vice President, R&D, Fujitsu America

THE BPI BLUEPRINT:

A STEP-BY-STEP GUIDE TO MAKE YOUR BUSINESS PROCESS IMPROVEMENT PROJECTS SIMPLE, STRUCTURED, AND SUCCESSFUL

Shelley Sweet

CODY-CASSIDY PRESS

The BPI Blueprint: A Step-By-Step Guide to Make Your
Business Process Improvement Projects Simple, Structured, and Successful

By Shelley Sweet
ISBN 978-0-9823681-3-8

Published by Cody-Cassidy Press, Altadena, CA 91001 USA
Contact
            info@cody-cassidy.com
            +1 (831) 685-8803

The author and publisher accept no responsibility or liability for loss or damage occasioned to any person or property through use of the material, instructions, methods, or ideas contained herein, or acting or refraining from acting as a result of such use. The author and publisher disclaim all implied warrantees, including merchantability or fitness for any particular purpose.

Library of Congress Subject Headings
Workflow -- Management
Process control -- Data processing -- Management.
Business -- Data processing -- Management
Management information systems
Reengineering (Management)
Information resources management
Agile software development

Cover design by Leyba Associates

This book is dedicated to my mother and father who encouraged me to do all that I wanted.

Bruce Silver

Principal, Bruce Silver Associates and BPMessentials

Author, *BPMN Method and Style*

I first met Shelley many years ago at a Business Process Management conference. At the beginning of the event, right before the keynote, they had one of those sessions in which each of the track chairs would pitch their particular track to the audience. My track was BPM Tools and Technology. I believed at the time that if you weren't using software to automate and monitor your business process, you weren't really doing BPM, and my pitch took that as a "given." Shelley was next up, and she wasted no time in setting me straight.

She asked the audience three basic questions:

1. In your process improvement effort, have you defined the roles and expectations of the Process Owner, Project Lead, and project team members?
2. At the start of each process improvement project, have you written down specific improvement target metrics, supported by actual baseline data with quantified goal values?
3. In analyzing your current state process for improvement, do you actually talk to customers and suppliers?

I was relieved, actually, that she didn't wheel around on stage and address those questions directly to me. My own consulting and training practice started from the assumption that the client or student knew in advance the steps of their current process, their objectives in improving it, and what an improved process would look like. My focus was on translating that information into models and process automation solutions.

But, of course, my assumption was mistaken. People doing BPM, even those who have been doing parts of it for a long while, *don't* have the right skills and experience in their project teams, *don't* have specific improvement objectives and metrics agreed upon at the start, and *don't* talk to all key stakeholders before defining those objectives. And, of course, you absolutely need to do those things if you want your process improvement project to be successful!

This book shows you how to do them:

- Who should be on the project team, the required skills and experience for each leadership and team role, and how those relate to the typical background of familiar job titles like Business Analyst, Business Architect, Project Manager, or Lean Six Sigma specialist.
- How to create the Project Charter, the document that establishes the project objectives, metrics, and team membership, used to secure management commitment to the effort.
- How to document the current state process, first as a High-Level Map and ultimately as a complete swimlane diagram using BPMN.
- How to establish metrics for success, including collection of actual baseline data and agreed upon goal values.
- How to perform the various required and optional analytical techniques for documenting process problems and improvement objectives.
- How to annotate the current state process diagram to create a Visual Analysis Map showing the problems and objectives graphically in the context of the current process diagram.
- How to use proven principles of redesign to guide creation of a To-Be process model.
- How to conduct all the sessions and workshops with the process improvement team so all this work progresses smoothly.

That's a lot of critical information, distilled from Shelley's many years of consulting practice working with process improvement teams. The book lays it all out, step by step.

There is a second aspect of this book that I am particularly happy about: its attention to blending traditional paper-based methods with use of 21st-century software tools. While the discipline of Business Process Improvement has been around for a long time, its practitioners have paid little attention to new tools, technology, and standards that could help them in their work. The focus is always on live face-to-face interaction among the project team members, where stickies on butcher paper taped to the wall is a time-honored tradition.

But as organizations gain maturity in BPM, they don't want project knowledge locked up in paper artifacts that make sense only to the original project team. They would rather preserve those artifacts as digital assets that can be referenced and reused by other project teams. And that in turn implies common standards, like BPMN, for the process models, modern software tools, and shared team repositories that allow cross-referencing, commenting, and model reuse. The book blends the traditional paper-based methods with use of modern tools, and includes an example of how to use one such tool – Blueworks Live from IBM – to implement the methodology even with project teams distributed in locations around the globe.

Shelley's book is a perfect complement to my own *BPMN Method and Style*. While my book focuses on how to make the process flow logic clear from the diagram, *The BPI Blueprint* shows you how to get that information from stakeholders, how to analyze it, and ultimately how to use it to improve your business process. That's a lot harder and certainly no less important. This book should be a reference for anyone doing business process improvement.

TABLE OF CONTENTS

PREFACE

I began to understand the power of process orientation when I studied Socio Technical Systems (STS) at National Training Laboratory in the 1980s. Since then, my work has focused on the process domain and my enthusiasm for a process culture has not waned. What fascinated me at first was how process gave a structure to the way people worked, and what continues to intrigue me is the importance of the intersection of process, people, and technology for making this domain successful.

I learned and used the various process improvement methodologies – quality improvement, STS, re-engineering, Six Sigma, Lean, Business Process Improvement and now the Business Process Management discipline – as I worked with organizations and teams on process improvement projects. I selected the best concepts and techniques for each client situation, and helped clients build their own methodologies. Today there is no universally accepted BPM methodology. The field encompasses numerous concepts, theories, and methodologies, many analytical techniques, and a wide variety of tools for process modeling, analysis, design, and decision modeling, many featuring collaboration and shared repositories. The scope and variety of options, even for me, a veteran of more than 20 years, can be overwhelming.

This complexity drove the need for a straightforward practical guide, a book that would make the Business Process Improvement field simple and accessible to managers and employees. And that's what this book is – a hands-on book for leaders and teams who are doing one of their first Business Process Improvement projects. These could be leaders who recognize the project need but don't know how to start, what role they should play, or whom else they should involve. It could be project managers or team facilitators that will be managing a team of subject matter experts to complete the process improvement work. It could also be subject matter experts, who bring content, technology, or data knowledge to the process improvement project team but also need to know what this type of project entails and how they should perform.

Some of these leaders and employees may have taken individual training courses in Business Process Improvement or even earned a certificate. But my experience in the field, with large and small companies across multiple industries, has taught me that there is a big step from initial training to doing real projects. My experience has been that once an organization sees the value of a process approach to improve efficiency, effectiveness, and customer satisfaction, they want to know what to do. They ask: What process should they start on? How do they scope the process? What results can they expect? How long will it take? How much will it cost? Who needs to be involved? What skills are needed? What is their role?

As I worked on Business Process Improvement projects with clients, they wanted to know specifically about their own projects. They wanted to know what to do and what to do next, what they needed to learn, how would it apply to their project, what to do if they stumbled, and how they could build leadership and employee capability in process management. I began by writing modules for different projects and specific requests, but soon I realized I needed a more comprehensive approach. My clients began to ask me to write a book; business employees told me they wanted to gain greater skills so they could grow professionally and work on future projects by themselves; technical employees wanted to know how to work with operational units better and form business and IT teams that could do Business Process Improvement projects together.

It was obvious that there was a need for a book that would guide leaders, employees, and teams through the process of selecting the right process to work on, defining a focus (the Project Charter) for the work, identifying the people to lead and be the process improvement team, and then using a simple methodology to get the project done. By 2008, technology became an integral part of process improvement, and the need was to incorporate specific tools into the methodology.

So this book was conceived. As I wrote it, I made sure to include the factors that make the blueprint not only simple but also structured and successful. The simple element is accomplished by identifying what is necessary and what is optional, by giving a clear sequence, and by providing practical procedures and template examples for the critical techniques. For structured, I show you how to schedule action learning workshops and team meetings to accelerate the project. I also show which specific modeling and analytical techniques are needed to achieve your project goals, and how easy it is to use modeling and analytical technical tools from the beginning for collaboration and consistency. To ensure success, the book identifies the critical leaders and team members, explains their roles and responsibilities, and shows how to engage them to foster synergy and ensure implementation. It also highlights red flags along the way and gives insights into how to deal with them.

After working with over 100 different teams and their processes, I have learned what the minimum critical specs are for a process improvement project, and I have laid them out in this book so your organization can follow them with success. This book provides the blueprint for that success.

Along the way there have been many client companies and individuals who have partnered with me in customizing the methodology and tools. I want to thank Liz Elliott, Delia Clark, Vera

Potapenko, Colleen Lewis, and JuneAn Lanigan specifically for their partnership, but there were many from other corporations, universities, governments, and non-profits as well. Their stories appear in the examples I use; their stories provide the background for why situations worked or didn't work; their stories show how process improvement really happens in the trenches; their stories make this book practical. You may see some aspects of your situation in them. I thank them all.

For this book in particular, I want to thank my two editors, Jerry Talley and Bruce Silver. Jerry read the first drafts and helped me rethink and clarify different concepts. Bruce read the following versions, and helped me focus the important themes, add elements for different audiences, and strengthen the use of technology tools throughout, especially seen in the IBM Blueworks Live chapter. He also brought clarity and consistency to the document wherever it was needed. The book would not be what it is without them.

Lastly, I want to thank my husband, who always encouraged me, and although he missed me, he knew I needed to spend a lot of time on the book. I appreciate his patience and love.

Shelley Sweet
January 2014

CHAPTER 1

PROCESS IMPROVEMENT—WHAT IS IT?

Twenty years of experience working in the field of business process improvement (BPI) have taught me the structures, methods, and approaches to ensure the greatest success. In this book I hope to pass along the lessons of all those years from all those clients.

This book is written for anyone who participates in a BPI Project, has struggled in a BPI Project, or who is about to do his or her first BPI Project: executives, leaders, facilitators, and team members taking on this assignment. It lays out the critical path for successful projects, and suggests what to leave out. It explains roles, needed actions, and coaching suggestions. With the framework and guidance provided, the reader will know what to do to work better, faster, and smarter.

The field of **business process management** (BPM) is broad and has been approached in a number of ways:

- **Business process improvement** focuses on improving the effectiveness and efficiency of individual processes for results that benefit the customer and the organization from a business perspective.
- **Process automation** is an IT-centric approach that seeks to improve internal efficiency, control, and business agility by applying technology to speed the workflow, integrate heterogeneous systems and databases, and enforce business rules.
- BPM as a **management discipline** seeks to manage and measure enterprise business performance from an "end-to-end" (customer-facing) process perspective and create a process culture for the organization as a whole.

All three approaches are important and they work hand in hand. This book concentrates primarily on the first element, business process improvement. It shows how to conduct process improvement using modern software tools, making it easy and collaborative for the business and IT. Business process improvement has a long tradition stretching over twenty-five years and many books have been written about it. But many of the tried-and-true techniques of practitioners are still rooted in the tools of the last century. Paper and pencil, whiteboards, and yellow stickies have their place in the information-gathering phase, but they are insufficient to handle a serious business process improvement effort. Their artifacts do not scale. They are not sharable, not searchable, and they are hard to maintain. They don't let you build links between models, standardize vocabulary, or do real quantitative analysis – to name a few important tasks. Today we have modern software tools, designed for business users, that update BPI for the 21st century, and this book shows you how to use them effectively.

The terminology used in process improvement – BPM, BPI, Lean, Six Sigma, Reengineering, and BPMS – is a frequent source of confusion.

BPM stands for Business Process Management. It is the predominant term used today for the overall category. As a business management discipline for the enterprise, BPM encompasses all three bullets above. When the organization is doing BPM, it is building an organizational process culture, with governance, consistent tools and techniques such as process modeling, metrics, analysis, and standardized applications tools; and it is using these to improve processes to increase operational performance and agility. But if the company is just starting its BPM journey, it may not yet have all these elements in place.

BPI is Business Process Improvement. It is a general term and can be used in narrow and wider arenas. BPI may or may not involve technology; it may not be enterprise wide; but it does imply a process methodology. This book is about BPI Projects and the methods for improving, redesigning, and transforming processes in your organization.

Lean, Six Sigma, and Reengineering are three different process improvement *methodologies*. All have overriding principles and use different techniques for modeling, analysis, and design. There is overlap between the three methodologies, and this book takes concepts and techniques from each in suggesting a simple and structured approach for success. They all focus on business process improvement, but often impact process automation and BPM as a management discipline as well.

BPMS stands for BPM Suite, a set of integrated software that enables organizations to automate the workflow, integrate business systems, apply business rules, and make process performance visible to the business in real time. A company does not have to use a BPMS to implement process improvement. In fact, it's not the best first step on the process improvement journey, and many process improvement efforts require no process automation at all. But BPM Suites can provide significant benefits both to improving individual processes and building a more mature process culture at the enterprise level.

There are many process improvement books in the literature. Some of them are focused on a single topic, like Bruce Silver's excellent *BPMN Method and Style*[1]; others are more comprehensive, like Paul Harmon's *Business Process Change: A Guide for Business Managers and BPM and Six Sigma Professionals*[2]; others provide a good overview of the concepts with some techniques, such as Artie Mahal's *How Work Gets Done*[3]; finally, a few are purposely introductory, such as IBM's *BPM for Dummies*[4] and Harvard Business Press's *Improving Business Processes.*[5]

What the field does not have yet is a book that tells companies and practitioners what is necessary and what isn't necessary for successful process improvement projects. That's what this book does. It lays out a methodology that can be applied to any process project, and tells you what are the required elements vs. the optional elements. It covers tools like process modeling tools, process diagrams, standard languages like BPMN, visual analysis tools, repositories for versioning and access control, linking between models, and simulation and design of the improved process model. It is pragmatic and provides lots of examples from client experiences.

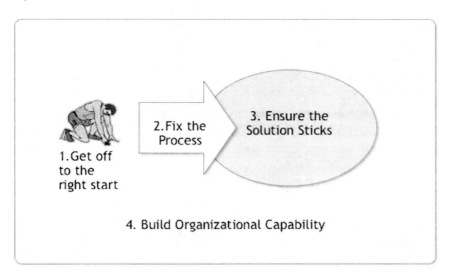

Figure 1. Elements of BPI Projects

[1] Silver, Bruce. *BPMN Method and Style*, 2nd Edition. Aptos, CA: Cody-Cassidy Press, 2011.
[2] Harmon, Paul. *Business Process Change: A Guide for Business Managers and BPM and Six Sigma Professionals*. Burlington, MA: Morgan Kaufmann, 2007.
[3] Mahal, Artie. *How Work Gets Done*. Bradley Beach, NJ: Technics Publications, LLC 2010.
[4] IBM. *BPM for Dummies.* http://ibm.co/1gNHUZD.
[5] Harvard Business Review Press. *Improving Business Processes*. Boston, MA, 2010.

This book provides a simple structured method for BPI Projects, the blueprint for what needs to get done. The basic elements of the method are shown in Figure 1: how to get off to the best start, what to do to improve a process, how to make sure the solution is maintained, and how to build organizational capability at the same time. The first two components apply to a single BPI Project; the third component takes the project into implementation and is a bigger oval because it impacts the entire business unit or possibly multiple functions. It also goes beyond a single BPI Project because it is about implementation and sustaining the process. The last component, build organizational capability, is something that starts with one project but grows to the whole box as the function or division improves and implements projects with many teams. The BPI methodology suggested uses a limited set of techniques so the reader can see what the minimal critical specs are for completing the project and moving toward success. Success comes with implementation and ongoing monitoring, and we touch on that as well.

BUSINESS PROCESS IMPROVEMENT METHODOLOGY

In order to have a simple, structured and successful BPI Project, it is critical to have a standardized methodology. Figure 2 is a graphic of the *BPM Process Methodology*. It has four stages, and they go in sequence. The first stage, *Process Selection*, involves choosing which process to work on first or next. The second stage is the *BPI Project* itself, and it has five phases. The third stage is *Implementation and Check*, which means implementing the improvements recommended and monitoring them to see how they are working. The last stage is *Monitoring and Sustaining*, which is the continuous improvement stage – reviewing the process after implementation, measuring its performance, evaluating emerging trends in the marketplace, and determining if additional improvements are needed.

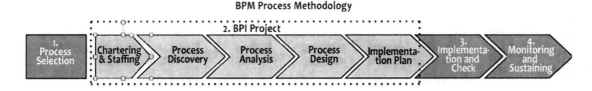

Figure 2. BPM Methodology and BPI Project

This book concentrates on the second stage, the BPI Project. In the BPI Project there are five phases. The first, *Chartering and Staffing*, sets the stage by developing a specific process charter for the project and identifying the leaders and team to do the project. The second phase is *Process Discovery*, documenting the current state process in a High-Level Map and subsequently in a more detailed Swimlane Diagram. Phase three is *Process Analysis,* which applies a set of defined analytical techniques and metrics and identifies Quick Wins to implement early. Phase four is *Process Design* of the new model, including application of some additional analytical techniques. Phase five is *Implementation Plan*, which is developing a plan to implement the improvements.

HOW THE BOOK IS ORGANIZED

This book is a pragmatic blueprint that explains the purpose and benefits of each phase and technique, as well as how to use the tools with a team. It covers the following:

Chapter 1: Process Improvement – What is It?

- Varied perspectives and names for process improvement
- Elements of process improvement projects

Chapter 2: Where Do We Start?

- Finding leadership
- Defining the scope and outcomes
- Selecting the process improvement team

Chapter 3: Who Does What and When?

- The leadership level
- The team level
- The different phases of a BPI Project

Chapter 4: Who's On First?

- The Business Analyst role
- The Lean Six Sigma Practitioner role
- The Project Manager role
- The Business Architect role

Chapter 5: Swimlane Mapping for Non-Swimmers

- Identifying the right instance to model
- Creating and documenting the swimlane model
- Gathering the initial issues, data, variances, and improvements at the same time

Chapter 6: What to Measure and Why?

- Identifying measures
- Gathering the needed quantitative data
- Where to measure

Chapter 7: How Do We Learn to Do All This?

- What training is necessary?
- Action learning and its benefits
- Structuring a BPI Project simply

Chapter 8: What Analytical Techniques Do We Need?

- Why analysis is necessary after process modeling
- How to use the four required analytical techniques

Chapter 9: Are We Done Yet? When is Enough Enough?

- What other analytical techniques are there?
- How do we know which ones are critical for our project?

Chapter 10: Standardization

- When standardization is needed
- Standardizing forms, subprocesses, and processes

Chapter 11: Time and Visual Analysis

- What takes up time in a process?
- Quantitative and qualitative methods of analyzing time
- The power of visual analysis models

Chapter 12: Errors and a Few More

- Finding the root cause
- Process roles and responsibility
- Assessing and managing risk

Chapter 13: How Do We Get to the New Design?

- What's valuable in the process?
- Using rules for redesign as a guide
- An innovative approach to create a new design
- Review of the new design

Chapter 14: Putting It All Together in IBM Blueworks Live

- What to look for in a BPI Project tool
- Organizing the team workspace
- High-Level Map and Project Charter
- Swimlane diagrams
- Process properties and Analysis Mode

Chapter 15. What's in an Implementation Plan?

- Building an Implementation Plan
- Change management
- Monitoring and Sustaining

Chapter 16. What Makes This Method Work?

- Keeping focused
- Engaging the right resources
- A standard methodology
- Structuring the project time

Although this book concentrates on business process improvement *projects*, it does not cover project management in detail. Rather it recommends a specific structured methodology for BPI Projects. There are, however, many aspects of project management in the method, and a good Project Lead must be organized and run the method like a project.

The method explains how to get the business and IT collaborating from the start. Having the initial BPI work completed by the business and then passing it to IT is detrimental to the overall enterprise. The method shows how to get them talking the same language, using a common process modeling format, and seeing the same big picture with common visual analysis. Such a business-IT partnership produces a sea change in the results – in the analysis, redesign, and implementation. Open communication between business and IT, when they share common goals and begin to use a common language, builds synergy and increases the return from the project overall.

This book is more than a compilation of techniques. You can't just purchase all the tools to build furniture and expect to be a cabinet-maker. There is a craft and you have to know what to look for when using the techniques. By understanding the five phases of a BPI Project, and determining what is right for the BPI Project at each phase, the reader will have a framework, guidelines for the appropriate steps, and examples that demonstrate successes and failures.

Together these elements will provide better, smarter, faster results for new process leaders and team members.

THINGS TO THINK ABOUT

HOW IT AND THE BUSINESS COLLUDE TO REDUCE ROI

Organizations have great expectations for ROI from business process improvement projects. But they often don't reach these expected returns because they...

- lack critical stakeholder participation
- have weak Executive Sponsorship
- rely on individual stories vs. gathering quantitative data to tell the objective story
- set new priorities overshadowing the project
- use experts to model and optimize the process instead of engaging a team of employee subject matter experts.

Here is another important barrier to consider:

- not having the business and IT work together.

In a sense, IT and the business unconsciously *collude* to reduce the return on investment. There are at least four ways that this happens.

1. The business throws requirements over the wall to IT. IT then struggles with the requirements and goes through multiple rework cycles with the business to understand and refine the requirements. The business dominates the relationship, saying, "Here's what we want. Now go do it." IT really comes in at a disadvantage. Also IT may have a long list of deliverables on their plate already and may not be able to get to this project for 12 months or more. If the business had discussed the need for the project and IT's workload, it could have avoided this difficulty.

2. The business outlines a specific feature or functionality it wants IT to provide in order to improve this process. IT does what the business asks, and then the business is not satisfied. The problem is that the business offered its solution without the full context. The proposed solution may be only a short-term fix, may negatively impact other stakeholders, may not get at the root cause, or there just might be better solutions. The business will get a solution but probably not the optimal one.

3. IT implements new technology without support from the business. In this case IT recognizes that new technology could offer more efficient methods for the business, and IT

buys or builds the technology. But without talking with the business and understanding its needs and usage, IT may not select the best application, may not build it for the most important use cases, or may neglect important stakeholder needs. Worst case is the business doesn't adapt the new technology, or buys a different version on its own, or uses it only minimally.

4.   The business uses a process improvement methodology to model and redesign the process and then brings in IT. The good news here is that the business has documented, analyzed, and improved the process using a systematic approach. But without IT involved, many opportunities for greater efficiency and effectiveness may never be considered – so the return will be less than optimal.

If these are four ways that the business and IT collude to reduce the ROI in business process management, what should they be doing instead? Here are four ideas I have used successfully.

1.   The business and IT prioritize projects together, looking at key criteria, such as alignment with the strategic plan or enterprise architecture, or more simply against a grid showing current performance vs. opportunity for several processes. It is important to know what processes the organization will work on first, understanding the anticipated return from optimization, and the likelihood of success based on the organizational culture.

2.   Include the business and IT on the team from the start. The business will provide most of the subject matter experts, and IT will provide technical expertise about the current process and new technologies. Together they create a dynamite team. They see different aspects of the current process and suggest different improvements based on a common goal.

3.   Make sure the Executive Sponsor and Process Owner are appropriate for the process. It is likely that the sponsorship will be on the business side but not always. It may make sense to have co-sponsors – either two different business executives or one business and one IT executive.

4.   Make sure that IT and the business have agreed to the resources needed, for (1) analyzing and improving the business process, (2) implementing the improvements and new technologies, and (3) sustaining the new process. A team can recommend significant improvements but without the implementing and sustaining stages the organization will not get the full return. If there are too many competing projects, the company often delays or forgets the BPI Project during implementation or sustainment.

But there is hope! IT and the business combined can be unstoppable. So get them working together early to get the full return for a Business Process Improvement project.

CHAPTER 2

WHERE DO WE START?

Getting off to the right start with a process improvement project is like preparing for a major remodel on a house – selecting an architect who listens to your needs, developing the plans, articulating a budget, seeing the plans in a visual format, and finding a contractor. If the homeowner gets off to the right start on the remodel, he feels confident in the leaders and team he has hired. He sees his desires turned into a plan that represents his wishes, and he can determine whether the plan will fit his budget and time frame. The initial phase enables the owner to work with the key players and test (1) the quality of the deliverables, (2) the capability, values, integrity, and commitment of the players he has hired, and (3) the working relationship he has with these players. The success of the first phase of a remodel provides an indicator of how the rest of the remodel will go.

Similarly, in a Business Process Improvement project, in order to get off to the right start it is necessary to choose the right process to work on. This is stage one of the BPM methodology. It is critical input to stage two, the BPI Project itself. The first phase of the BPI Project is Chartering and Staffing. This phase creates a key deliverable, the charter, which identifies leaders and team members, clarifies their roles and responsibilities, and establishes a timeline for the improvement project.

Over 54% of process improvement projects fail for one of three reasons[6]:

- Scope creep
- Resistance by the end users and key stakeholders
- Lack of executive sponsorship

---

[6] 2011 BPM.com State of the Industry survey. Bpm.com primary research (a survey of approximately 500 firms).

All three of these failures can be managed positively by getting off to a good start, marked by five critical criteria:

1. A clear business need
2. A Project Charter
3. The right leadership
4. A cross-functional improvement team
5. Quantitative baseline data

A recommended approach for achieving these criteria is presented below.

PROCESS SELECTION: A CLEAR BUSINESS NEED

Associating the BPI Project with a clear and recognized business need is absolutely critical. There are many ways to do this, but I encourage organizations to use some combination of the following:

1. **Align with strategy**. Determine what BPI Projects are needed to support the strategic plan for the business unit or enterprise.

2. **Prioritize candidate processes**. Analyze multiple processes using a nine-box matrix, with current process performance on the vertical axis and potential return or opportunity on the horizontal axis. This helps you select which processes are the best candidates to work on now.

3. **Identify executive sponsorship.** Find an Executive Sponsor and Process Owner eager to initiate a BPI Project important to them. The Executive Sponsor and Process Owner, along with a Project Lead and Team Facilitator, are specific leadership roles in a BPI Project. Their duties and required skills are discussed at length in Chapters 3 and 4.

All three of these methods have a common thread – first, deciding what is most strategic, either for the organization as a whole or for a specific function or business unit, and then identifying a project that supports the strategy.

Align with Strategy

If the selection of processes is being driven from the top down, the executives will review the overall strategic objectives for the organization, business, or functional unit, along with the processes important to implementation of the strategy. Then the executives will identify and use criteria to select which processes are the important ones to work on first. Often the organization has not thought about which processes are necessary for a particular strategy, and so it will be necessary first to list the processes relevant to it. There may be overlaps where a process is relevant to more than one strategic objective.

Once the BPI Project is selected, its leaders – specifically the Process Owner and Project Lead – must communicate to managers and process stakeholders about how the process improvement effort supports the organization's strategy and Executive Sponsor's key initiatives. The Process Owner articulates the alignment with the business need, and confirms it with the Executive Sponsor. Then the Executive Sponsor, Process Owner, and Project Lead all must continuously communicate to project team members and other stakeholders the business need and how the project supports organizational priorities. Specific skills and duties of the BPI leadership roles are explained in detail in Chapter 3.

Books on BPM architecture sometimes refer to the enterprise's *process portfolio* and its alignment with the company's overall business strategy and capability maps. But our focus here is on process improvement at the individual project level. In my experience, most process improvement projects do not involve analysis of the enterprise process portfolio, but rather use the methods described in this chapter.

Once processes are aligned with strategies, the next step is to prioritize them as candidates for a BPI Project.

Prioritize Candidate Processes

One good method for prioritizing candidate processes uses a nine-box matrix, with *Current Performance* on the vertical axis and *Importance* on the horizontal axis. Such a matrix is useful for comparing multiple processes to determine where the most urgent need is, and to see if fixing a single process will be meaningful to the organization.

First, define criteria for Performance, such as cost, cycle time compared to competitors, or customer satisfaction rating, and criteria for Importance, such as profit or value to the strategy or brand. Next, evaluate each process under consideration using those criteria, rating it High, Medium, or Low in both the Performance and Importance dimensions, and place each process on the matrix to show where it falls (Figure 3). Now look for processes in the bottom right corner – underperforming and of high importance – such a numbers 1 and 5 in Figure 3. These are normally the best processes to start on unless there is an additional constraint, such as the cost is too high or it will take too long, or there is not enough bandwidth to work on that one now.

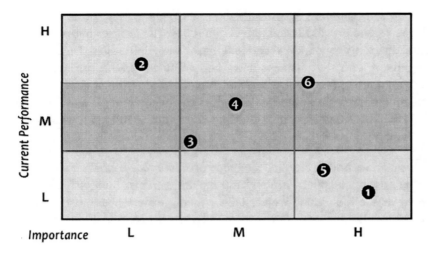

Figure 3. Nine-box matrix

Identify Executive Sponsorship

Another way to select an initial BPI Project is to find an Executive Sponsor and Process Owner with a process improvement project in mind that is critical to the success of their business or function. It's great if the Executive Sponsor or Process Owner identifies the need for the project directly, but it's also OK if the Project Management Office, a BPM professional support group, or a middle manager identifies the need. In that case, the person identifying the need needs to talk with the potential Process Owner and Executive Sponsor, explain the need, how it will benefit them and the organization, and get their support and commitment.

If this is one of the first BPI Projects in a function or division, the Executive Sponsor and Process Owner are by default BPM "early adopters" and their actions will be key. The whole company will be watching them, to see what they do, to see if this project really succeeds, to hear if they are advocates or naysayers, to see what happens when hard decisions come up, and to see what happens with the BPI Projects when push comes to shove. They need to be believers and strong supporters of the BPI Project in order for it to succeed.

Here's an example where it didn't work. We had the support of the head of IT and were working on key IT processes such as configuration management. But when the company needed to devote more resources to product development, resources for the BPI Project were pulled off. In this case, the Executive Sponsor and Process Owner did not follow through on their responsibility to support the BPI Project and make sure it had the necessary resources.

The first BPI Projects usually occur in a department, function, or division, while the rest of the organization is watching. Once several BPI Projects have been completed in various functions

---

or divisions, the enterprise may move toward an Enterprise BPM culture. Evolving toward higher levels of process maturity means taking a wider look using a standard BPM methodology, standardizing tools and roles more consistently across the enterprise, identifying key metrics and comparing them enterprise wide, and maybe having a BPM Center of Excellence. This book focuses on BPI Projects that typically start in individual business units, but they are often part of a nascent enterprise effort.

CHARTERING AND STAFFING PHASE

Once a process has been selected, we move into the BPI Project itself. Phase 1 is called Chartering and Staffing. The Chartering and Staffing phase includes three of the elements needed to get off to a good start: the Project Charter, the right leadership, and a cross-functional improvement team. It begins the work of developing quantitative baseline data. This phase also initiates the working relationships among the players.

In the Project Charter meeting, the Executive Sponsor and Process Owner formulate the vision and Improvement Targets, which provide direction and key values to the process improvement project. The Project Lead knows the content of the process the best and will carry the weight of the process improvement project effort. The Team Facilitator (who could be either an internal person or an external consultant) helps facilitate this meeting that creates the first draft of the Project Charter.

Success Criteria, Warning Signals

Look for the following quality indicators during the Chartering and Staffing phase:

- Clear priorities should be set for the project.
- The four leaders are actively supportive rather than suspicious of the project.
- There is a compelling business need.
- A clear charter is formulated and agreed upon, with specific Improvement Targets, baseline data categories, and scope articulated.
- Team members are designated and leaders made responsible for enrolling them in the project.
- The leaders are candid about any political complexities; any rocks that need to be turned over should be brought up.

On the other hand, the Project Charter meeting and the Chartering and Staffing phase may provide early warning signals of problems ahead. These warning signals include the difficulty of getting the Process Owner to participate in the charter meeting, assigned team members who complain of competing work priorities, leaders who have excuses for why this BPI Project won't work, or a business need that is ambiguous or uninspired. Failing to get off to the right start can lead to unfortunate consequences later in the project, such as:

- Needing to change Process Owners in midstream
- Wasting time focusing on the wrong goals
- Not involving the right resources
- Missing critical information and making poor decisions
- "Buying" the technology solution

Here is an example. In one company, the CIO had established an overall process improvement initiative. He and his executive group prioritized which process improvement projects to start on, wrote initial Project Charters, and selected the work teams. But the Process Owners for each team were not part of the executive session, did not agree with the Project Charters, and were not sure the projects were going to be successful. So the organization had to backtrack to get everyone aligned, assign Executive Sponsors and Process Owners again, and redefine the Improvement Targets in the Project Charters. The company wasted about two weeks of each team's time, and the project did not get off to a good start.

The Project Charter

The Project Charter is the foundation of the BPI Project, the blueprint for what is expected. Like the Constitution, it has several components and will be revised over the life of the project. It starts as a draft and is iterated as the team gathers critical quantitative data, hears from the customer, and analyzes the current process.

Different BPM methodologies use different starter elements for the project. For example, Lean uses a high-level value stream map with key data on it. Six Sigma uses a SIPOC (suppliers, inputs, process, outputs, and customer) model. The 8 D method starts with Defining the Problem.

Instead, I suggest starting with a Project Charter. The Project Charter combines several elements and puts them all in one place. In contrast, methodologies like Lean or Six Sigma focus on a single element and leave out critical elements of the Project Charter, or spread them over a variety of places, making it difficult to refer to them together on a regular basis.

Project Charter development is completed in a meeting with the Executive Sponsor, Process Owner, Project Lead, and an internal or external Team Facilitator. The Project Charter meeting is really a launch meeting for the four leaders, and it builds and confirms the focus and improvements as well as forming the relationship among the four leaders.

Sometimes the Executive Sponsor is not able to attend the Project Charter meeting. That's too bad, but the meeting should proceed anyway. If the Executive Sponsor can't attend, then the

Process Owner needs to go back to the Executive Sponsor and review the draft Project Charter and make revisions. Do not proceed with the Project Charter meeting, however, if the Process Owner can't come. In that case, you need to reschedule.

The Project Charter meeting takes from 60 to 90 minutes. I usually allow 90 to ensure that the initial Project Charter is finished in one sitting.

Here are the critical elements of the Project Charter.

1. Name of the Process
2. Key Challenges (in the current process)
   - Operational (to be completed now)
   - Customer (to be completed after customer interviews)
3. High-Level As-Is Map
4. Scope
5. Technology and Data Sources (in the current process)
6. Improvement Targets
7. Metrics and their Values
   - Baseline value (identify measure category now and then gather the real quantitative value for the current situation in the next few weeks)
   - Goal value (what the measure should be after improvements; stipulate after quantitative value for baseline is gathered)
8. Process Vision
9. Staffing Needs (description of roles and selected managers and employees for roles)

Facilitating the Project Charter Meeting

At the Project Charter meeting, the elements of the Project Charter should be discussed in the order listed above if you want the meeting to flow, be organized, and stay focused. The Team Facilitator runs this meeting; the others are all contributors to the content. If the Team Facilitator does not structure the meeting, it's easy to get waylaid in extraneous conversations or personal stories and lose over 30 minutes of the time.

The Project Charter meeting can be conducted over the phone or in person. It is helpful to send an agenda ahead. Attach the Project Charter template with suggested team members filled in, and provide a completed Project Charter for another process as an example.

1. Name of the Process

Start by asking the Process Owner and Project Lead what process they have decided to improve and have them name it. Encourage them to give it a simple name that says what it is and does – Paying Employees, Servicing Technical Issues, Developing New Products, Developing a Web Portal (for external clients), or Servicing Pension Plans – to name a few. Beware if they say something like "the Communication Process." Communication is often part of a process, not the name of the workflow to be analyzed and improved.

2. Key Challenges (in the current process)

- Operational (to be completed now)
- Customer (to be completed after customer interview)

Have the Process Owner and Project Lead tell the group why they chose to work on this process and what the current challenges are with the process. They will have plenty to say, possibly more comments than are needed. The Project Lead is likely to tell you in detail about all the problems that exist. The Process Owner may know a few critical problems. The Executive Sponsor will relay the few he has heard. This information provides a useful context, but don't let them go on for more than 10 minutes or the meeting timing will be shot.

Note that the Project Charter has two parts in the Key Challenges section, Operational and Customer. Record the Operational challenges at this Project Charter meeting. You will fill in the customer ones later after doing customer interviews.

3. High-Level As-Is Map

Then move on to the High-Level Map, a diagram in 6-10 steps showing the process. The Process Owner and Project Lead are the major contributors to this discussion. However, High-Level Maps can be difficult for some Project Leads who will want to give too much detail. Tell the Project Lead that the team will develop a detailed swimlane model of the process later on. If the High-Level Map turns out to be 12-18 steps, the Team Facilitator may combine some steps when he documents it.

The High-Level Map helps in three important ways:

- It scopes the process by defining the beginning and end of the process.
- It suggests who should be on the team, because the team needs subject matter experts who together know every step in the process.
- It visualizes the process graphically so people begin to see process steps and decisions vs. reading a procedural list or hearing anecdotal stories about the process.

The High-Level Map is the starting point of the process model used to fully document and analyze the current state process. The process is visualized as a diagram with rectangular boxes and arrows representing the flow of steps, or *activities*. In the more detailed swimlane models created later in the BPI Project, it is best to use an industry standard notation called BPMN for these diagrams, and we will discuss this in Chapter 5. But when assembling the Project Charter, it is not critical that the High-Level Map exactly follow the rules of BPMN. In Chapter 14, you will see how BPMN swimlane models can be generated automatically from the High-Level Map using a popular business-oriented tool from IBM called Blueworks Live.

The Team Facilitator should follow these steps to build a High-Level Map with the Executive Sponsor, Process Owner, and Project Lead. Put the name of the process at the top. Under it write it *High-Level As-Is Process*.

1. In the diagram, use oval shapes to denote the start and end of the process. Ask what is the first step of the process. Following the start shape, insert a rectangular box for the first activity, and label it with an active verb followed by a noun. Then ask for the last step and insert it similarly before the end shape. Confirm that this start and end truly mark the scope of the process. Is that where they want it to begin and end?

2. Now go back and fill in the steps in between, and any branching in the flow that may occur. Branch points are diamonds in the diagram. Label the diamonds as yes-or-no questions and label the outgoing flows *yes* and *no*. (The *no* flow may go to a new step or back to a former step.)

3. Go back and review the steps in the High-Level Map if this is being done over the phone. Then remind everyone that the Team Facilitator will send a copy for review.

4. Scope

Define what is in scope and what is out of scope.

Scope identifies the areas the process improvement project will cover and will not cover. The high-level process map showed the scope from a process standpoint, by designating the first and last step of the process. Scope also includes what demographics, channels, and other use case categories will be included. For example, the scope stipulates if the process improvement team should focus on certain types of invoices or all invoices, particular market segments or all market segments, all use cases or specific use cases.

For the hiring example:

- In Scope: All full-time employees in all locations; start point of the process is *Submit hiring request* and end point is *Start work*.
- Out of Scope: *Part-time employees, summer interns*

5. Technology and Data Sources (in the Current Process)

Ask for the key systems that are accessed or used in the process. Make a list of them. These include both desktop applications like Excel or Access and enterprise systems like HR or Financials. Document the major ones involved in the process. Ask about the databases where information is stored. All of these will be shown on the more detailed swimlane As-Is model. At this point, it is useful to make the key leaders aware of the applications, enterprise systems, and databases that interact with the process.

6. Improvement Targets

The Improvement Targets are provided by the Executive Sponsor and Process Owner. They articulate the goals for the process improvement project; initially they may be general statements about the focus of the project, but once data is collected they should have baseline and goal values.

Examples of Improvement Targets with baseline and goal values are:

- Reduce time to hire from the current range of 12-18 months to 3-6 months.
- Reduce billing errors from 300 per month to 50 per month.

To elicit Improvement Targets, a good question for the Team Facilitator to ask is "What two or three improvements do you want to see in this process?" Develop two or three Improvement Targets only. Just a critical few are needed to provide a focus. Ideally, Improvement Targets have quantifiable data for the current process and identify the quantitative goal desired for the improved future state process. Often, however, the actual data is not known at the Project Charter meeting, so the Improvement Targets may begin as qualitative goals, such as

- Reduce time to hire
- Eliminate billing errors

You can accept these qualitative Improvement Targets for now, but tell the group that once the team gathers the baseline data, it will be necessary to go back and quantify the Improvement Targets in the Project Charter.

7. Metrics and their Values

Metrics refer to specific measurements aligned with the Improvement Targets. They should include both baseline and goal values.

- Baseline value: Baseline data is reference data for the way the process runs now. The value will quantify the current state of the Improvement Target.

- Goal value: The goal is the quantitative number that the Process Owner sets as a target for the team to achieve. The goal value should measure the same data used for the baseline, but showing the value for the process after improvement.

It is hard to get quantitative values in the first Project Charter meeting, so talk about them generally. The Executive Sponsor and Process Owner can provide approximate numbers or articulate data categories. I recommend that the Team Facilitator or Project Lead have one or two measures to suggest for the process being discussed. They can offer these if the Executive Sponsor and Process Owner cannot name measurement categories for each Improvement Target on the spot. That will start the conversation going.

Once the measurement categories have been articulated, remind the Executive Sponsor and Process Owner that the team will gather this quantitative data for the baseline values and you will bring it back to them. Then they will review it and determine the goal values that they want to set for each metric for the BPI Project. The actual values for baseline and goals are then documented in the next iteration of the Project Charter.

For example, for the Improvement Target **Reduce time to hire,** one measure could be:

- The current total time to hire from the hiring manager's request to acceptance of offer

For another Improvement Target **Eliminate billing errors**, two measures could be:

- The total of billing errors per month for the last 6 months
- The unresolved billing errors at the end of the current month (Sept.)

Once the actual data is gathered, the quantitative values for the baseline are inserted in the Project Charter, such as:

- The total time to hire from manager's request to the acceptance of offer is currently 12-18 months.
- The total billing errors per month for the last 6 months ranged from 205 to 441
- The unresolved billing errors at the end of September were 428.

8. Process Vision

Have the Executive Sponsor state what the process will look like when it is perfect. The Team Facilitator can ask, "What would this process look like when it's really working?" And then the Team Facilitator waits and Executive Sponsor will answer in a bit. (Give him time to think!) The vision should be stated in the present tense as though it is already happening. Here's an example of a vision for the Hiring Process from one client:

- We hire employees that meet the organization's requirements and demonstrate the organization's values.

A vision usually expresses key values of the organization and does not have quantitative data. It differs in that regard from the quantitative goals of the Improvement Targets. Both are needed in the Project Charter.

I often ask the Process Owner and Executive Sponsor how this vision and the Improvement Targets relate to their strategic initiatives and the company's strategy. It helps to get them to articulate this alignment. I had been having this discussion informally, and I now see it is useful to make it more explicit. If they cannot articulate the alignment, it could mean several things: (1) this project is not really that important to them; (2) they have not thought about it; (3) they know how the BPI Project relates to their own area but not to the larger organization. Then the Project Lead and Team Facilitator will need to come back to this question and address it again with them, maybe with some suggestions. It is important for all these leaders to be able to communicate how this process and the BPI Project relate to key strategies.

9. Staffing Needs

The Project Charter should describe the BPI Project Team roles and list the employees selected for those roles, and their managers. See Chapter 3 for a full description of BPI Project team roles.

The team consists of the following roles in addition to the Project Lead and Team Facilitator: subject matter experts (SME) who work in the process, an information technology person who brings technical expertise, a data person, an outsider who asks, "Why do we do it this way?," a documenter, and an optional customer or supplier.

Discussing Roles with the Leadership Team

Before charging into the suggested names for the team members, the Team Facilitator should pause and go over the roles and responsibilities of the leaders who are in the meeting: the *Executive Sponsor, Process Owner, Project Lead,* and *Team Facilitator*. These are listed in the Project Charter, so enumerate them and give specific examples. Describe how often each role will be involved in meetings and what their roles are at different phases of the project. It is also helpful to clarify the differences between the roles of the Executive Sponsor and Process Owner, and between the Project Lead and Team Facilitator. Although the Executive Sponsor and Process Owner are quite different, it is useful to get each of them to state their responsibilities in their own words. That helps to articulate what each person sees as important.

It is useful for the Team Facilitator to provide the leaders with a document that delineates their roles and responsibilities, and those of the team as well. You can use the sample provided at the end of Chapter 3, or create your own. Provide a time estimate of the commitment for each role. Finally, ask if the leaders have any questions or concerns, and whether they think their role is doable for them.

After the initial discussion about the leaders' roles, discuss other needed resources for the project: team members, time, and potential budget for improvements. The team is critical and members should be nominated by the Executive Sponsor and Process Owner themselves. Who should be on the team? The High-Level As-Is Map in the Project Charter suggests the SMEs. The BPI team should include employees and managers who perform the activities in the High-Level Map. It is also necessary to think about representation from different regions, as well as the range of authority levels of the different team members.

It helps if the Project Lead and Team Facilitator bring a list of names of employees or managers they recommend be on the team. During the Project Charter meeting, the Team Facilitator should review the suggested team members with the leaders to determine if the selected members are the right ones, and if any more are needed.

The Process Owner extends the invitation to each team member and asks for his commitment, explaining expectations, roles, why this person was selected, the necessary time commitment, and schedule. When the invitation and explanation come directly from the Process Owner, team members see the project as important and understand the commitment.

I really encourage organizations to form an ongoing *cross-functional team* to do the business process improvement project. That means that people working hands-on in various parts of the process should be actual members of the BPI Project team, not just contributors of information to it. If you just use a business analyst to interview subject matter experts to collect process information, analyze it, and then redesign the process, you don't really have a cross-functional team. The advantage of a team is that all the stakeholders get to view the end-to-end process together, air different points of view in one room, and work them out. Their work together gets the group aligned behind the Improvement Targets and committed to executing on the optimized process together.

Summary

The Project Charter contains nine critical elements:

1. Process Name
2. Key Challenges
3. High-Level As-Is Map
4. Technology and Data Sources
5. Improvement Targets
6. Metrics and their Values

7. Scope
8. Process Vision
9. Staffing Needs

Some organizations may want to add elements that are part of a standard company charter, possibly developed in the Project Management Office (PMO). Use whatever makes sense from a company charter, but don't make the BPI Project Charter too long. The point is to create a viable usable document that has the necessary elements and not much more. Start off with this template and use it five or six times; then revise it based on the learning from experience in your own company.

The Project Charter is an important starter because it:

- Establishes a blueprint for your work
- Builds the first High-Level Process Map, thus moving away from anecdotal stories about problems and toward the actual current process
- Designates the goals, scope, and vision of the process improvement effort
- Matches the team members to the process improvement effort
- Defines roles and responsibilities
- Provides focus to the team members who will work on the project

If some of the Project Charter elements are not yet included, make sure the BPI team goes back and adds them as it works through the process. I have had teams who left out key team members and when they recognized it, they added them quickly. I have had teams with the wrong Process Owner; sometimes they changed the Process Owner midstream or they found a different Process Owner for implementation and ongoing monitoring. I have had a few colleagues who said their company would not tolerate a Project Charter. If that's the case, don't call it a Project Charter, but define all the elements and document them. If you have all the elements, you're off to the best start!

EXAMPLE OF A COMPLETED PROJECT CHARTER

The following pages contain an example of a completed Project Charter from Santa Clara University Law School. (Certain sections may be omitted because they were not part of the Project Charter elements at that time.)

Academic Record Keeping

Published on: [date]

Draft Prepared by [Team Facilitator]

Further revisions prepared by [Project Lead]

Executive Sponsor	
Process Owner	
Project Lead	
Team Facilitator	

PROCESS PURPOSE – WHAT IS THE REASON WE DO THIS PROCESS? (OPTIONAL)

Maintain student paper files and electronic records and track academic progress from matriculation through graduation. Provide reports to outside institutions like the State Bar. Provide reports to faculty and administration when required.

KEY CHALLENGES – WHAT ARE THE BIG PROBLEMS WITH THIS PROCESS NOW?

Customers' Standpoint: (Customers – student body and faculty) (This section was inserted later after the Customer Scorecards were completed. It is not part of the initial Project Charter, because it is important to wait to hear from the customer directly.)

STUDENTS:

- Students are not always ready to absorb the information that is being shared with them.
- Information is not always shared in ways that are most useful to students.
- The admissions process is too long.
- LLMs do not feel included.
- Students need a better understanding of the Wait List process.
- Students are unsure about which classes qualify for the writing requirement.
- The students would like to be treated as professionals. One/some students interpret the tone of the office as condescending at times. 1/3 of the class may need a lot of individual attention.

FACULTY:

- There is a lack of clarity of faculty's role in the process, timing, rights, etc. (What can faculty access online for themselves?)

OPERATIONAL STANDPOINT:

- We tend to have deadlines that come in clusters so there are peak periods for larger volumes of work vs. a workable steady flow.
- Maintaining a steady workflow while managing frequent requests from students that require a quick response can be challenging.
- A lot of our work is really manual and it would be better to have it automated. (E.g., SAWR, Letters, Wait List)

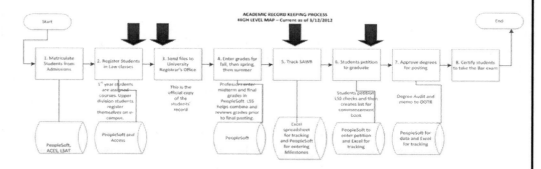

Indicates processes targeted for redesign/improvement:

1. First-year registration
2. Wait List
3. Grading
4. SAWR (Supervised Academic Writing Requirement)

IMPROVEMENT TARGETS (WHAT ARE 2-3 IMPROVEMENTS THE EXECUTIVE SPONSOR AND PROCESS OWNER EXPECT?)

Overall Goals for Our Function

- Examine the workflow and find a way to reduce the workload (but not reassign the work to other groups).
- Achieve a department that is less stressed with the delivery of a set of services that matches the agreement we set.
- Create a more effective process.

Improvement Targets for This Process

- Make the process more streamlined through automation.
- Use automation to provide self-sufficiency for students.

METRICS (BASELINE FILLED IN AFTER WORKSHOP 1; NEED 1-2 METRICS PER IMPROVEMENT TARGET)

Improvement Target: Make the process more streamlined through automation.

Baseline Values
- There are approximately 21 steps in the supervised analytical writing subprocess. The process takes approximately 235 hours of staff time per year.
- There are approximately 21 steps in the wait list subprocess. It currently lasts 5 - 7 weeks and takes approximately 195 hours of staff time per year.
- There are approximately 27 steps in the 1L registration subprocess. The process takes approximately 75 hours of staff time per year.
- There are approximately 28 steps in the grading subprocess. The process takes approximately 690 hours of staff time per year.

TOTAL – 97 steps and 1195 hours of staff time per year.

Goal Values - DRAFT
- Reduce # of steps in these processes by XX% and staff time by XX %.

Improvement Target: Use automation to provide self-sufficiency for students.

Baseline Values
- Students have access to a degree audit to show them what requirements are remaining, but things like the writing requirement are not really reflected in real time so their viewing is not up to date.
- Students use these forms on line:
  Registration Forms: Add/Drop Request Form, Consortium Agreement Application, Criminal Justice Externship Application, Criminal Defense Expungement Application, Civil and High Tech Externships, Individual Research Form, Late Add Request Form, Law Clinic Application, Moot Court Enrollment Form, Pass/No Pass Request, Special Student Application, Wait List Petition.
  Other Forms: Division Form, Exam Reschedule Request, General Petition Form, Letter Request, Nondisclosure Request, Petition to Graduate J.D., Petition to Graduate LL.M., Transcript Requests, J.D. Graduation Requirement Worksheet, LL.M. Graduation Requirement Worksheet.

Goal Values
- X % of all functions that currently require the student to submit a form and LSS to process manually are available to students on e-campus. E.g., enrollment verifications could be moved over to e-campus to eliminate manual processing.
- X % of current hard copy files will be online.

Scope

In Scope:

- Academic Record Keeping services for all students.

Out of Scope:

- Nothing that we can identify at the moment

Process Vision — When the process is really working, what will it look like?

Academic Record Keeping services are delivered in an effective, efficient and timely manner while maintaining a positive and balanced workplace for the employees.

Staffing Needs

Executive Sponsor

The Executive Sponsor authorizes and legitimizes the business process improvement initiative. He approves and supports the vision and Improvement Targets set by the Process Owner for this process. He suggests team members for the team as needed and provides influence in getting their agreement to work on the project. He identifies and appoints the Process Owner. He provides monetary and other resources as needed. He reviews project progress periodically with the Process Owner. He may assist with decisions on requests for scope changes. He advocates for the process improvement methods and team recommendations. He is responsible for influencing implementation in the organization, especially across divisions that may be beyond the authority of the Process Owner.

Process Owner

The Process Owner articulates the process vision and its value to the organization and customer. He sets the Improvement Targets and scope. He gets approval from the Executive Sponsor for the vision and the Improvement Targets. He identifies and appoints Team Facilitators, the Project Lead, and all team members. He attends all leadership sessions with Project Lead and Team Facilitator to learn BPI principles and tools. He provides resources for the project – budget and team members time. He reviews project progress regularly with the Project Lead and Team Facilitator. He attends portions of team meetings and/or workshops. He reviews project progress periodically with the Executive Sponsor. He helps identify measures for the Improvement Targets. He discusses and helps resolve issues and concerns from the Project Lead or Team Facilitator. He is responsible for resolution of interpersonal problems. He makes decisions on requests for scope changes. He is accountable for achieving the desired outcome and success of the overall initiative. He advocates for the process improvement methods and team recommendations. He communicates the success of project to others. He is responsible for driving implementation in the organization. He monitors process results monthly or more often if needed. He uses metrics and quantitative values to identify problem areas and suggests corrective action.

Project Lead

The Project Lead ensures the project has clear direction and support. He attends the Leadership training sessions. He strategizes with Team Facilitators on BPI tools that are needed for this process improvement. He provides subject matter expertise to the team on the current process and their organizational unit. He puts the documented team outputs from each meeting in the shared repository. He plans and conducts Process Owner meetings with the Team Facilitator. He helps resolve project problems and conflicts. He identifies if team ideas are beyond the original scope and brings these needs to the Process Owner. He ensures that the project's outcome meets the business objectives. He operationalizes the process improvement changes in the workplace during the Implementation and Check stage. He continues to monitor the process after the BPI Project and suggests revisions or additional improvements over time in the Monitoring and Sustaining stage.

Team Facilitator

The Team Facilitator assists the team in developing the project scope and suggesting the Improvement Target measures. He assures the quality of the business process improvement process. He helps the team select tools for the Process Discovery, Process Analysis, and Process Design phases. He moves the team toward the Improvement Targets using the BPM methodology. He facilitates weekly working team meetings and team sessions in the daylong workshops, and assists the team in reviewing the "lessons learned." He raises issues and concerns with the Project Lead and Executive Sponsor. He ensures that all team members' points of view are heard. He is not responsible for implementation in the organization, nor resolution of interpersonal problems.

Team Member

Team members fully participate in achieving the project objectives. They bring knowledge and ideas to their teams from their own experiences. They are open to ideas from different stakeholders in the meetings. They look for the strengths and weaknesses of the current process, and are eager to make improvements. They develop and implement a communication process. They develop an Implementation Plan and may help in its installation in the organization. They advocate for improvements.

Subject Matter Experts (SMEs)

Subject matter experts perform the work of the current process. There should be enough SMEs to have someone who knows all the activities in the process. They represent the roles in the process and should represent the different locations that perform the process as well.

Maverick

The maverick asks probing questions, suggests different perspectives, challenges statements such as "we've always done it that way." The maverick does not work the process. He is an outsider. He brings a fresh outsider view to the improvement effort.

IT

The technology person brings ideas and reality to discussions about what is possible with current and future technology solutions.

Data

The data person is a team member who encourages the team to identify and gather quantitative data, and will spearhead this effort for the team.

Documentation

One team member documents meeting ideas, action items, and diagram models for current and future state processes.

Project Role	Name	Functional Role/Title	Anticipated Commitment
Executive Sponsor			x hours
Process Owner			y hours
Project Lead			z hours (for workshops, team meetings, sponsor meetings, coaching sessions, and offline work)
Team Facilitator			z hours (for workshops, team meetings, sponsor meetings, coaching sessions, and offline work)
Subject Matter Experts			
Team Member (SME)			s hours (for workshops, team meetings, and offline work)
Team Member (SME)			s hours (for workshops, team meetings, and offline work)
Team Member (SME) and Data person-			s hours (for workshops, team meetings, and offline work)
Team Member (SME)			s hours (for workshops, team meetings, and offline work)
Team Member (SME)			s hours (for workshops, team meetings, and offline work)
IT Team Member			s hours (for workshops, team meetings, and offline work)
Maverick			s hours (for workshops, team meetings, and offline work)
Documenter			s hours (for workshops, team meetings, and offline work)

Figure 4. Staffing Table in Project Charter

Where Do We Start?

FIVE WAYS TO GET EXECUTIVES EXCITED ABOUT PROCESS

Our executives...

- Can't spell "process" and predict it will just slow us down;
- Think Business Process Management is just another program of the month;
- Get bonuses based on the results so they hesitate to tackle cross-functional process improvement where they have less control over the outcome;
- Wonder if there will really be any tangible business results.

So how do you get executives interested in process improvement work?

NOT – a PowerPoint presentation of 60 slides to explain the benefits of process improvement

NOT – Skill training for all employees over 6 months with an overview for executives

NOT – Defining and modeling As-Is core business processes using a modeling tool

First, get the executives to identify critical problems they see and then get them excited about solving that business problem in a new way, using business process improvement methods.

Remember you can drag a horse to water but you can't make it drink, and forcing your executives to drink could be career limiting for you. So here are five ideas that can work.

1. **External Customer Data.** If the executive knows that customers are complaining and efforts to date haven't worked, process improvement can help. I worked with one company whose customers told them that their website had lots of information, but they could not find the information on the website. This helped the organization move from the siloed website with different information and prices by division, product line, and customer segment to an integrated website focused for the customer's benefit.

2. **Discussions with peer executives**. Executives in other companies who have benefited from process improvement can speak to your executives about the benefits and challenges of a process improvement approach. They will speak realistically, at the same level as your executives, telling them the actual returns, the time and resources it took, and their role. These peers could be executives from your company in another region or in companies in similar industries.

3. **Competitive threat.** Fear can be a strong motivator to get your executive's attention. If a competitor is doing something and you aren't, your executive will recognize the urgency to take action. Maybe you are a global company and are growing rapidly but you won't be able to scale to meet the new opportunities if you don't gain the efficiencies of standard processes across different regions; this is a potential threat. Quantitative data can pinpoint the need even more by showing how much your organization is behind or will lose market share. For example, competitor X brings a product to market in 30% less time than you do, or your ratio of administrative staff to total staff is 15% higher than other companies in the industry.

4. **Short YouTube Video** (2-3 minutes only). There is nothing like the power of seeing it to get your point across. Go out in your organization and video-record how the process happens in your organization today. But think carefully about what you want to show and how you will tell the story. It's better that the video is homegrown, but it must have evidence that shows what's not working. You can insert a few graphics to display key performance indicators that aren't up to snuff. If you know of best performing examples of what the process could be, it would be great to have those as a teaser, but not necessary. Think about a catchy title or a final provocative question for the video too.

5. **Internal Quantitative Data**. Gather quantitative baseline data on key performance indicators for two to three core processes that are critical to the executive. Use the quantitative data to "surprise" the executive about how the process is currently performing. He may not know how the cumbersome pharmacy record process is delaying getting product to market or that 400 backlogged customer inquiries are impacting customer retention. Do some investigative work on processes that are important to the executive and then let the data do the talking.

MACRO MAPS HELP YOU CHOOSE PROCESSES

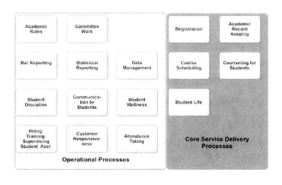

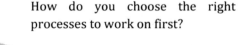

How do you choose the right processes to work on first?

- A leader raised his hand and said, "Let's start with this one."
- IT bought some software and needed to install it.
- The process was key to the strategic plan.
- The organization used criteria to choose from its portfolio of processes.

All of these methods will work (and there are different advantages and disadvantages to each), but if you know the portfolio of processes and have defined criteria, you can determine which one to choose from among the full list.

A Macro Map is a graphical rending of an organization as a portfolio of processes. (Many thanks to my colleague Jerry Talley (www.jltalley.com) for initially developing this concept of a Macro Map. He and I have been using it and improving it ever since.) Here's an example:

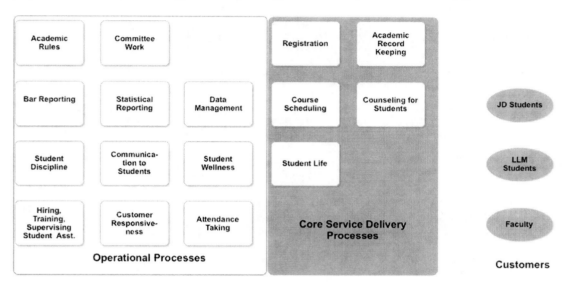

Figure 5. Macro Map of Process in Student Services

How Do You Build a Macro Map?

I suggest starting with a small group of executives/managers who know the work of the department. Build the first draft of the Macro Map with them, and then take it to staff and have them verify it and add to it. Below are some specifics to help you with the process.

With the managers:

1. Begin with listing the customers – the people who receive or use the output.

2. Then list the core products or services delivered by the department.

3. Next, list the key stakeholders, who could be internal or external. These are people who are essential to listen to, but they are not your customers.

4. Now, what are the processes that support the delivery of the core products? They could be planning, scheduling staff, research, or securing resources. (I put these items on the graphic

right away. Jerry makes a documented list of the elements and then turns it into a graphic overnight.)

To create a fuller Macro Map, you can add four other areas: management processes, infrastructure processes, capability building, and maintenance. A first draft of the full map could look something like this (Figure 6):

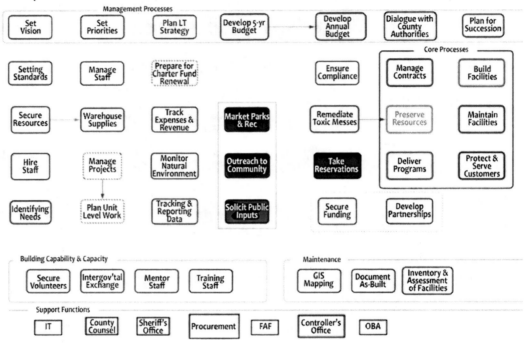

Figure 6. Macro Map of Parks and Recreation with additional elements. Source: Jerry Talley

Then take the map in graphic form to a representative staff group.

- Explain how you built the first draft of the map with the managers, and what its components are.
- Start with the core processes and ask them if anything is missing or needs revision.
- Then go to the support processes.
- Ask them if they can see the components of their job in different places on the Macro Map. What components of their job are missing?
- Keep adding and revising the map as suggestions are made.

How the Map is Used

The map provides a list of the portfolio of processes for the department or organization.

- These processes are categorized, so it's easy to see which are the core ones supporting customer deliverables, and what other types of processes there are. (Then it's clear which ones are the most important to the customers.)
- Add quantitative data to the Macro Map. The Macro Map below is the same one as shown in Figure 5, but now it has data showing number of hours worked on each one and the customer satisfaction ranking. It is obvious which ones demand the most employee time. And for this organization, where the goal was to streamline processes, reduce workload, and not hire additional employees, it was obvious which ones to work on first.

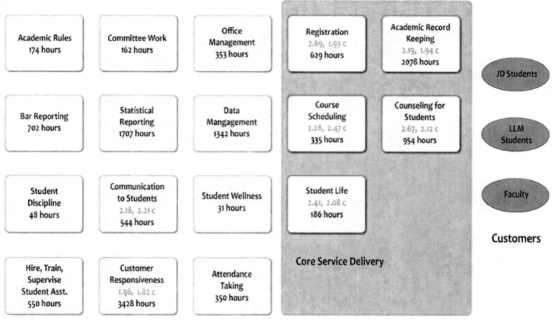

c = Customer survey rankings means for 2010 then 2011, based on 5-point scale
1- Very Satisfied, 2- Satsified, 3- Neutral, 4- Dissatisfied, 5- Very Dissatisfied
Hours = Total hours for Student Services Staff activities by process for year

Figure 7. Student Services Macro Map with Data

The Macro Map is a wonderful infographic to display and categorize all the processes. It also gets executives and employees engaged in thinking about the big picture by process, and helps each one relate it to his or her own work. And it doesn't take that long to build. Try it!

CHAPTER 3

WHO DOES WHAT AND WHEN?

FOUR LEADERSHIP ROLES AND SEVEN TEAM ROLES

The critical staff resources for each BPI project are the Executive Sponsor, Process Owner, Project Lead, and Team Facilitator – collectively called the *leadership roles* – and the BPI Team members. Figure 8 depicts how the leadership and team member roles interrelate during the BPI Project.

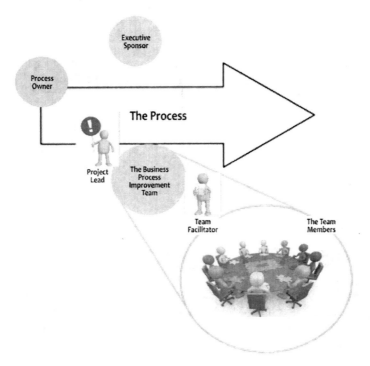

Figure 8. Roles on the BPI Team

The BPI Leaders

The people leading the BPI Project are just as important as the steps. The BPI Leaders (Figure 9) drive the project, provide resources, communicate and engage others, and manage the work of the project. They should be chosen based on their organizational authority, skills, and experience with the process. It's important to have leaders who can provide focus and support for the project and the team, as well as influence others in the organization, especially during implementation.

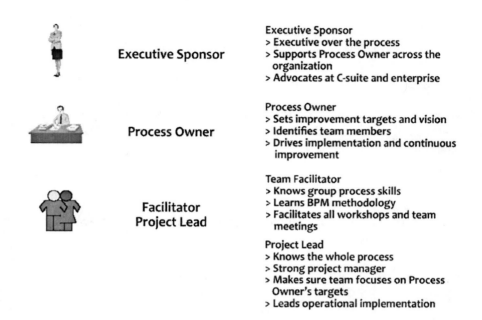

Executive Sponsor

Executive Sponsor
> Executive over the process
> Supports Process Owner across the organization
> Advocates at C-suite and enterprise

Process Owner

Process Owner
> Sets improvement targets and vision
> Identifies team members
> Drives implementation and continuous improvement

**Facilitator
Project Lead**

Team Facilitator
> Knows group process skills
> Learns BPM methodology
> Facilitates all workshops and team meetings

Project Lead
> Knows the whole process
> Strong project manager
> Makes sure team focuses on Process Owner's targets
> Leads operational implementation

Figure 9. The BPI Team Leadership

In addition to the work of the BPI Project, the leaders initiate the transformational work of the BPM Process Methodology, including process implementation and ongoing monitoring. The leaders provide the goals, alignment to the strategy, and articulation of the results and benefits. In other words, they give the case for change, and continue advocating for the improvement effort. Then during implementation, they are instrumental in influencing other areas of the organization that may be impacted by changes but may not have been involved in the team's work.

The *Process Owner* is a business manager accountable for the process from initiation of the improvement effort through modeling, analysis, and redesign. He is also responsible for driving implementation of the improvement and then continuing to monitor the process in an ongoing fashion for the corporation.

The *Executive Sponsor* is an executive above the Process Owner, who has this process within his authority. The Executive Sponsor and Process Owner are the top leaders for the process and the specific BPI Project.

The *Project Lead* is a manager who has experience with the work of the specific process. He reports to the Process Owner on this BPI Project and is the day-to-day leader of the process improvement team.

The *Team Facilitator* is an individual experienced with the BPM Methodology, but who may not know the specific process well. Using strong group process skills, he guides the team members through the steps of the BPI Project, as explained in this book. If the organization has no staff to fill this role, the Team Facilitator may be an outside consultant contracted for the project.

People are selected for these leadership roles during the Chartering and Staffing phase of the project. This chapter will explain the criteria for selecting players for each role, and the responsibilities they have in the different phases of the BPI Project and in the post-project stages of the BPM Methodology. A more detailed table of roles and responsibilities for the leaders and team members follows at the end the chapter.

BPI Team Members

BPI Team members (Figure 10) include subject matter experts, an IT person, a Maverick, and optionally a representative of the Customer or Supplier.

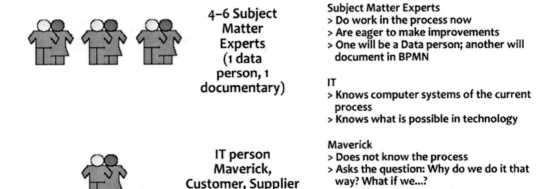

4–6 Subject Matter Experts (1 data person, 1 documentary)

IT person Maverick, Customer, Supplier (optional)

Subject Matter Experts
> Do work in the process now
> Are eager to make improvements
> One will be a Data person; another will document in BPMN

IT
> Knows computer systems of the current process
> Knows what is possible in technology

Maverick
> Does not know the process
> Asks the question: Why do we do it that way? What if we...?

Customer or Supplier (optional)

Figure 10. The BPI Team Members

Indicators for Measuring Success – Here's How You Know When You Have the Right Leaders and Team

- The players see the benefits of the BPI Project for themselves and the organization.
- They are eager to learn new skills and concepts.
- They are open to new perspectives and speak willingly about challenges they see.
- The scheduled sessions have good attendance, often 100%.
- There is team synergy, which builds better ideas than any individual's contribution.
- They think cross-functionally toward the overall goal.
- People have fun and step up to do the work; they manage the accelerated pace.

TIPS FOR SELECTING THE FOUR LEADERSHIP ROLES AND TEAM MEMBERS

Executive Sponsor

Outside of the BPI domain, the project "sponsor" means the overall leader. At one time in my practice, each BPI Project had a single such sponsor, but I found that a single sponsor was not sufficient, for several reasons. First of all, the term "sponsor" is too generic. Managers think they know what a sponsor does, based on other projects, and often they don't feel the need to find out how a BPI Project might require different responsibilities. Second, when sponsors lead a process improvement effort, once the improvements are recommended and implemented, the sponsor's attention goes away. He returns to other aspects of his ongoing executive role. For these reasons, I now recommend splitting the generic "sponsor" role into two separate roles: Executive Sponsor and Process Owner. Both are critical.

The Executive Sponsor and Process Owner bring different strengths to the BPI Project. The Executive Sponsor has wider authority and recognizes enterprise opportunities and challenges for the particular BPI Project. He is oriented outward to the full organization. He represents the project in the C-Suite, and advocates for it across the organization and to customers or suppliers. The Executive Sponsor may have many processes and Process Owners under him and may not be able to give a high level of attention to your particular project. Be aware that the Executive Sponsor role in a BPI Project will usually go away after the initial improvement effort is completed, although hopefully the executive remains as an enterprise BPM advocate.

The key functions of the Executive Sponsor are as follows:

- Authorizes and legitimizes the process improvement initiative

- Identifies and appoints the Process Owner
- Provides monetary and other resources as needed
- Provides the voice for the process and project in strategic discussions
- Is oriented outward, communicating about the process to the customers, suppliers, the market, and the full enterprise
- Influences implementation across divisions that may be beyond the authority of the Process Owner

Process Owner

The Process Owner, by contrast, not only leads the phases of the BPI Project from the start but also drives the implementation of the redesigned process. He is also the person accountable for sustaining the process after the improvements from the BPI Project have been implemented. In other words, while the Executive Sponsor serves mainly during the BPI Project phases, the Process Owner continues through all stages of the BPM Methodology.

The Process Owner is oriented inward toward the process. It is not enough that the Process Owner sees his role as a leader for this single BPI Project. He is the ongoing leader accountable for the improved process going forward. Without Process Owners, no one is minding the store, and processes can slip back to where they were before.

Below are listed the key functions of the Process Owner.

- Articulates the process vision and its value to the organization and customer
- Sets process Improvement Targets and scope
- Identifies the Business Process Improvement (BPI) team and has resources to support the BPI effort
- Is oriented inward toward the process, leading the process improvement effort at an executive level, driving its implementation, and monitoring it for continuous improvement
- Helps identify baseline and goal metrics
- Drives implementation, influencing key leaders in the organization
- Is accountable for achieving the desired outcome of the overall initiative

Many organizations do not have the term "Process Owner" in their lexicon. This is both bad and good. It is good since Process Owners want to read their "job description" before agreeing to the task. It is bad because there are often no easy candidates for Process Owners and no experienced Process Owners for others to use as mentors.

So how do you identify candidates for Process Owners? Ideally, Process Owners should have *responsibility and authority over all the steps in the High-Level Map developed in the Project Charter*. In other words, these process steps should be under the direction of the Process Owner person on the org chart. But if processes are cross-functional, no one person may meet this authority requirement. Then what? Here are a few suggestions:

- Choose the person who is responsible for most of the steps and decisions in the High-Level Map (although it may not be all).
- Split the role and choose two Process Owners to start (not my preference, but it can help with implementation).
- Choose an individual who has responsibility for the output.

Since the role of Process Owner may be new to the company, it is important to be aware of the political tensions it can cause. Functional department heads may be threatened by this new role. They may wonder what authority a Process Owner will have over people in their functional area when these people are working on a process. They may also wonder what the pecking order will be when Process Owners and Functional Leaders sit together in the organization and vie for priorities and resources.

Relationship of Process Owner to the Organizational Hierarchy

There are four or five organizational models relating functional owners and Process Owners in an organization. A few companies have Process Owners reporting directly to the CEO and managing all the company resources by process. More commonly, companies assign the tasks of the Process Owner as an additional role to a Functional Leader or Business Unit Leader, but this matrix management does imply organizational matrix benefits and concerns.

Some companies identify all their core processes to start, and name Executive Sponsors and Process Owners for each process and critical subprocess. Then all Executive Sponsors and Process Owners in the organization learn about their new roles and responsibilities through documented job descriptions and maybe a specific orientation session. Since these process roles are new roles, however, the Executives Sponsors and the Process Owner need to do real work to understand their role and demonstrate the needed leadership behaviors. Instead of naming all these executives to these roles across the enterprise, I recommend identifying three Executive Sponsors and three Process Owners who have real processes to model and improve now, following the criteria and roles above, and getting started on a few real projects.

Project Lead

The Project Lead and Team Facilitator are the hands-on leaders of the BPI team. They work together to plan team meetings and determine what BPM tools will be helpful.

The Project Lead keeps the team on track moving toward the Process Owner's goals without getting into the minutiae that team members sometimes tend to explore. The Project Lead should know this process well and have the authority and commitment to lead the team and implement the improvements. He is usually a manager in the organization, and becomes the manager of the BPI Project. The Project Lead performs some project management duties as well, such as scheduling meeting rooms, maintaining the team documents on a shared repository, inviting participants to meetings, monitoring the tasks being accomplished by team members, and scheduling and conducting the regular meetings with the Process Owner and Executive Sponsor. If the process is small and contained within one or two departments, it is likely that the Process Owner and Project Lead could be the same person; for larger processes that are more complex and span several functions, the Process Owner would be responsible for the process outcomes overall, and the Project Lead would be the day-to-day person who manages the process.

Listed below are the key functions of the Project Lead:

- Knows the whole process and works in or manages the process; he is a strong subject matter expert
- Is a strong project manager
- Makes sure the team focuses on the Process Owner's targets
- Leads operational implementation

Team Facilitator

The Team Facilitator guides the team toward the BPI Improvement Targets by using the BPM techniques with the team.

The Team Facilitator knows the BPM methodology and runs the meetings using the BPM tools and techniques. He has good group process skills and neutrally facilitates sessions and meetings with the team, making sure that agenda objectives are accomplished, time is wisely used, and team members all participate. The Team Facilitator does not need to know the workings of the process. In fact, do *not* choose someone who works in the process. It can be someone in the same department or unit, but not someone who would have any desire to influence the solution in a particular way. Instead choose someone with strong BPM knowledge and good facilitation skills. The Team Facilitator can be an internal role, or an outside consultant may be hired specifically for this project.

The key functions of the Team Facilitator are:

- Knows (or learns) BPM methodology
- Knows group process skills
- Facilitates all workshop and team meetings
- Maintains a neutral position relative to team outcomes

If the Executive Sponsor and Process Owner are new to BPM and this is their first or second BPI effort, the Team Facilitator may need to coach them in BPM skills and technologies. I often prepare a cheat sheet for them, which has questions for the Executive Sponsor/Process Owner to ask the Project Lead in their regular meetings. It also has recommended actions for them at each stage of the process. Clearly the Executive Sponsor and Process Owner need to have access to the shared repository, and the Team Facilitator and Project Lead should make sure the current process diagram, data, and analytical techniques are in the repository to discuss at each meeting.

The Team Members

Subject Matter Experts

The team needs two to six subject matter experts (SMEs) in addition to the Project Lead. The SMEs as a group need to understand all the activities in the High-Level Map. So one SME could represent activities 1-3, another SME knows activities 5-8, and a third SME activities 3 and 4. That means SMEs will have a variety of roles in the company, representing the employees and managers actually doing the process. The number you need is dependent on the complexity of the process and the size of the company. If the process is completed in multiple locations or globally, it is helpful to have some SMEs from each area represented. Additionally, the SMEs should represent the different divisions of the company that use the process. So if the process is recruiting, which is done across the whole company, the team should have representatives from several divisions. In a recruiting and hiring process shared by 15 divisions, it would not make sense to have SMEs from all the divisions, so a small representative sample would be selected.

The SMEs you select should be the best and the brightest, not just people who are available, and they should be eager to improve the process. It is fine to have one naysayer in the group, but if several of the SMEs are naysayers, forward progress will be difficult. Once I worked with a small team with a Process Owner, Project Lead, Team Facilitator, and five team members (three SMEs, IT), and a Maverick. Only the Project Lead and Maverick were positive; the three SMEs and IT were naysayers. It was very hard to make any progress; the SMEs kept saying this wouldn't work.

Maverick

The Maverick asks probing questions, suggests different perspectives, and challenges statements such as "we've always done it that way." The Maverick does not work in the process. He is an outsider. He brings a fresh outsider view to the improvement effort.

A good choice for the Maverick is someone in another department, or someone who works in a related process but not the one being improved. Most important, the Maverick should be someone who "thinks differently" and asks good questions. In the beginning of the BPI work, the Maverick will be listening and learning about how the process operates today, but later on there will be plenty of opportunity to ask, "Why do we do it that way?" or "What about considering this?" This is a fun role, and a person from a totally different area who wants to learn more about process improvement and has an inquisitive mind would be a good choice. I have one colleague who calls this role the Free Radical.

Anyone on the team can ask Maverick questions, and that naturally begins to happen on the team. But, it is still helpful to have that role represented individually on the team.

Information Technology (IT)

The technology person on the team brings ideas and pragmatism to discussions about what is possible with the current technology and could be possible within future technology solutions.

The team member in the IT role is not usually a developer, but a business analyst or an enterprise architect who knows the current systems and databases involved in the process and can suggest ideas for technology improvements in the process. The IT person can really help with thinking about the integration needed with other systems and databases. He doesn't have to be able to do all that work – that comes later in preparing for execution – but his understanding of what is needed and what is possible provides real value to the team.

IT people usually love being on the team. They get to see the process end-to-end and can make more valuable improvement suggestions with that perspective. They help the team understand what is easy from an IT perspective and what will take longer to develop. Often the IT person will say, "We have the functionality to do that right now. It's just not turned on, and maybe you didn't know about it." Terrific, that's a Quick Win!

Data

The data person is a team member who encourages the team to identify and gather quantitative data, and will spearhead this effort for the team.

The data person just has to love data and speak up when quantitative data might be useful. This person does not have to gather all the data and analyze it himself; rather, he just raises data issues to the team. Of course, it helps if he is good at data analysis too. It's important that the person in this role know something about the process so that he understands the process's current and future data requirements. Sometimes this role can be combined with a SME to keep the total number of team members smaller.

Documentation

One team member documents meeting ideas, action items, decisions, and models for the current and future state process.

It is most efficient to have someone on the team capture the process diagram models in real time on a laptop while the team is creating them on a large whiteboard or butcher paper. But it is also possible to create the documentation after the session. A few other items need to be documented after each session as well. This role can be combined with another team role too. The documenter is responsible for entering the documents into the team repository in the filing system that the Project Lead has established.

Customer and External Supplier (Optional)

The customer is the person who receives or uses the process output. It can be either an internal or external customer. It's ideal to have a customer on every team, but that's not always practical because of the time commitment required. The customer brings the customer perspective to every team conversation. Of course, the team has to remember it is just one customer, and other customers with different demographics might have different points of view.

The Process Owner and Project Lead decide if the team should have a customer and, if so, who to recommend. In some cases it can be useful to have a customer on the team; in other cases, it may not. In one process I worked on, which was studying prospect identification and information, the team decided to include a customer, an internal fundraiser, on the team. They found it was helpful to hear what information and timing the fundraiser customer needed. In another example, a team was analyzing the process of course credit evaluation for transfer students entering in their junior year. The team decided to ask a transfer student at the university to participate as the customer. The student not only advocated for what was important to transfer students from a value and process standpoint, but let the more experienced SMEs know when some of the methods were not up-to-date or not needed by today's students. In a third example, working with a Tech Support process, the customer can be any user with problems or requests in the company. In this case, it is not worthwhile to have a customer serve on the team full time. There are probably too many types of customers, and the time working with the team would be excessive for their use of the process.

In the same vein, an external supplier could become part of the team. In one situation, the team included an external supplier from the Department of Defense. This person had many roles in the process – external supplier, auditor, and provider of funding. He knew the DOD perspective, which meant that the practicality of ideas could be tossed about in real time.

But don't worry. If you don't have a customer or external supplier on the team full time, there are other times to address their needs and concerns. Customer interviews will be discussed in

Chapter 8, and one of the optional analytical techniques, Input Evaluation (for internal and external suppliers), is noted in Chapter 9.

The Best Size for the Team

The ideal team would be seven to nine people including the team members, Project Lead, and Team Facilitator, and they could be configured as follows:

- 7 people = Project Lead, Team Facilitator, IT, Maverick, SME combined with data, SME combined with documenter, SME or customer/supplier
- 9 people = Project Lead, Team Facilitator, IT, Maverick, SME combined with data, SME combined with documenter, SME, SME, and customer/supplier

Here are some easy ways to think about whom you need on the team and how to combine roles:

- Try to find SMEs for all the steps in the High-Level Map.
- Seek representatives from the various divisions and geographic areas that use the process.
- The documenter can be a combined role, usually performed with the SME role or IT role.
- The data person can be a combined role, usually performed with the SME role, as it is helpful to have someone who knows the process.
- The Team Facilitator may be the Maverick – not my preference, but I have seen it work.
- Do not combine the Team Facilitator and Project Lead. The Project Lead is the SME who knows the most about the process and needs to contribute content to the process improvement effort. The Project Lead is also the operational lead for the project, and may be the manager of some of the SME team members and might restrict open discussion. The Team Facilitator needs to be neutral and engage all members as well as to know the BPM methodology well.
- The customer and supplier are optional.

The Process Owner and Project Lead decide who should be on the team, getting the best people possible. The Process Owner recruits them and helps provide the time to do the work. If the needed team members are outside his functional area, the Process Owner helps influence the employee's manager in order to enlist a particular team member.

The smallest team I have ever worked with had five people: a Project Lead (who was a strong SME), two other SMEs, one of whom was from IT, and a Maverick. I was an external consultant and had the Team Facilitator role. This was a simple customer service process for internal website changes and improvements. We did it all by videoconference – the workshops, the team meetings in between, and the meetings with the Process Owner. It worked fine. The size of the team was appropriate for the need of the project.

The largest team I have ever worked with had 16 people. It had a Project Lead, 10 different SMEs, two IT people, a Maverick, and a customer. I was an external consultant and was the Team Facilitator. It was a complex process that spanned several divisions. There were lots of SMEs because they had people from different divisions who participated in the process – doing the work at the beginning, middle, or end, creating reports, and working with customers. There were probably more people than needed, but the company wanted full representation. When there are large teams and they have an internal facilitator, I suggest they use two facilitators. Two facilitators really help to keep the team on track, pay attention to all the team members, and can relieve the pressure often felt by the single facilitator.

So, look at the High-Level Map to see what SME roles are needed because they do the work of the process. Then think about what levels of roles (manager, worker, assistant) are needed and the different departments or divisions that should be represented. Add the specific roles as well. Don't leave out any roles. Combine the roles if you want to make the team smaller.

DOMAINS OF EXPERTISE AND INFLUENCE NEEDED

The domains of knowledge, skills, and authority that are needed for a BPI Project are pictured in Figure 11. What is essential is that the leaders and team members cover all the domains. It is possible to vary who performs effectively in the domain as long as he or she has the skills, experience and authority to be helpful and successful.

The rounded rectangles in Figure 11 depict four domains of relationship to the process: knowledge of the process content, experience working in the process, ownership of the process, and operational leadership of the employees carrying out the process. The ovals show knowledge and skill domains needed: BPM concepts and techniques, group process, project management, and special expertise for certain roles like IT, documentation, data, the supplier or the customer. The parallelogram shapes are domains of organizational influence, such as the political clout to influence resources and decisions across the enterprise, the ability to see and influence cross-functional needs and work, and the ability to see how a BPI effort should be aligned with strategy or other processes in the organization.

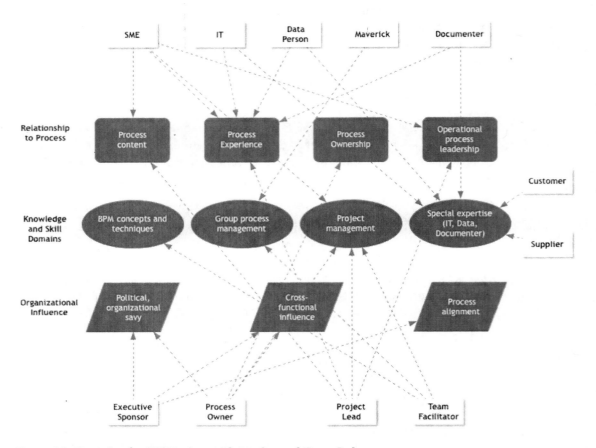

Figure 11. Domains for BPI Project with Leader and Team Roles

The graphic maps these various domains to each of the BPI Leaders and team members. For the leadership roles, the Executive Sponsor can probably fulfill all three organizational influence domains. The Process Owner will probably be able to fill all three organizational influence domains as well, and also fills the process domain of Process Owner. He may also have project management skills and be able to fill that skill domain. (For smaller processes, the Process Owner and the Project Lead could be the same person.) The Project Lead needs to know the process, have some project management skills, and be the operational leader for implementation and the ongoing work of the process. The BPM Team Facilitator needs to know BPM and have group process skills. He could have project management skills as well, so he could take on the project management tasks, but he could not be the Project Lead because he does not know the process and will not be the operational process leader.

An SME can have many roles. He can provide process content because he knows the process from the content and experience domains; he may have project management skills, and he may be the head SME, so that would make him a good candidate for the Project Lead. He also could play a dual role as the documenter or data person. The IT role brings special technology experience and so fills the special experience domain; he should know the process by contributing to the work of the process as well. The Data person is similar to the IT person; he brings skills of knowing about data, and he should do work in the process. This role is one that is easy to combine with SME or IT. The Maverick should be an outsider, and he best fills the domain of group process, in that he is asking the Maverick questions within the group. The Documenter should work in the process and has the special expertise domain skills of a documenter (which would be doing BPMN capture as well as preparing other notes).

The graphic presents a comprehensive picture of the domains that leaders and team members fill. The organization can devise different combinations as long as all domains are matched appropriately with a BPI role.

THE BPI PROJECT WORK DURING PROCESS DISCOVERY, PROCESS ANALYSIS, PROCESS DESIGN, AND THE IMPLEMENTATION PLAN

The ongoing BPI Project work is the work following the Chartering and Staffing phase (Figure 12). It includes BPI workshops with the team, team sessions, and meetings with the Process Owner and Executive Sponsor.

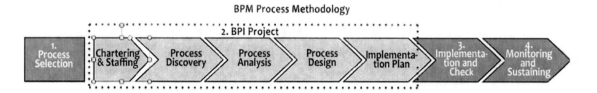

Figure 12. BPM Methodology Stages and BPI Project Phases

Regular Meetings with the Process Owner and Executive Sponsor

Together the Project Lead and Team Facilitator should hold regularly scheduled meetings with the Process Owner and Executive Sponsor. These meetings are not just status meetings. They are meetings to review key findings with the two executive leaders, get their input on certain items, ask for their help with other executives in the company, discuss challenges and suggest solutions. These meetings are important for ensuring that the senior leaders give input while the BPI Project is progressing and not only when it is finished. I like to say to senior leaders,

"When the BPI Team comes with its redesign and recommendations, I don't want to you approve or not approve this project. I want you to adopt it, although you may have some slight suggestions and revisions. The team does not want to spend all this time working on the BPI Project only to have it be turned down. So the Project Lead and Team Facilitator should be connecting with the senior leaders regularly."

The Project Lead runs these meetings, and the Team Facilitator learns perspectives that can help in planning for and facilitating the team sessions. (See Chapter 7 for how to coordinate Leadership sessions, BPM workshops, Process Owner and Executive Sponsor meetings, and Team sessions.) Sometimes Executive Sponsors cannot, or choose not to, attend these regular meetings. Then it is the Process Owner's responsibility to keep the Executive Sponsor updated.

Workshop Sessions and Team Meetings

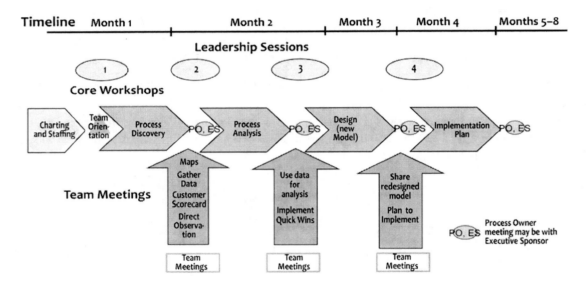

Figure 13. BPI Leadership Sessions, Core Workshops, and Team Meetings

I recommend a structured method for leadership sessions, workshops, team meetings, and Process Owner/Executive Sponsors meetings. I have used this method successfully with over 100 BPI Projects over the last ten years. Leadership sessions (Figure 13, large ovals toward the top) prepare the four leaders for the upcoming work with the teams. Workshop sessions (chevrons) are full-day sessions with an experienced BPM instructor conducting the workshop and two to three BPI teams, each with their Project Lead, Team Facilitator, and team members attending. The instructor sets the agenda, conducts small teaching modules, and the teams apply the concept or technique on their own process improvement projects. Workshop sessions can be half day as well if that makes more sense for the client schedule. Team Meetings (up arrows at the bottom) are weekly meetings of 90 minutes to 2 hours where the team meets with the Team Facilitator and Project Lead working on assignments out of the workshops. These assignments represent the steps in the BPI Project, such as diagramming additional instances of the As-Is Diagram, interviewing customers using the Customer Scorecard, going out in the workplace to observe the process firsthand and talking to other employees doing the process, or gathering quantitative data. The Executive Sponsor/Process Owner regular meetings (small ovals) are the 30-60 minute meetings as described above.

IMPLEMENTATION AND CHECK

At the end of the BPI Project, the Project Lead and Team Facilitator build a draft Implementation Plan. They revise it with the team in the last workshop or meeting. (Chapter 15 has helpful ideas on the Implementation Plan.) Then, in the *Implementation and Check* stage of the BPM Methodology (Figure 12), the baton is passed from the BPI team that developed the new design and Implementation Plan to the team performing the actual implementation.

Some roles from the BPI Project continue into this stage. The Process Owner and Project Lead remain in the same roles during Implementation and Check. The Project Lead is responsible for operationalizing the improvements incorporated into the new design during implementation. The Process Owner drives implementation. He supports the Project Lead but works at a higher level. The BPI working team may remain intact during Implementation, or the Project Lead and Process Owner may decide to add new members to the team, which now is called the *Implementation Team*. It is best to keep a core group from the BPI team on the Implementation Team because it helps for a smooth transition.

Here are some important actions that should occur during Implementation and Check:

- The Process Owner regularly monitors the Implementation Plan against the milestones or prototype iterations. This can be scheduled every two weeks or monthly. (See Chapter 15 for more details.)
- The Process Owner reports implementation challenges and successes to the Executive Sponsor or a Steering Team.
- The Process Owner supports the Implementation team with resources, influence, and coaching. The Executive Sponsor assists if the Process Owner needs more influence across the organization.
- Change Management is an important element of this stage. The Change Management plan is part of the Implementation Plan, and incorporating it occurs during Implementation and Check.

Sometimes, after the Implementation Plan is approved, the original Process Owner may not be the right choice for the new process. Then it's necessary to change to a new Process Owner appropriate to the scope of the redesigned process. The start of Implementation is a good time to select a new Process Owner. A transition is needed, and the Executive Sponsor and Project Lead can bring the new Process Owner up to speed. The Process Owner is responsible for monitoring and improving the process in an ongoing fashion, so get that person in place now. That way the Process Owner will have participated in implementing the process, since he did not get to design it.

Both the Executive Sponsor and Process Owner have a role in the Implementation. Get their active support and commitment. Since more areas of the organization will be impacted by the changes in Implementation and Check, the Executive Sponsor and Process Owner can help influence these groups.

MONITORING AND SUSTAINING

The last stage of the BPM Methodology, *Monitoring and Sustaining*, is managed by the Process Owner and the employees doing the process. This stage is outside the scope of this book, but here are a few tips that breed success. These involve paying attention to implementation, ensuring it is successful, and continuing to use the project management and data monitoring practices of Implementation and Check in Monitoring and Sustaining.

Identify Measures

- Identify ongoing metrics for (1) the outputs of the process, and (2) the leading indicators within the process for signals of problems or health. The Project Lead and Process Owner may also want indicators for personnel needs, inventory, time, or wastes. Don't create too many metrics. It's helpful to collect the metrics in real time or close to the event. The point is to be able to make decisions and take action on them quickly. Use real-time BPM data to identify bottlenecks, rebalance workloads, identify negative trends, and monitor outputs.
- Identify how measures will be gathered. It is best when done automatically by the process, but someone should still be accountable.
- Agree on the frequency of monitoring data and an escalation process when leading indicators suggest action is required.

Monitor Continuously

- Using data, monitor how employees are performing the new process. Then, if there are problems, let the employees and Project Lead figure out how to make corrections. Remember to separate process metrics from employee performance metrics. In one situation where the company was measuring productivity of employees and teams against a target metric, they used results to identify best practices and improve worker productivity overall.

- Watch technology and market trends for changes that impact the process, either positively or negatively.
- Have a clear succession plan for how to replace the Process Owner and operational leader to provide for job changes.
- Keep at it. Don't improve the process and just let it slip back to where it was before.

SUMMARY

This chapter explains the functions and responsibilities of the four BPI leadership roles and the team members in each phase of the BPI Project as well as in the Implementation and Check and Monitoring and Sustaining stages that come afterward. Other stakeholder roles may be important adjuncts to the ones discussed here, but these are the key ones. These leaders and the team will be successful if they follow the suggested roles and responsibilities. Some variations are possible, but keep it simple and structured.

There are several benefits to using these roles in your BPI Project:

1. These leaders represent the governance of the process for this initial BPI Project, and the Process Owner and Project Lead become the governance for the process during ongoing Monitoring and Sustaining. Clear governance is important for the success of the project and for building a process culture.

2. The BPI members become a team while working toward the goals of the improvement project. No longer are individual employees promoting the needs of their individual functions or business units; rather they are working toward the outcomes and benefits of the process for the customer and the organization. When the team is a strong one, they carry their understanding and enthusiasm into implementation, enhancing the returns in the organization.

3. The leaders and team members gain skills and build new professional capabilities. Before their first BPI Project, many leaders do not know much about what BPM is and what their role should be as a leader in an improvement project. By attending leadership sessions, helping formulate the Process Charter, participating in regular meetings with the Project Lead and Team Facilitator, and observing segments of team meetings and workshops, they learn to use the tools of business process measurement. For the team, they learn the modeling, analysis, redesign, engagement, and implementation tools and apply them to the process. For all the leaders and players, these skills will carry over to other projects, either BPI-specific ones or different types of projects.

Appendix: Detailed Selection Criteria and Role Descriptions for Leaders and Team Members by Phases of the BPI Project

---

Executive Sponsor

Criteria for selecting an Executive Sponsor
- Has hierarchical authority over the process
- Is personally motivated by the business need behind this effort
- Sees this effort as important to his goals
- Can influence outside suppliers and other divisions in the organization
- Is committed to a process orientation for this project

Responsibilities

Project Initiation: Chartering and Staffing
- Authorizes and legitimizes the process improvement initiative
- Approves/supports the vision and Improvement Targets set by the Process Owner for this process
- Suggests team members for the team as needed, and provides influence in getting their agreement to work on the project
- Identifies and appoints Process Owner
- Provides monetary and other resources as needed

Supports Ongoing BPI Project Work: Process Discovery, Process Analysis, Process Design, Implementation Plan
- Reviews project progress periodically with the Process Owner
- May assist with decisions on requests for scope changes

Implementation and Check
- Advocates for the process improvement methods and team recommendations
- Is responsible for influencing implementation in the organization, especially across divisions that may be beyond the authority of the Process Owner

Monitoring and Sustaining
- Regularly hears from the Process Owner on process health and developments.
- Suggests enterprise-wide connections for this process with other processes
- Supports BPM effort overall.

Figure 14. Details, Executive Sponsor

Process Owner

Criteria for selecting a Process Owner
- Has responsibility for most steps in the High-Level Map
- Is committed to a process orientation and this effort
- Is respected and influential in the organization
- Sees this effort as important to his goals
- Will continue to monitor and improve this process after the initial project

Responsibilities

Project Initiation; Chartering and Staffing
- Articulates the process vision and its value to the organization and customer
- Sets process Improvement Targets and scope
- Gets approval from the Executive Sponsor for the vision and the Improvement Targets
- Identifies and appoints Team Facilitators, the Project Lead, and all team members

Supports Ongoing BPI Project Work: Process Discovery, Process Analysis, Process Design, Implementation Plan
- Provides resources for the project – budget and team members' time
- Attends all leadership sessions with Project Leads and Team Facilitators to learn process improvement principles and tools
- Reviews project progress regularly with the Project Lead and Team Facilitator; attends portions of team meetings and/or workshops
- Reviews project progress regularly with the Executive Sponsor
- Helps identify baseline measures, goal values, and ongoing metrics
- Discusses and helps resolve issues and concerns from the Project Lead or Team Facilitator, including interpersonal problems
- Make decisions from Project Lead on requests for scope changes

Implementation and Check
- Drives implementation in the organization
- Is accountable for achieving the desired outcome and success of the overall initiative
- Advocates for the process improvement methods and team recommendations
- Communicates success of project to others

Monitoring and Sustaining
- Monitors process results regularly
- Uses metrics to identify problem areas and suggests corrective action
- Watches leading indicators for signals of needs for resources or support for the process
- Stays abreast of market and technology changes to identify needed improvements for the process

Figure 15. Details, Process Owner

Project Lead

Criteria for selecting a Project Lead
- Is highly respected in the organization
- Has responsibility for, or influence over, much of the process
- Knows the steps in the process well; is a strong subject matter expert (SME)
- Has strong project management and organizational skills

Responsibilities
Initiation and Ongoing Work: Chartering and Staffing; Process Discovery, Process Analysis, Process Design, Implementation Plan
- Ensures the project has clear direction and support
- Attends leadership sessions
- Strategizes with Team Facilitators on BPM tools that are needed for this process improvement
- Provides subject matter expertise to the team on current process and organizational units
- Plans and conducts Process Owner meetings with the Team Facilitator
- Helps resolve project problems and conflicts
- Identifies if team ideas are beyond the original scope and brings these needs to the Process Owner
- Ensures that the project's outcome meets the business objectives
- Finds administrative support for room scheduling, equipment, and logistical setup
- Keeps the documented team outputs from each meeting and stores in shared repository
- Develops an Implementation Plan with the Team Facilitator

Implementation and Check
- Leads and operationalizes process improvement changes in the workplace.

Monitoring and Sustaining
- Continues to monitor the process and suggests revisions and additional improvements over time

Figure 16. Details, Project Lead

Team Facilitator

Criteria for selecting the Team Facilitator
- Experienced in both process improvement methods and group facilitation
- May or may not be a member of the process being analyzed

Responsibilities
Initiation and Ongoing Work: Chartering and Staffing; Process Discovery, Process Analysis, Process Design, Implementation Plan
- Assists the team in the development of the project scope and quantifying project objectives
- Assures the quality of the business process analysis methodology
- Helps the team select tools for the process improvement modeling, analysis, and redesign
- Moves the team toward the Improvement Targets using the BPM Process Methodology
- Develops an Implementation Plan with the Project Lead

Group Facilitation
- Facilitates weekly working team meetings and team segments of the day-long core workshops.
- Raises issues and concerns with the Project Lead and Process Owner
- Ensures that all team members' points of view are heard.
- Is not responsible for implementation in the organization, nor for resolving interpersonal problems.
- Assists the team in reviewing "lessons learned"

Implementation and Check
- No formal responsibilities, although the Team Facilitator could choose to stay on to work with the Implementation team in a similar role.

Monitoring and Sustaining
- No responsibilities

Figure 17. Details, Team Facilitator

Team Members

The team includes 6-10 employees/managers with a maverick, technology person, data person and possibly a customer or supplier.

Criteria for selecting each team member
- Is a key stakeholder in the process
- Is among the best and the brightest employees
- Works in the process now or is a customer or key supplier to the process
- Is eager to improve the process

Responsibilities
Initiation and Ongoing Work: Chartering and Staffing; Process Discovery, Process Analysis, Process Design, Implementation Plan

Subject Matter Experts and Team Contributors
- Fully participate in achieving the project objectives
- Bring knowledge and ideas to their teams from their own experiences
- Are open to ideas from different stakeholders in the meetings
- Look for the strengths and weaknesses of the current process, and are eager to make improvements
- Develop and implement a communication process
- Develop an Implementation Plan and help in its installation; advocate for improvements

Specific Roles
- **Maverick:** The maverick asks probing questions, suggests different perspectives, and challenges statements such as, "We've always done it that way." The maverick does not work the process. He is an outsider. He brings a fresh outsider view to the improvement effort.
- **IT**: the technology person brings ideas and reality to discussions about what is possible with current and future technology solutions
- **Data**: The data person is a team member who encourages the team to identify and gather quantitative data, and will spearhead this effort for the team. This could be a dual responsibility with a subject matter expert.
- **Documentation**: One team member documents meeting ideas, action items, decisions, and BPMN models for the current and future state process
- **Customer and external supplier** (optional)

Implementation and Check
- Often a few subject matter experts and the IT person become part of the Implementation Team
- Additional appropriate team members are added

Monitoring and Sustaining
- The subject matter experts execute the process as part of their job.
- Identify problems in the process and suggest additional improvements

Figure 18. Details, Team Members

CHAPTER 4

WHO'S ON FIRST?

ORGANIZATIONAL ROLES RELEVANT TO PROCESS IMPROVEMENT

If your organizational role or job title is Business Analyst (BA), Lean Six Sigma Practitioner, Project Manager, or Business Architect, your skills and experience bring real value to a BPI Project and allow you to play a variety of project roles. A hybrid organizational role, the Process Improvement Expert, combining the skills of the BA, Lean Six Sigma Practitioner, and Project Manager, is actually ideal. On the other hand, you may not have experience in any one of these organizational roles but nevertheless have been assigned a leadership role in a BPI Project. If you are a leader, it will also be helpful to know more about how these four common organizational roles relate to BPI Project roles, as you will be evaluating and selecting leaders and team members for the project.

Specific duties of the leadership and team project roles are detailed in Chapter 3. But these roles are rarely actual job titles or even permanent assignments. This chapter discusses four job titles found in most organizations – Business Analyst, Lean Six Sigma Practitioner, Project Manager, and Business Architect – and relates their typical functions, training, and skills to suitable project roles in a process project. You will see what value each brings to a BPI team, what they typically know, what they need to learn, and the BPI Project roles best suited to their skills and experience.

Let's consider them one by one.

BUSINESS ANALYSTS

What a Business Analyst does varies by size and type of company, and whether the position reports to IT or the business. The International Institute of Business Analysis (IIBA) says the BA's function can range from executing business or IT projects, to guiding them, to strategically creating them. Their primary function is to provide "business requirements" for some kind of change, typically to solve a business problem with an IT solution.

Below is a sampling of job requirements for the Business Analyst. This role is different in each organization, but the sampling below is a good representation of the skills, activities, and perspectives that the organizational role needs, and many are related to business process improvement.

Skill Sets

- Ability to translate complex business inputs from Business and Operations into technical solution requirements
- Solid subject matter expertise in areas such as business intelligence, business rules, data analysis, data integration, specific organizational functions or products, ERP Systems, and other specific applications
- Ability to apply a focused set of techniques to resolve complex business problems. These techniques include business rules analysis, data modeling, process modeling, Agile, Lean Six Sigma, metrics and key performance indicators, change management, communication, use cases, and implementing operational improvements.

Critical Activities

- Facilitate subject matter experts, end users and other stakeholders to identify business requirements, recommend solutions, and conduct user acceptance testing and training
- Assist in object-oriented analysis and design; system integration requirements; process, use case, and data modeling; and BPM tool evaluation
- Monitor implementation and ongoing operations

Perspectives

- See the link between business need and IT capabilities and user satisfaction
- Articulate how short-term improvements align with business goals

To develop their skill set, Business Analysts take individual courses at universities, online or in person, and would probably follow the curriculum suggested by the IIBA and laid out in *A Guide to the Business Analysis Body of Knowledge.*[7] Many schools offer Business Analyst certificates after the completion of several courses in different categories. The IIBA has two professional

---

[7] IIBA. *A Guide to the Business Analysis Body of Knowledge.* Toronto, Ontario, Canada, 2009.

certificates – the Certified Business Analysis Professional (CBAP) and Certification of Competency in Business Analysis (CCBA). These are granted once individuals have met specific educational, experience, and knowledge requirements, which are listed on the IIBM site (www.iiba.org).

LEAN SIX SIGMA PRACTITIONERS

Lean Six Sigma job titles identify an employee who has skills, knowledge, and experience in both the Lean (or Toyota Production System) and Six Sigma methodologies. These are well-known process improvement methodologies.

Lean originally grew out of the Toyota Production System (TPS) for manufacturing in Japan. It was brought to the United States by James P. Womack and Daniel T. Jones after their study, together with Massachusetts Institute of Technology, of TPS in Japan. The TPS concept and name Lean became known with the publication of their book, *The Machine That Changed the World*,[8] initially published in 1990. Today there are corporate courses and courses at universities that offer training in Lean methodology, but the ultimate training would be working at Toyota for several years to understand the TPS/Lean culture, philosophy, and when and how to use specific techniques. Although Lean started with a focus on manufacturing, it is now applied to the service industry as well.

Six Sigma, on the other hand, was a programmatic name for a continuous improvement methodology developed by Motorola in 1985; it became more widely known when Jack Welch, the CEO of General Electric, made it a part of his overall business strategy in 1995. GE trained hundreds of employees, certified Green Belts, Black Belts, and Master Black Belts through numerous Six Sigma projects it conducted and tracked.

Today training for Six Sigma is available at universities, within corporations, and through private training companies. Certification at different levels, from the simplest Yellow Belt, to Green Belt, Black Belt, and Master Black Belt, involves a standardized test, completion of one or more projects, and demonstration of a certain dollar value improvement for each project. Only the initial and relatively new Yellow Belt does not require a project.

The Lean methodology focuses on increasing flow through the process, thus reducing cycle time and eliminating wastes in the process. The culture has senior management supporting the worker, with the philosophy that the worker gets the core work done for the customer. Employees and managers learn the methodology through participating in it, recommending and

---

[8] Womack, James P., Jones, Daniel T. and Roos, Daniel. *The Machine That Changed the World: The Story of Lean Production*. New York: Productivity Press, 1990.

making improvements, experimenting, and getting coached by their managers and sensei, or specific Lean coaches in the organization.

Six Sigma focuses on identifying and removing the causes of defects and minimizing variation in the process. It uses two project methodologies: DMAIC (Define, Measure, Analyze, Improve, Control) for improving existing processes, and DMEDI (Define, Measure, Explore, Develop, Implement) for creating new process designs where there is not a current process. The governance structure requires strong executive leadership and commitment and encourages all leaders to have Green Belt or Black Belt training.

Lean and Six Sigma have different historical origins, points of emphasis, and terminology, but neither is well integrated with the mainstream of BPM tools and technology. While Lean and Six Sigma differ in focus, their overall objectives are largely the same: improve work processes using data, customer insight, and workflow understanding, focusing on removal of wastes, defects, or problems. Many corporations, practitioners, and authors have now combined the two methodologies into Lean Six Sigma. What that really means is they are using the principles and techniques from both methodologies together, and apply what's relevant to their practice or organization. Although this blurs the original focus of each methodology, it is practical to combine them.

The qualifications for both Lean and Six Sigma practitioners are well established, and many job positions list Lean Six Sigma in the title. Other job titles that don't include the words "Lean Six Sigma" have similar requirements listed in the postings. These include Industrial Engineer, Quality Engineering Systems Director, Customer Support Project Manager, Shift Manager, Operational Excellence Site Champion, Quality Manager, and Productivity Manager.

Sample job requirements for the Lean Six Sigma Practitioner include:

Skill Sets

- Solid understanding and experience in DMAIC (Define, Measure, Analyze, Improve and Control), DMEDI (Define, Measure, Explore, Develop, Implement), and Toyota Production System "House" frameworks
- Strong problem-solving skills with the ability to acquire, assimilate, and analyze data from multiple systems and data sources
- Project management skills, including time management, planning, resource tracking, information summarization, budgeting, and establishing workflow

Critical Activities

- Determines critical business metrics; uses business logic and technical skills to structure dashboards, and other metric systems
- Collects, validates, and analyzes data required to understand the root causes of problems, or the key drivers of required business results
- Provides leadership, direction, and facilitation to cross-functional teams empowered to execute the Lean Six Sigma strategy for process improvement, productivity improvement, and cost reduction
- Communicates team progress to champions, business leaders, and Master Black Belts

Perspectives

- Sees organization as a set of processes that produce improvement opportunities
- Sees strategic roadmap for process improvement
- Views process improvement as a requirement to organizational performance and customer experience

PROJECT MANAGERS

"Project Manager" is a common term in business these days. On the simplest level, a Project Manager can be an individual in charge of a plan that was developed on a cocktail napkin or a simple spreadsheet. For a more complex project, the Project Manager can be an employee in the Project (or Program) Management Office, be certified in Project Management by passing the rigorous PMI test, create sophisticated work breakdown schedules using software, and manage enterprise projects from beginning to end for the organization. The Project Manager I am talking about in this section has responsibilities like the second (complex) type, but may not always work on enterprise projects; instead he might also work on medium or large projects.

According to the Project Management Body of Knowledge (PMBOK), a project is a "temporary endeavor undertaken to create a unique product, service, or result."[9] And Project Management is "the application of knowledge, skills, tools and techniques to project activities to meet the project requirements."[10] The PMBOK then goes on to say that there are 42 logically grouped activities that the Project Manager does in five Process Groups. All of these Process Groups are relevant to the phases in business process improvement projects.

---

[9] Project Management Institute. *A Guide to the Project Management Body of Knowledge.* Newton Square, PA: Project Management Institute, 2013, p. 5.
[10] Ibid., p. 6.

A "project" in the project management sense ends with implementation, but a process continues as part of the ongoing operation and needs monitoring. There is no element of Project Management for ongoing monitoring, since a project by its definition is temporary.

Project managers are usually trained through courseware in universities or corporate educational programs, and earn certificates from completing a course curriculum. The Project Management Institute often teaches these courses in organizations, in universities, or directly, and they are by far the most respected project management institution in the field. They have also developed the PMI certification test, which is difficult and highly regarded. After the initial test, there are 'continuing education courses' necessary to maintain certification and become more advanced in the field.

There are many activities in Project Management that are similar to the activities of a BPI Project. Project Managers prepare a charter and identify the needed staff for leadership and the team similar to a BPI Project. For the BPI phases of Process Discovery, Process Analysis, Process Design, and Implementation Plan, they use similar project management techniques to plan and execute the project (such as define activities sequence, develop schedule, manage project execution, manage project team, etc.) In fact, the 42 project management tasks are more extensive than what is needed for most BPI Projects. But the task sets also differ in that Project Management activities do not include the specific BPM techniques (such as process modeling, waste analysis, time analysis, rules for redesign, etc.) that are needed for the focus on process improvement. Monitoring and Controlling occurs in Project Management within a project (e.g., monitor work, control scope, control costs). In a BPI Project, monitor work, control scope, and control costs occur within the project, but, as shown on the BPM Process Methodology model, ongoing monitoring and controlling also takes place after Implementation, as the process continues in the operational environment once the project is done.

The point is that a business process improvement project is a PROJECT that models, analyzes, and improves a business process. But then a process workflow continues once the improvements are recommended and implemented, whereas the project ends.

Below is a sampling of job requirements for the Project Manager.

Skill Sets

- Demonstrated expert analytical and technical abilities and task management skills
- Experience in multiple methods of estimating time and resources for task assignments and resource leveling
- Experience using Project Management tools such as Microsoft Project Professional, and Microsoft SharePoint

Critical Activities

- Provides hands-on management and delivery of multiple projects to meet technology and business requirements on time and within budget
- Influences and executes project management methodologies and standards, such as those from the PMI PMBOK
- Undertakes such detailed tasks as developing/managing/maintaining comprehensive, accurate project plans and schedules, performance estimation, forecasting, planning, analysis, issue/risk/change management, escalation management, meeting facilitation, variance analysis, and status reporting
- Is proactive in the identification and resolution of issues that may negatively impact a project.

Perspectives

- Sees the comprehensive interrelated work of a large initiative
- Is committed to the success of this one-time project effort the first time

BUSINESS ARCHITECTS

Business Architects prepare "a blueprint of the enterprise that provides a common understanding of the organization and is used to align strategic objectives and tactical demands."[11] The Business Architect works with executives to align business strategy with operational priorities, promoting business transformation and continuous improvement.

Business Architects bring transparency to the business by integrating models and information to enable the business to see duplication of efforts, systems, or information across the enterprise. They usually begin with value streams of core business processes, and show the relationship of those value streams to capabilities, information, and the current organizational structure. Then they assist the business in creating roadmaps from the portfolio of value streams to align business and IT initiatives toward the strategy objectives. Business Architects usually report within the IT function but their role is to serve as coaches to business executives.

The Business Architect is a relatively new role (4-5 years old) in the organization. There are now training classes in some universities, and the Business Architecture Guild recently

---

[11] Object Management Group, Business Architecture Working Group, http://bawg.omg.org.

developed and published *A Guide to the Business Architecture Body of Knowledge (BIZBOK™).*[12] The Business Architecture Guild is becoming a key professional organization for employees and consultants in this role.

The baseline blueprints that Business Architects use are listed in the BIZBOK, and include

- Business Strategy Mapping
- Capability Mapping
- Value Mapping
- Information Mapping
- Initiative Mapping
- Product Mapping
- Stakeholder Mapping

In addition to the above list, there are a number of hybrid blueprints that provide, for example, cross-mappings between value streams and capabilities or between business units and capabilities. Many of these blueprints or templates could be used by one or all of the other three roles in this chapter, although they might not be called by the same name. But Business Architects are likely to use them all in their effort to assist in developing the roadmap for the enterprise that is aligned with an overall strategy.

This type of systemic work implies that the organization wants to work enterprise-wide, and that may or may not be realistic for an organization. When assessing the process maturity of an organization, it is useful to use a process maturity framework. There are many process maturity frameworks, but the one I reference is the CMMI process maturity framework pictured in Figure 19.

---

[12] Business Architecture Guild. *A Guide to the Business Architecture Body of Knowledge,*™ version 3.1.1 (BIZBOK™) 2012.

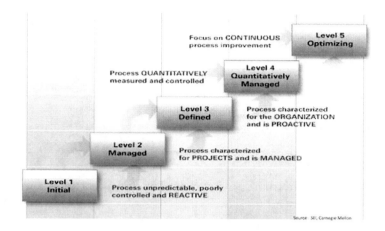

Figure 19. CMMI Process Maturity Levels. Source: SEI, Carnegie Mellon

Most organizations today are operating at Level 2 or early Level 3. At Level 2, process improvement initiatives can come from single functions or business units in the organization. At Level 2, it makes sense to focus on BPM initiatives that are important to specific business leaders, not on end-to-end processes across many units. Over time, however, there will be duplication of effort and sub-optimization of processes across the enterprise by focusing on these narrower processes in silos. Recognition of this redundancy by C-suite executives leads to choosing processes that are more enterprise wide, setting BPM practice standards across the organization, and assigning Process Owners to all processes, all of which are characteristics of an organization at Level 3. Business Architects may encourage executives to take a more comprehensive approach at the enterprise level, but the culture, skills, and resistance of middle managers who are at Level 1 or 2 will provide challenges.

Job descriptions for Business Architects can vary based on the background and skills of the individual needed. Some Business Architects play a major role in blueprint development but may not have the background to apply the blueprints within the context of certain business initiatives. Other Business Architects have the skills required to align these blueprints to strategy, initiatives, business processes, value streams, or IT architecture. For each of these more specific roles, the Business Architect is likely to focus on particular aspects of the job. They may operate in a Center of Excellence in a business unit or from a corporate Center of Excellence.

Sample job requirements include:

Skill Sets

- "Basic understanding of blueprint structures (such as capability maps and value streams) necessary for capability, organization, value, and information mapping."[13]
- Ability to incorporate blueprints into various tools.
- "Business subject area expertise appropriate to the role and areas being mapped."[14]

Critical Activities

- Analyzes the organizational landscape to determine redundancies and find opportunities to minimize complexity of technology environment
- Conducts business process and requirements analysis and advises clients on key architectural decisions concerning the platform and the supporting technologies
- Determines priorities for when new business solutions need to be implemented and deployed

Perspectives

- Provides insights on domains of business, information, application, and technology and how they interconnect
- Sees how the business, technology, and information perspectives can be aligned to improve the business

Below is a helpful graphic from Bill Ulrich, a Business Architect, and co-founder of the Business Architecture Guild.

---

[13] Ibid., p. 219.
[14] Ibid., p. 219.

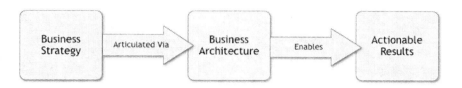

- Mission and Vision
- Policy, Rules and Regulations
- Goals and Objectives
- Executive Priorities
- Customer Requirements
- Strategy and Tactics

- Organizational Alignment
- Business Capabilities
- Information Concepts
- Value Streams

- Well articulated business priorities
- Business-driven roadmaps & funding
- Collaborative initiatives
- Framework for requirement analysis, business designs
- Synchronized business-driven IT transformation
- Strategy and Tactics

Figure 20. Building and Using Business Architecture. Source: William Ulrich, TSG, Inc., 2013

LEADERSHIP ROLES FOR THE BUSINESS ANALYST, LEAN SIX SIGMA PRACTITIONER, PROJECT MANAGER, AND BUSINESS ARCHITECT IN BPI PROJECTS

The easiest way to see what BPI Project roles each of these four organizational roles could play is to look at the domains first discussed in Chapter 3. Figure 21 shows that the four organizational roles can fill many domains based on their skills, experience, and place in the organization. Let's look at them one by one.

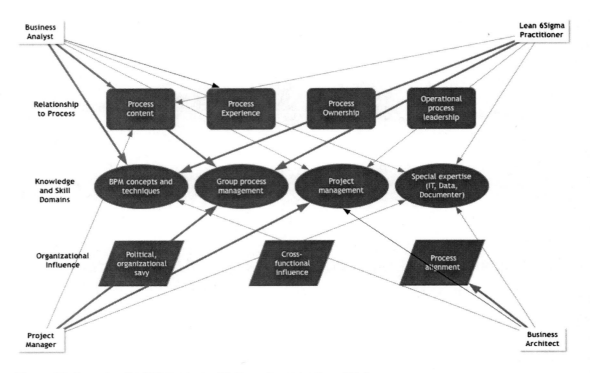

Figure 21. Domains for BPI Project with Four Organizational Roles

Business Analyst

A Business Analyst can fill many of the domains needed in a BPI Project. He probably has some group process management skills from his role in working with groups as a BA. Depending on the process and the BA's background, he might possess content knowledge and even work in the process now or recently. He may also have project management skills. A BA often brings knowledge of some of the BPM concepts, and techniques. He may also have special expertise, such as an understanding of technology, data analytical skills, or documenter skills. As an individual performer, he could be a SME, the IT Person, the Data person, the Documenter, the Maverick, or a combination of these. He could be the Project Lead if he intends to stay on and implement the improvements. He could be the BPM Team Facilitator. He could not be an Executive Sponsor or a Process Owner, because he would not have that type of position in the company.

In some companies, the BA runs "solo," taking the BPM techniques out to individual leaders, SMEs, and stakeholders and gathering their input individually, combining it, and forming a summary. I do not recommend this approach because it takes longer and does not allow all the

SMEs to see varied points of view, work through their differences and tensions together, and form a team recommendation vs. just giving input to the BA. But it can work, and the BA might gather the information individually and then bring an SME group together for consolidation discussions.

Lean Six Sigma Practitioner

An experienced Lean or Six Sigma practitioner could easily fulfill the BPM concept and techniques domain. He usually has significant project management skills and could fulfill that domain. An individual Lean Six Sigma practitioner may have process content knowledge or even past process experience. He also has strong special expertise in data.

So what BPI Project roles would be appropriate? He could play team roles such as the Maverick, Data person, or Documenter. But it is more likely that he would have a leadership role. Both Project Lead and BPM Team Facilitator are possible. For the Project Lead role, he could provide the project management skills. In this situation, I suggest that the Process Owner designate a Head SME who is on the team who will implement the improvements with the Lean Six Sigma's project management help and become the ongoing operational process leader. The Lean Six Sigma practitioner would then move on to another project. If an SME on the team is not responsible for leading implementation and becoming the ongoing operational leader, the likelihood of project failure increases.

A person with strong Lean Six Sigma skills and group process skills makes an excellent candidate for the BPM Team Facilitator. But that individual would need to make two adjustments in the change from a pure Lean Six Sigma project to a BPI Project: (1) He would have to bring his Lean or Six Sigma techniques to the BPI effort only where appropriate and use other techniques where appropriate. (2) He would need to assume the role of a facilitator, not the Lean Six Sigma expert. The BPM Team Facilitator does provide BPM expertise, but he does not run the team, or follow up on assignments; instead he guides the team members to use BPM techniques, coaches the Project Lead to keep the team on track toward the Process Owner's objectives, and supports the team when they are doing modeling or analytical work.

The most senior Six Sigma Practitioner, the Master Black Belt, would have the capability to provide guidance to executives in the domains of process alignment to strategy, influencing cross-functionally, and providing political or organizational savvy. There is no role on the BPI Team for these capabilities, although strong managers who have been Process Owners or BPM Team Facilitators many times and have both BPM knowledge and experience through former BPI Projects could take on this larger enterprise role and advise the Process Owner or Executive Sponsor.

Project Manager

What domains can the Project Manager contribute to? He has strong project management skills and group process management skills. He may know the process content and could have worked in the process before.

The most obvious BPI role for the Project Manager is Project Lead, because of the similarity of names and the project management skills needed. But the Project Manager is missing two important domains of the BPI Project Lead – namely, being an SME with process experience currently and taking on the domain of operational leadership during the project, during implementation, and in an ongoing fashion. The Project Lead in a BPI Project should be the chief subject matter expert for the process, the leader of the BPI team, accountable to reach the Process Owner's goals, and should be responsible for making the new process operational in the workplace. So in this situation, as with the Lean Six Sigma Practitioner, I would recommend that the Process Owner select a Head SME who would work with the Project Manager during the project, and the Head SME would become the Operational Leader during Implementation and ongoing for the process. During the BPI Project, the Project Manager would focus on managing the project aspects of the BPI work, and the Head SME would focus on modeling, analyzing, and improving the process.

A Project Manager could also take on the BPM Team Facilitator role, although it is likely that he would have to learn several BPM concepts and techniques. He could be the Documenter, Data person, or Maverick on the team as well. These team roles are smaller in scope than the Project Lead or BPM Team Facilitator role. The Project Manager might perform them to learn more about the BPM Methodology or because the Process Owner wanted him on the team for some reason such as his creative skills as a Maverick. But the mostly likely role for a Project Manager would be BPI Project Lead or BPM Team Facilitator.

Business Architect

The Business Architect has a strategic consulting role in helping the company with Portfolio Management and Relationship Management. In Portfolio Management, he assists executives in envisioning the processes in the portfolio, aligning them with the overall strategy, and then prioritizing process projects and monitoring their success. In Relationship Management, the Business Architect brings IT and the business together, encouraging working relationships vs. silos, enabling technology and operations to build operations and systems in sync. Therefore, the Business Architect could fulfill the process alignment domain and advise on the two others – political or organizational savvy and cross- functional influence.

A Business Architect is likely to have project management skills and some special expertise, probably data analytics, possibly technology, and Maverick questioning so he could fulfill those domains. But, although the Business Architect could fulfill the special expertise roles on a BPI team, it is unlikely he would do so. And he cannot be Executive Sponsor or the Process Owner because he does not sit in that type of business leadership role. Instead it is more likely that the Business Architect would be an advisor to the Executive Sponsor or Process Owner.

Initially, senior executives and the Business Architect would establish the blueprints and then identify the process portfolio. Then, once the processes in the portfolio have been prioritized based on the organization's strategy, individual BPI Projects could begin.

Then the Business Architect could help in the development of the BPI Project Charter. He could also assist the Process Owner in aligning the Project Charter Improvement Targets and vision with the overall strategy, or he could just review these items in the Project Charter to ensure alignment. He may also help identify or concur in the choice of key leaders and team members for the team. The Business Architect is likely to know key cross-functional employees who should be tapped for the team, both from the Business and IT side. The Business Architect would not likely be a leader or team member, but an important outside resource.

SUMMARY

The four job titles discussed in this chapter, Business Analyst, Lean Six Sigma Practitioner, Project Manager, and Business Architect, play key roles in most companies today. If you are in one of these roles now, or want to move into one of them, this chapter shows what skills you can bring to process improvement. However, the individual in any of these job categories must candidly assess his expertise and practical experience in each domain and identify new skills he will have to learn for whatever role he takes on within the BPI team. The materials in the book will help build many of those skills.

CHAPTER 5

SWIMLANE MAPPING FOR NON-SWIMMERS

The next critical piece after the Project Charter is creating a diagram of the current process. The process diagram uses a flowchart type of notation. It shows the beginning and end of the process, the sequence of steps and decisions in between, and the performers doing them. When the document is complete, the team has a visual picture of how the process is done today (called the *As-Is* or *current state* model) which depicts the flow of the work and information in "swimlanes."

WHY DIAGRAM THE AS-IS PROCESS?

The ostensible purpose of diagramming the current state is to document, in a standard format, how the process flows today, prior to improvement. But diagramming has many benefits in addition to documentation. Importantly, a diagram transforms the process description from a long text document into a picture that is easily shared and understood. Anyone who looks at the process diagram can see the order of the steps and who performs each one. That moves the process description from one individual's anecdotal story, which can skip all over the process and leave out important steps, to a display of how the process really works. Another benefit is that the As-Is diagram itself can be analyzed, indicating the step count, the handoffs between task performers, the approvals and decisions, and so forth. Chapter 8 provides a variety of ways to use this information to analyze the current process.

There are emotional benefits as well to capturing the process in a diagram. For example:

- The team usually gets very excited about seeing the swimlane process diagram finished. Team members will comment, "It is great to see the whole process. I never knew much about what happened after my part." Or, "Wow, I can see how what I do really makes an impact on the process." "Now I see what the customer really gets from this process."

- Once it is documented in a diagram, the process begins to be seen as something independent of specific employees that perform its activities. Blame for problems begins to shift from a particular department or person to the process itself. This new behavior is important in building a process culture—having employees and managers ask, "What's wrong with the process?" instead of "Who messed up?" or "Who was accountable and didn't do what was needed?"
- The As-Is process diagram can be annotated to highlight the team's analysis in the context of the activity flow. For example, you can add wastes – anything that adds inefficiency to the process – to the diagram, or display a Notched Timeline to show how long steps take and the wait time between them. You can add customer comments and needs, and show relevant measures. (Chapters 8-11 show examples and explain tools that are critical in the analysis phase.)
- Building the As-Is model is also a team-building exercise. Team members get inspired about the diagram and about adding comments and ideas to the parking lot lists. When the diagram is complete, someone often says, "I didn't know you needed that. I can get that for you right now." Here is the first Quick Win.

THE HIGH-LEVEL MAP

Recall that the purpose of the High-Level Map is to create a shared visual understanding of the current state (As-Is) process. For that purpose, I recommend using a simple flowchart with 6-10 steps. (See Figure 22 for the basic flowchart symbols used.) You could actually create this diagram in PowerPoint, but I usually do it in Visio for the first High-Level Map.

A flowchart is better than a bulleted list of the activities. Lists are overwhelming and harder to comprehend than a diagram. In order to move toward a process orientation, it helps to have a diagram that everyone can see on the wall or screen, and that shifts the focus away from just one person talking.

- **The map should use flowchart symbols, not chevrons.** Chevrons are a popular way of showing concepts or process stages at a very high level. They serve that purpose well, but I would not use them here because you want the organization to begin to see what a process map is – a picture of the flow, using a few standard symbols and the directional arrows. Chevrons could be used to represent the roadmap of what will be happening in the overall BPI effort; I use them to depict that.
- **Don't embellish with your own creative symbols.** If you use special shapes and symbols that you personally like, you will then have to explain the whole map, and you will be the only person who really knows what the symbols mean. The High-Level Map is a good place to introduce the basic flowchart notational symbols. If you want to do something creative, construct a storyboard, but do not call it a High-Level Map. The storyboard might better

represent a story about today's process and some of the challenges. But I really do not recommend it here; in fact, you would still need the High-Level Map for the Project Charter.

- **Don't use a Lean value stream map**. Lean notational symbols may be unfamiliar to folks on the business side. If your organization has adopted Lean as a whole and employees and managers have had training on the Lean tools, then you might want to use a high-level value stream map. I love the data on the value stream map, but it is too detailed at this stage of the BPI methodology.

- **It is probably too early for BPMN.** BPMN is similar to flowcharting and has many advantages over it, but unless your BPI leadership team has experience with the language, the High-Level Map is too early to adopt it. Using it properly is more complicated than is needed for this Project Charter element. I suggest leaving the BPMN diagram until a bit later in the methodology, but under some circumstances a simplified form of BPMN may work here, as we shall see in Chapter 14.

Reviewing the High-Level Map and Other Project Charter Elements with the Team Before the Team Starts on the Process Diagram

Once the Project Charter is finished and the Team Orientation has been conducted, it is time to document and discuss the current state process in the form of a detailed swimlane diagram. Begin by reviewing the high-level current state map with the team. Since this map was created during the Project Charter session with the Process Owner, Executive Sponsor, Project Lead, and Team Facilitator, the team has not seen it. It's important to start with the High-Level Map because it defines the scope of the process, helps the team to understand the flowchart symbols and process diagram construction, and encourages the team members to offer input on the accuracy of the steps.

Here's a sample plan outline for discussing key Project Charter elements with the team. It should take about 40 -60 minutes.

1. Review the High-Level Map with the team. Each member should have a copy, or it can be projected on the wall.

2. Read the Process Owner's Improvement Targets.

3. Read the Process Owner's vision

In this plan, the Team Facilitator and the Project Lead share the task of leading the meeting. The Team Facilitator explains the flowchart symbols (activity, decision diamond, and directional flow arrow), and then the Project Lead reviews the High-Level Map, going through each step. The Project Lead is the best person to do this review because he knows the steps through experience, whereas the Team Facilitator usually does not.

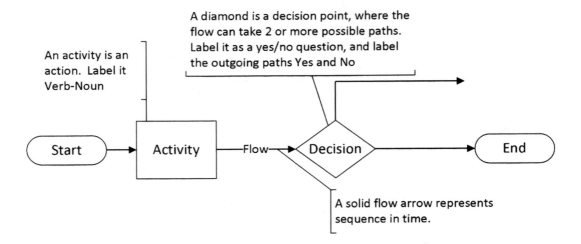

Figure 22. Flowchart symbols in the High-Level Map

Next, the Team Facilitator asks the team, "Are these the right starting and ending points? Should we start earlier or extend it further?" Changes to the starting and ending points of the process have two important implications: (1) the project scope gets larger or smaller, and (2) it may be necessary to add other people to the team. Encourage the team to consider the advantages of an alternative start or end point. With some teams, this is a short discussion; with others it is a heated discussion. Although the start and end points provide alternative choices these points set the scope of the project. Typically the Process Owner has already considered the start and end points appropriate for achieving the Improvement Targets, whether the process should span several functions or be more contained, and whether he wanted to tackle the full end-to-end process or only a segment of it at this time. If the team decides to recommend changes to the scope, the Project Lead and Team Facilitator need to take the recommended changes back to the Process Owner for acceptance or revisions.

I once had a team that continually discussed expanding the scope in the first three working sessions. The Process Owner listened carefully to all their considerations presented in different iterations. Finally the team decided the original scope was the best one. The scope discussion is an important one. If the team and the Process Owner can't come to an agreement, there will be contention throughout the whole process, and the team will get off track more often.

As the Project Leads explains all the high-level steps, the Team Facilitator asks the team to look for steps that need to be added or moved, and any wording that needs to be changed. The Project Lead should try to go through the whole High-Level Map before the team starts to comment. (This will be hard to do!)

Usually the team wants to include additional steps so their own work shows up in the High-Level Map. Reassure them that they will be creating a much more detailed swimlane process diagram soon, and this one is limited to the high-level, with just 6-10 steps. Often I accommodate the team's need for more detail and write their comments as bullets under the high-level model task (subprocess) where the more detailed task would go. But don't take a lot of time with this review by trying to get a comprehensive list of all these details. The details will go in the swimlane map.

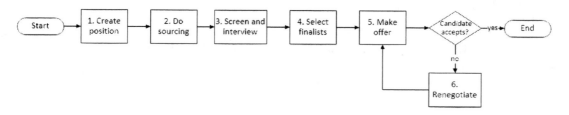

Figure 23. Hiring process, As-Is High-Level Map, in Visio Basic Flowchart

Instead, focus the team on the major steps. They may want to reword them. Sometimes they are in the wrong order, or an important step may have been left out. Make sure the Documenter is noting these changes on the initial version of the High-Level Map so these revisions can be documented after the session.

Next, the Team Facilitator reviews the Improvement Targets and vision provided by the Process Owner and Executive Sponsor. It's wonderful to have the Process Owner at this session, actually giving his thoughts about the challenges in this process and why he selected the Improvement Targets and vision. Allow the team to make recommendations for changes to the Improvement Targets and vision if they want, but don't get into petty wordsmithing.

In one client situation, the Process Owner wanted to improve the registration process for students transferring from community colleges in their junior year, and had the following two Improvement Targets and vision:

Improvement Targets

1. Increase the accuracy of reporting prior educational units (for basic requirements and major requirements) for transfer students before the Orientation session.

2. Decrease the time for students to identify total incoming credits from 8 months to within 1 month after Orientation.

Vision

Transfer students have access online to their own degree credit information early and completely so they are able to make informed choices about course selection.

As the team talked about these Improvement Targets and vision, a transfer student on the team mentioned another important goal. He said that transfer students should have the same privileges as regular students, but many transfer students felt they were treated more like second-class citizens. They came to a public university and could not get into critical classes for their major because sophomores had filled them up earlier in the spring. He suggested we add to the vision, "Give ongoing and transfer students the same opportunities." The Process Owner agreed.

By establishing the start and end points of the process, the High-Level Map helps determine what team members are needed. It also gets the team on the same page about the process. While the team reviews the process, they see it at the overview level, understand its scope, and make comments from their own perspective and experience.

WHICH PROCESS DIAGRAMMING NOTATION SHOULD WE USE?

So far, we have created a High-Level Map of the current state process as part of the Project Charter using a few basic flowcharting symbols. Soon we will create a more detailed swimlane diagram. Should we continue with the flowchart notation of the High-Level Map, or should we move to a similar but richer standard notation, such as BPMN? Does it really matter? Here are my recommendations.

I have been using the terms *process map*, *process diagram*, and *process model* somewhat interchangeably. Business people tend to use the word *map*, while IT tends to use the word *model*, and both take the form of a diagram. The swimlane flowchart, which originated in the 1980s, is the most common form of process diagram in use today. In a swimlane flowchart, *activities* (actions) are represented as rectangular boxes arranged in parallel rectangular areas – the *swimlanes* – representing the *actors* performing them. Solid arrows represent the activity flow. Diamond shapes, called *decisions* in flowcharting, represent branch points in the flow: under some conditions, the *yes* path is taken, while under other conditions the *no* path is taken. The presence of these decision diamonds illustrates that different *instances* of the process may take different paths from start to end.

These flowcharting shapes and symbols are familiar to virtually everyone who has used process diagrams. Swimlane flowcharts can be drawn by hand and are supported by any general-purpose drawing tool, such as Microsoft PowerPoint or Visio. But while the basic meaning of these traditional flowcharting symbols is understood, their precise meaning – as well as the meaning of other shapes and symbols in the diagram – is not well defined. The meaning is actually based on the personal interpretation of the person creating the diagram and, in some cases, on the tool used to create it.

For detailed documentation, visual analysis, and collaboration with IT, a more precise notation is needed. To be business-friendly, it should adopt the basic look and feel of traditional swimlane flowcharts, and ideally should be an open standard, not linked to one particular software tool. Fortunately, such a business-friendly standard notation for business process diagrams exists and is widely adopted: the *Business Process Modeling Notation*, or *BPMN*. While BPMN looks very similar to traditional swimlane flowcharts, the precise meaning of all the shapes and symbols is well-defined in a specification. Certain details, such as whether an activity is performed by a person or is automated, are indicated by specific icons and markers drawn inside the basic shapes. For that reason, while BPMN diagrams can be drawn by hand, it is far more common to use a software tool. Many BPMN tools are available, and process improvement teams are slowly learning how to use them.

BPMN Pluses and Minuses

With BPMN, the meaning of a process diagram does not depend on the tool used to create it, nor does it depend on the personal interpretation of the process modeler. The precise meaning of each shape and symbol is defined in a specification. BPMN has rules about what can connect to what, and exactly what those connections mean. But that has a downside as well, because it increases the chances that the modeler is using the notation incorrectly. Many BPMN tools let you validate your diagram in a single click, but to avoid errors, modelers can't simply fall back on their previous experience with flowcharting. They need to learn the basics of this new language. Certainly, at the start of your BPI Project, many team members, including the leaders, may not have this knowledge. However, it is a good idea to have at least one team member, perhaps the Documenter, the Team Facilitator, the IT person, or a borrowed resource with BPMN knowledge.[15]

You sometimes hear that BPMN is too complicated for business people, but it's not really true. It is true that the language contains a large number of icons and markers that convey special meaning to the basic shapes, but you can safely ignore most of them. The spec actually calls out a basic working set of shapes, symbols, and icons, called the *Descriptive element set* or, more commonly, the *Level 1 working set*. While Level 1 BPMN is a small fraction of the total element set and in fact is very similar to traditional flowcharting, it covers anything you will need in your swimlane diagram. Business people can use BPMN successfully!

While learning the basics of BPMN does impose an additional hurdle in your BPI Project, there are significant advantages in using BPMN for the swimlane diagram. First and foremost is clarity in visual communication: the process flow is described precisely in a way that is both

---

[15] There are many good books and training courses on BPMN available. See www.bpmnstyle.com and www.bpmessentials.com, for example.

tool-independent and modeler-independent. BPMN is also widely used by IT, so it serves as a common language shared by business and IT in the requirements for implementation. Moreover, BPMN provides a standard interchange format between tools, so you can employ one tool for business-oriented documentation and analysis, a separate one for more technical analysis such as simulation or process mining, and a third one for automated execution on a BPM Suite, with faithful translation of the model from one tool to the other.

The basics of BPMN Level 1 appropriate for the As-Is process model are discussed at the end of this chapter.

Tools for Process Modeling

Any drawing tool that can create boxes, diamonds, circles, and arrows can, in principle, be used for the High-Level Map. This includes tools like Microsoft PowerPoint or Word, for example, which you probably already have. Tools like Microsoft Visio, using its Basic Flowchart template, provide a bit more standardization of the common flowcharting shapes and symbols.

BPMN tools are more specialized. Visio 2013 Pro provides a BPMN template, while add-ins like Process Modeler for Visio from itp commerce[16] BPMN-enable all editions of Visio 2007, 2010, or 2013. Cloud-based tools like IBM Blueworks Live[17] and Signavio[18] provide BPMN modeling through a web browser and have a built-in team repository, which is extremely helpful for BPI. All of these tools are good and business-friendly. In Chapter 14, we'll show you how to use Blueworks Live to create and analyze the As-Is process model.

BPM Suites – process automation tools like IBM Business Process Manager or Oracle BPM Suite – also frequently include a BPMN tool that is nominally "business-oriented." If your company has standardized on one of these, you can use it for creating the As-Is process model, but they are not as business-friendly as the tools just mentioned.

Transitioning to BPMN

Weighing BPMN's advantages and disadvantages, I recommend introducing BPMN at a high level after the first Project Charter. I suggest using traditional flowcharting symbols to do the High-Level Map with the leaders. It is simple, using only a few symbols, and will get everyone looking at a process diagram. It is possible that the High-Level Map may change from the first map to a second iteration because the Process Owner or Project Lead has changed the scope of

---

[16] www.itp-commerce.com
[17] www.blueworkslive.com
[18] www.signavio.com

the project or the names of some activities in the process. That is fine. The Project Charter is iterating as it should. Both of these versions should be reviewed with the leaders and the BPI team.

When the team is ready to create the swimlane diagram, I recommend using BPMN Level 1 and developing a BPMN Level 1 diagram at the high level. The symbols are very similar to flowcharting, but you will need a tool that specifically supports BPMN, as described previously. In Chapter 14, we'll see how to use a nice cloud-based tool from IBM called Blueworks Live, which simplifies diagram creation by generating the BPMN automatically from a simple list of activities and actors. It is possible that the organization may choose to stick with a tool that does not have BPMN, but I find more and more are going to BPMN now, and I recommend that you make it part of your knowledge investment.

Figure 24 shows the BPMN high-level model prepared by the BPMN designate. Figure 25 is the Project Charter High-Level Map in flowcharting notation.

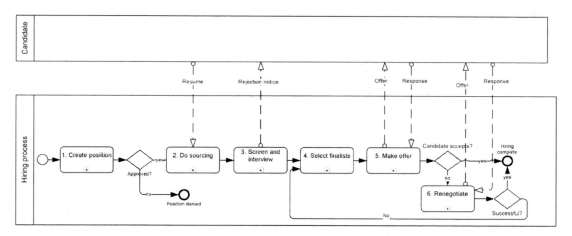

Figure 24. High Level Model in BPMN – Hiring Example

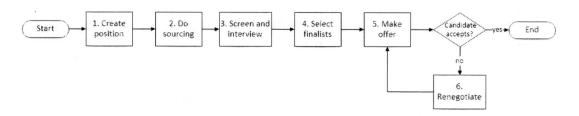

Figure 25. High-Level Map in Flowcharting Notation – Hiring Example

Note that the BPMN diagram (Figure 24) has many similarities to the High-Level Map the leaders originally created using flowchart symbols (Figure 25), with a few important differences:

1. The top-level BPMN diagram reveals the significant exception end states in addition to the normal success, or "happy path," end state. The High-Level Map in the Project Charter will only have the happy path end state.

2. The high-level BPMN diagram shows the interactions between process activities and external entities such as the Customer, in the form of dashed connectors called *message flows*. This places the process in an overall business context that includes the Customer, service providers, and other processes in the organization. These entities are represented in rectangles called *black-box pools*. The High-Level Map does not show these interactions.

3. In further iterations of the model, the BPMN diagram will be elaborated with swimlanes to denote the actors performing the activities. While flowcharting supports swimlanes, I omit them in the High-Level Map for simplicity.

Also note that in Figure 24, each activity has a [+] marker at the bottom center, signifying it is a *subprocess*. A subprocess is an activity that contains details that can be described as a process flow from start to end – basically, what is happening inside that activity. As the team creates a detailed As-Is process model, it will be adding those details.

Now it's time to create the real As-Is process diagram with the team.

The Project Lead should explain the BPMN high-level diagram to the team once any changes have been made to the flowchart from the team input. The team members and leaders will not find it hard to read BPMN if they have a little help the first time once the new symbols and meanings have been explained.

CREATING THE SWIMLANE DIAGRAM

I can't tell you how many clients have said to me, "It takes us 5-8 hours to document the current state process." It doesn't have to. Remember the process diagram is just a document of how the work flows today; it captures the current state. The team is going to look at it and see what is working and not working. They are going to analyze it to identify the underlying problems and find opportunities for improvement. It is similar to a drawing of your house as it currently exists before you do a remodel. There's no need to get every piece of it perfect because it is going to change. But it is helpful to know the steps in the current process, who the performers are, and where the bottlenecks are.

Here is a general timeline that I find works. Bring the team together and set aside 2 hours. It's important to finish this task in one sitting, so don't cut the time short. Allow 3 hours if you are nervous. The Project Charter elements review, described earlier, and diagramming the As-Is instance can be done together in half a day (3.5 hours). Alternatively, you can do the Project Charter review ahead of time, and then the current state swimlane model will take only about 2 hours. I prefer to do them together.

Start with a Single Process Instance

In order to make developing the swimlane model go smoothly, it is helpful to select a *single process instance* – the way that the process worked on one occasion – that the team will follow. When the team follows a single instance, the diagramming goes more quickly. Capturing one instance of a real completed process makes it easy to complete the model in 90 minutes or less, and it won't have the spaghetti look of a process model showing all the exceptions. It shows what happened in that one instance.

For optimum results, pick an instance to start with...

- that is an actual use case of the process and is completed
- that represents a common example of the process
- that had some obstacles but was not the case from hell
- that many team members were involved in

Don't pick one...

- that just one person knows
- that is still going on with the outcome still unknown
- that had lots of special problems

I often ask the Team Facilitator and Project Lead to talk about instance ideas ahead of time and have some suggestions for the team. The Project Lead can even gather some real data about the instance, such as emails or information telling how it started, about specific challenges, or showing sequence flow and how long things took. This is great specific information but will not be a showstopper if the Project Lead is not able to do it.

More instances? Ultimately, the process improvement team will want to model some other instances beyond the original one, but not right away. For example, you will need to capture instances that include each of the exception end states. You also may want to capture additional instances for different levels of complexity, different customer groups, or variations in process at different company locations. Carefully decide which additional instances are useful. Often, after discussing a few instances, the team begins to see what sections of the process are consistent and what sections are not. The consolidated current state model can be the first step in standardizing the improved future state process. Chapter 10 has more information on how and when to create a consolidated model.

I-4 Lists

Remind the team that the objective of this session is to document the instance. Since lots of ideas will come up as the team diagrams the instance, the Team Facilitator captures those ideas using a four-quadrant box called an *I-4 List*. These lists are actually the first cut at analysis of this particular As-Is instance and the current state process in general. Use the I-4 Lists as a parking lot for ideas from the team. Write them on a flip chart for all the team to see.

Issues	Improvement Ideas
Indicative Data	Instance Differences

Figure 26. I-4 List Template

- **Issues** are any challenges or problems that team members relate while the As-Is instance is being documented.
- **Improvement Ideas** are any ideas that come up that are recommendations for changes to make the process better. They could become Quick Wins or part of the redesigned model.
- **Indicative Data** is quantitative data that would be helpful to collect to identify how the process is working at present.
- **Instance Differences** are examples of different ways the process is completed in other regions of the company, by different individuals or teams, for different use cases, or for different market segments. The team is diagramming one instance of the process model, but team members may mention that the way they do it is different, or in this situation the process was different from the instance being captured.

The team will be tempted to go off on several tangents as they explain each step of the As-Is instance. The Team Facilitator's role is to keep them on track, and I-4 Lists are an easy way to do that. When the team names a problem or recommendation, acknowledge it on the I-4 Lists, but do not let them discuss it or try to solve it at that time.

Recording the Activity Flow

The Team Facilitator runs the session and captures one instance of the process. Get a long piece of butcher paper (about 4 feet by 9 feet) and hang it on the wall ahead of time. I like big butcher paper because it engages the full team the best. Have plenty of stickies and a black felt-tip marker for writing on the stickies.

I like to record the activity flow simultaneously in two ways:

1. Using stickies on a large piece of butcher paper (4 feet by 9 feet) in the BPMN format.

2. In a BPMN tool with a scribe experienced with the tool and the notation.

Creating the As-Is Instance using stickies on butcher paper is a light-touch way of documenting a current state model. The team has fun, gets the model done, and identifies issues, data, and improvement ideas quickly. It is very easy to make changes – just throw out and rewrite the stickies.

I find the best approach is to have the BPMN scribe simultaneously capture the process model on his laptop. That way, the BPMN model is done in real time and there is no time delay, but the team is paying attention to the stickies on the butcher paper. Having the team interact in real time with the butcher paper, rather than with BPMN projected from a laptop, avoids several problems:

- The Team Facilitator doesn't have to simultaneously facilitate the group and operate the BPMN tool.
- You don't have to struggle with BPMN from the tool projected onto a screen, which will often have text and symbols too small to read easily.
- Team members won't be distracted by the novelty of the BPMN tool rather than focusing on the process flow.

When the team is ready to diagram the As-Is map using the selected instance, take the following steps to create a simple plan.

1. Write the name of the process at the top. Label it *AS-IS Process*.

2. Select the instance you will capture. Write the instance name under the title.

3. Represent the customer or other external requester at the top in a separate empty ("black-box") pool labeled with the name of the entity. (In the Hiring Process of Figure 24, it is called *Candidate*.)

4. Below it, draw a pool for the process, and label it with the name of the process. Subdivide it into lanes representing the performers and systems.

---

5. The process starts on the left and flows to the right. Insert a BPMN *start event* (circle) to represent the process start, consistent with the High-Level Map. If the process begins with a customer request, label it to indicate the type of request.

6. Insert a BPMN *end event* (circle) on the other side of the paper. It is also on the High-Level Map. Label it to indicate the end state, such as *Job Opening Filled*.

7. Insert a BPMN *activity* (rounded rectangle) for each step in the process, labeled with an active verb and noun, such as *Screen Applicants*. An activity could be either a *subprocess* (denoted with [+] marker) or a *task* (no [+] marker). The only difference between them is that a subprocess contains a sequence of internal steps that will be described later on in the model, while a task does not. Use either one here.

8. Insert a BPMN *gateway* (diamond) for each potential branch point in the flow. Even though we are now following a single instance, make note of points where it is possible that a different path might be taken, and insert a gateway there. Label the gateway as a yes-no question, such as *Offer Accepted?*, and label the outgoing flows *yes* and *no*. After adding the gateway, continue to model the flow followed in this instance. Later on, you will go back and add the other path out of the gateway. By focusing on one instance here, the group stays focused, and it is easier to complete a model in a two-hour sitting. When the team goes back to fill in the other side of each gateway, they ask the question, what would happen if the path did not go the first way? The other path may loop back to a previous activity, skip ahead to a downstream activity, or lead to a special activity only needed under certain conditions. This other path implies a different instance, but we do not want to fully diagram that instance now.

9. As you capture the activity flow, the team will provide additional information about each step that you will record in *I-4 Lists*, described in detail later in this chapter. Keep the I-4 Lists as you go.

10. When the process diagram for the first instance is finished, go back and insert the other path out of each gateway, and possibly insert additional activities performed in that case. But don't spend too much effort on those details.

11. Review the model as a team and make sure all activities have both incoming and outgoing *sequence flows* (solid arrow connectors). Add any message flows connecting activities to or from the external customer if they were not done earlier.

QUESTIONS THE TEAM WILL ASK ABOUT THE PROCESS DIAGRAM

How should BPMN be used? When the team is developing the instance for the As-Is map, I prefer to use butcher paper to show the whole diagram at once, and I use stickies for activities and gateways with pencils to draw the connectors and a few other symbols. So the Team Facilitator should draw the diagram with a black-box pool at the top for any external customer, another pool below it for the process, and put lanes in that for the actors. Develop the instance across the paper using Level 1 BPMN, but don't get too hung up on getting the BPMN diagram perfect. (The BPMN designate will fix it later.) The important thing is to let the team visualize the whole process at once. Using BPMN Level 1 notation and terminology here will begin to get the team familiar with the language and concepts.

If you prefer to document the process diagram on a computer and project it on a screen in the room or need to show it over the Internet to several people, use a software tool that supports BPMN. Show all the steps of the instance and do not worry at this point about how they relate to the subprocesses in the high-level BPMN diagram. That will be adjusted later by the BPMN designate. Make sure the BPMN designate is proficient with the tool, however, as there is nothing worse than having problems with the software to slow down the diagramming.

(Note that some of the examples in this book taken from my client work are done with flowcharting notation, not BPMN. That is because I have been using BPMN with clients only for the last three years and have fewer examples of those.)

How detailed should this diagram be? The As-Is swimlane diagram shows the main steps and decisions in the process and who does them. It is not so detailed that a new employee could come in, follow it, and perform the process perfectly. It does not tell you each field to fill out on an electronic form. Yet it is far more detailed than the High-Level Map. Most processes I have worked on with teams entail 30-60 steps. But major end-to-end processes, such as order to cash, could be much longer, up to 160 steps or more.

Who are the performers? A swimlane – BPMN calls it a *lane* – is inserted for each actor (performer role) in the process. The start event is normally placed in the lane of the actor who initiates it or receives the initiating request. Lane names should be *roles*, like "Human Resources Director," "Accounting Supervisor," or "Business Analyst," not departments or personal names. Departments are at too high a level for lane names, and department names frequently change with reorganizations. Departments include many roles; if you use roles for lane names, you get to see all the handoffs better.

Use a lane for each system that is part of the process. However, if a person is required to interact with the system – even if it's just pushing a single button – put the activity in the lane of the person's role. In the system lane, use a database "can" symbol – in BPMN it's called a *data store* – and attach it to the human activity with a dotted line connector called an *association*. If the system performs the activity automatically with no human involvement, such as *Send all benefit changes to the Benefits Specialist every Friday*, put the activity in the system lane. Don't worry about getting this part exactly right; a designated BPMN expert in the organization can fix it later.

Key Phrases for the Team Facilitator

The Team Facilitator leads the mapping session. All the team members and the Project Lead participate. Here are some key phrases the facilitator uses:

- Ask, *How does the process start?* Begin with a start event symbol with a label. Use the High-Level Map as a reference to remind you where to start. The start event is the triggering event that initiates the process. It could be a customer call, an internal staff trigger, or a regularly recurring event, such as the day each month that the payroll process begins. The label is phrased as noun-adjective, such as *Hiring request received.*
- Then ask, *What is the end of the process?* Again, look at the last step on your High-Level Map to remind you of how the process has been scoped. Insert an end event with a label and put this on the far right side of both the butcher paper and electronic model. The end event represents the *end state* of the process, and should be labeled as noun-adjective, such as *Hiring complete.*
- Now go back to the beginning and ask, *What happened when the process first started?* The answer will be the first activity in the diagram, which will relate to the first step in the High-Level Map.
- *What role performed this step?* Label that swimlane and put the activity inside it. Keep adding swimlanes as they come up in the process. You don't have to list all the swimlanes to start.
- *What happened next?* is the most critical recurring question for the Team Facilitator. It constantly reminds the team that they are recording what actually happened in this instance. Sometimes a team member says, "Well, we do this next," or "And the next thing that happens is...." Stop and ask the team member what actually happened in this instance, not what can happen in some other instance.
- *Should we put that idea on the I-4 Lists?* These log Issues, Improvement Ideas, Indicative Data, and Instance Differences.
- *That sounds like a choice point or decision.* What is the choice here? We need to use a gateway here.
- *What happened in this instance after the gateway?* (It could go a few ways, but initially follow the way that the instance went.)
- *Can you state that activity using an active verb and noun?* This question reminds the team to use an active verb and noun, and helps the Team Facilitator write it more succinctly.
- *Could you summarize that?* This is helpful if you get lost as the Team Facilitator. Or you may summarize yourself and say, "Is that what you said?" Try to use the team member's words, but don't get too long-winded.

When the map is finished, the Team Facilitator reviews the whole diagram with the team to make sure it captures how this instance worked. Make needed revisions, and add more notations on the I-4 Lists as needed. During the review, add the other path out of each gateway.

In the instance just finished, the team mapped the diagram following one path. Now as you review, ask, "Where does the process go when it does not go that way?" Usually the sequence flow will loop back to a task before the gateway that is already on the diagram or skip forward to a later task, and it may be necessary to add one or two other tasks.

Team Facilitator Tips for Recognizing I-4 List Items

In addition to recording these steps and decisions, the Team Facilitator keeps a keen ear out for comments that members are stating directly or as asides about a step or the process as a whole. Examples of these phrases and how to deal with them are given below.

When the team says, "It should have happened this way," that's a clue that there is an improvement idea. Note that to the team, and write the improvement idea on the list.

When a team member says, "That doesn't happen very often" or "That's a big problem," that's a signal that you want to get real data. Write that item on the Indicative Data list. Write something like "Find out how many customer service issues are in backlog on a daily basis" or "Identify how many input requests arrive incomplete." Later, as a team, you will review this Indicative Data list and see which items are the most important to collect.

When a team member says, "We don't do it that way," that's a signal for an Instance Difference. Note it on that section. The purpose of keeping the Instance Differences is twofold:

1. To stay on track and keep the process diagramming moving

2. To identify other types of instances, since you are diagramming the first one the team chose

Diagramming Instance Differences

After the initial process diagramming session, the team should review the list under Instance Differences to see if other instances are important to document or not. Sometimes a team decides that other instances may be quite different, and they complete additional process diagrams of them separately; sometimes the team decides the instances are pretty similar and there is no need to do that. The team might also feel that a certain subprocess is handled differently, and they want to document the difference of just that subprocess.

In the working session, the Team Facilitator honors that there is an instance difference and writes it down, but does not include it in the process diagram. I have found that when teams try to include all the instances in a single diagram to start, they get very confused, it takes them much longer, and they can end up creating "spaghetti diagrams." It is easier and faster to start with one instance.

Finishing Up

There are a few steps left to finish up these process diagrams.

- Distinct end states of the process – how did it end, successfully or in some exception condition? – should be represented by separate end events. Each end event should be labeled with the name of the end state, typically a Noun-adjective phrase, such as *Hiring Complete* or *Position Cancelled*. Check to see if this instance includes all the exception end states of the BPMN top-level model. If it does not, choose another instance that ends in the exception state, and add it to the first instance to show just the major steps (not fine detail) leading to the exception end state.
- Now add *message flows* (dashed connectors) to and from the customer, who should be represented by a *black-box pool*, as shown in Figure 24. Label each message flow with the name of the message, a noun, such as *Hiring Request*. The message flows connect to the boundary of the Customer pool and to activities (plus Message start event) in the process. You may have to go back and review these and adjust after completing the additional instances.

The As-Is Swimlane Map

The resulting As-Is Swimlane Map using BPMN is shown in Figure 27. So-called "flat" models like this that show all the individual steps in a single diagram are most readily viewed on large butcher paper taped up to the wall. In a digital tool you need to pan and zoom to see it all. For readability, we've split it into two separate Figures here.

A few things to note in this diagram:

- The Candidates are not shown as a lane inside the process because in BPMN they are technically outside the process. Instead they are represented as a black-box pool interacting with process activities via message flows.
- In BPMN, gateways do not "make" decisions; only activities do that. Gateways merely test a condition, often the result of a decision made in the preceding activity. The condition determines which path is taken out of the gateway. For example, an activity *Approve Position* makes the decision whether or not to approve. A gateway following that activity splits the flow into two alternative paths representing the conditions *Approved* and *Rejected*.
- The success and exception end states of this process, *Position Filled* and *Position Denied*, are indicated as separate end events labeled with the name of the end state.
- The HR System has been given its own swimlane, but in it we do not have activities. The activities that interact with the HR System are shown in the lanes of their human performers because they are the ones that initiate the action. In the HR System lane we

use a *data store* shape to indicate the information that is either queried or updated by that activity. The dotted line connector from the activity to or from the data store is called a *data association*. Data associations into the data store indicate updates; data associations out of the data store represent queries.

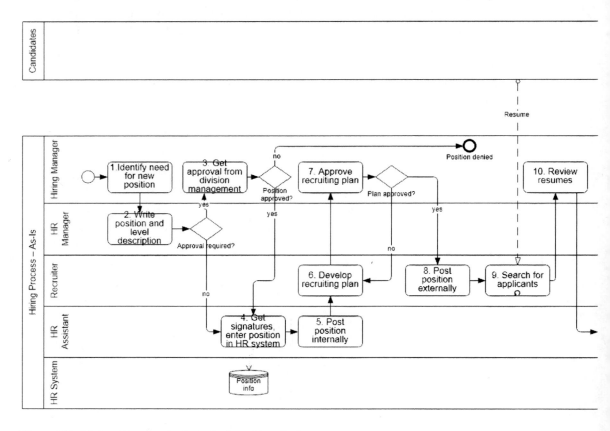

Figure 27. Hiring Process, As-Is Swimlane Map (left)

This diagram was created in Process Modeler for Visio from itp commerce. In Chapter 14, we'll see how to create it in a different tool, IBM Blueworks Live.

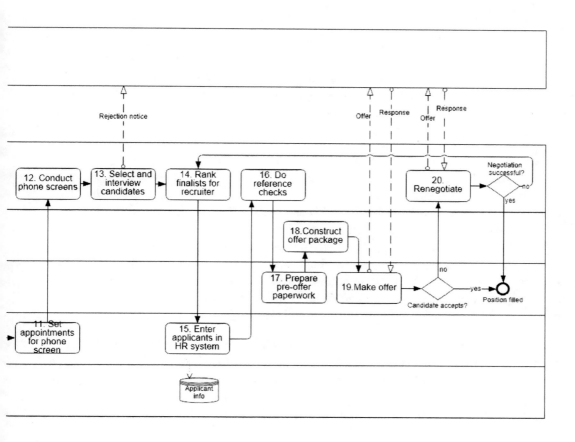

Rejection notice

Offer   Response   Response

Offer   Offer

12. Conduct phone screens

13. Select and interview candidates

14. Rank finalists for recruiter

16. Do reference checks

20. Renegotiate

Negotiation successful?

no

yes

18. Construct offer package

17. Prepare pre-offer paperwork

19. Make offer

no

Candidate accepts?   yes   Position filled

11. Set appointments for phone screen

15. Enter applicants in HR system

Applicant info

MAKING THE MODEL HIERARCHICAL

Flat models like the one in Figure 27 usually do not fit on a standard sheet of paper or computer screen, and when you scale it down to fit, the text is illegible. In the live working sessions with the BPI Project team, that's OK, since the team is going to use the large butcher paper as an instance example and then for initial process analysis. But as the team eventually standardizes and improves on the process, it is important to turn it into a more shareable, long-lived digital asset, leveraging the BPMN model in the software tool.

To do that, it is best to transform the flat model into a *hierarchical model* using subprocesses. The top-level diagram, like the High-Level Map, contains only 6-10 activities, in this case subprocesses. Details of the flow inside each subprocess are modeled in separate *child-level diagrams*, each a process flow from start event to end event. The top-level diagram provides a simple high-level view of the end-to-end process, including interactions with the Customer, and you can drill down to see any level of detail via the child-level diagrams. For maintainability, this is better than creating separate models for high-level and detailed views, with the challenge of keeping them in sync as the process model is refined. Thus, hierarchical BPMN better preserves the process model as a long-lived digital asset, and makes it more shareable outside the immediate project team and between business and IT.

Properly structuring the hierarchy takes a bit of experience and practice with BPMN, and it should not be the focus of the BPI Project team. It is better left to a designated BPMN expert in the organization after the initial documentation and analysis is complete, before creating an improved future-state process. Bruce Silver's book *BPMN Method and Style*[19] describes a procedure for creating it, which I briefly summarize here.

The procedure takes as its input the flat process diagram we have just completed, and reorganizes the information in a top-down manner. By top-down, I mean that the process is first decomposed into 6-10 activities – just like the High-Level Map. This is the *top-level BPMN diagram*. Typically each activity in it has a [+] marker in the bottom center, indicating it is a *subprocess*, an activity containing child-level details. Then each of those subprocesses is similarly decomposed into 6-10 activities, each in its own *child-level diagram*. In most BPMN tools, subprocesses are connected via hyperlinks to their corresponding child-level diagram, but as we shall see in Chapter 14, IBM Blueworks Live can expand each subprocess in place, essentially combining the flat and hierarchical models into one.

The procedure for going from a flat model to a properly structured hierarchical one sounds simple, but it can be tricky and takes some practice. For example, when an exception flow loops

---

[19] www.bpmnstyle.com

---

back to a previous step in the flat model, that step must be the first one in a subprocess in the hierarchical model. It's best not to do this conversion live with the team. Instead, have someone familiar with BPMN do it on their own, starting from the flat diagram created by the team. Creating the top-level diagram is similar to creating the High-Level Map, with the additional constraint that every activity in the flat model must be included somehow within one of the 6-10 top-level activities. The flat-model activities implicitly contained in each subprocess in the top-level BPMN will be shown explicitly in the child-level diagram for that subprocess. As it turns out, the translation from a flat model to hierarchical with the Hiring example is not very complicated.

Normally, we do not use lanes in the top-level diagram, because each top-level activity typically contains child-level activities performed by multiple roles. The High-Level Map in BPMN, such as we created in Figure 24, is a good starting point for the hierarchical As-Is model, where it becomes the top-level diagram. Figure 28 through Figure 32 illustrate the entire hierarchical model. Top-level activities Make offer and Renegotiate have no further detail, so no child-level diagrams are required for them.

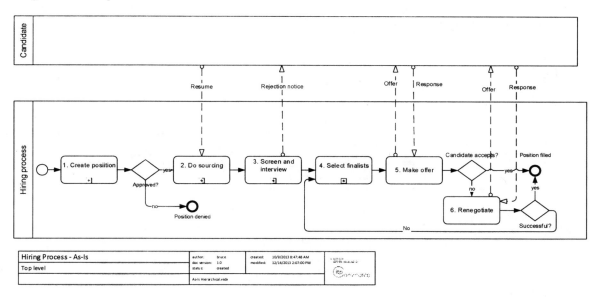

Figure 28. As-Is Hierarchical Model, Top Level

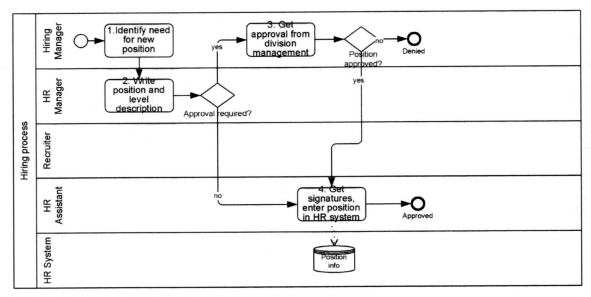

Figure 29. As-Is Hierarchical Model, Child Level *Create Position*

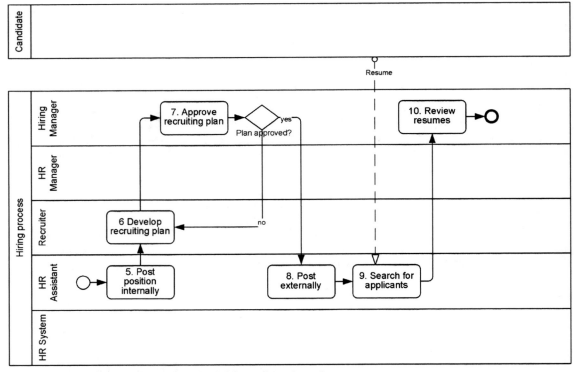

Figure 30. As-Is Hierarchical Model, Child Level *Do Sourcing*

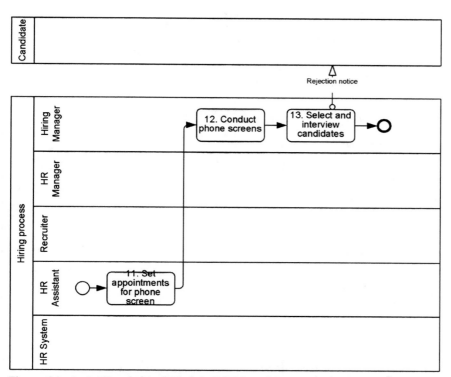

Figure 31. As-Is Hierarchical Model, Child Level *Screen and Interview*

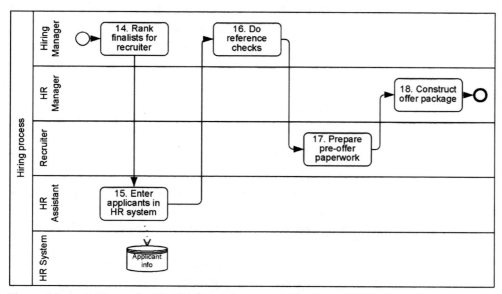

Figure 32. As-Is Hierarchical Model, Child Level *Select Finalists*

For more discussion on hierarchical modeling in BPMN, I refer you to *BPMN Method and Style*.

Completing a detailed swimlane diagram of the current state process is a lot of work. When you are done, how will you know your efforts have been successful? Here are some key indicators.

Indicators for Measuring Success of Documenting Current State Diagrams

- The team reviews it and says that's what happened.
- Others can follow the symbols and relate the same workflow, using the appropriate notation from the chosen modeling tool.
- All sections of the process are accurate from the SME performer's view.
- Other employees affirm the items on the I-4 Lists and add some additional examples of their own.
- During the swimlane diagramming session with the team, employees begin to think in terms of process.

SUMMARY

The As-Is process diagram provides a graphic of the current process, which is the basis for the team's analysis. When the team starts with a single instance and uses the I-4 Lists, they can complete this diagram in 2 hours or less. And the team gets to see what the process is and how a model is developed. Key elements for a productive modeling session are:

- Choosing a relevant instance
- The Team Facilitator keeping the team on track
- Finishing the model in one sitting
- Using the I-4 Lists to document the ideas
- Using a standard language for diagramming – BPMN

The team and organization benefit from...

- Mapping the process together, seeing the end-to-end process visually, clarifying what they do and what others do, and contributing ideas
- Moving to a process orientation by seeing work as a process vs. blaming individuals or holding specific departments accountable for errors
- Engaging the cross-functional team together so that they begin seeing the problems in the current process and begin working as a group for the benefit of the organization vs. staying positioned in their silos

---

- Recommending improvements to streamline the process that will make it more efficient and effective across stakeholder boundaries. These can be longer term improvements or Quick Wins that come up just from doing the process diagram.

Because BPMN is a standard, your swimlane model can be communicated and shared not only within the immediate process improvement project but also across the organization to other teams, and to IT, even if they use a different modeling tool. I can't tell you how often clients tell me, "We have already modeled our current state processes." I always say, "Great. We will build off that work." But later when I look at these models, I often don't understand them. The person who created them used flowchart symbols and other symbols in a "creative" way, and only he or she can read the model.

So create As-Is models describing the process flow using stickies on the wall, and capture it in BPMN simultaneously. Then go back and review the BPMN process diagram with the team. Even though they may not be able to build it themselves, the team will soon be able to read the BPMN diagram easily. And the BPMN process model conveys the logic of the process unambiguously from the diagram.

THINGS TO THINK ABOUT

BPMN BASICS

If you want to learn more about BPMN, I recommend Bruce Silver's book *BPMN Method and Style*,[20] his live-online course of the same name,[21] or his gamification-based eLearning app bpmnPRO. [22] More information on these is available on www.brsilver.com and www.BPMessentials.com. All of them teach you not only the meaning and usage of the BPMN shapes and symbols you need to learn (and the ones you can ignore) but, in addition, prescriptive guidance that ensures that the meaning of your process model is clear and complete from the diagram on its own.

In the meantime, below is a very brief introduction to the notation of BPMN Level 1.

---

[20] www.bpmnstyle.com
[21] www.bpmessentials.com
[22] www.brsilver.com/bpmnpro/

Activity

An *activity* (Figure 33), represented by a rounded rectangle, represents some work performed in the process. Every activity is either a *task* or a *subprocess*. The only difference between them is that a task has no internal steps that are defined in the process model, whereas a subprocess does. A task requiring a person, called a *User task*, is denoted by a head-and-shoulders icon in the upper left corner of the rectangle. A task that is performed automatically with zero human involvement, called a *Service task*, is denoted by a gears icon in the upper left. There are additional task types, but the BPMN Level 1 working set includes just these two.

Subprocesses can be represented in one of two ways. Some tools, like IBM Blueworks Live, can toggle between them, but most cannot. A *collapsed subprocess* is marked by a [+] icon in the bottom center, indicating that the activity contains internal steps described in the model in a separate child-level diagram. The child-level diagram looks just like a process, a flow of activities from start event to end event.

Alternatively, an *expanded subprocess* is an enlarged rounded rectangle with the child-level flow drawn inside it on the same page.

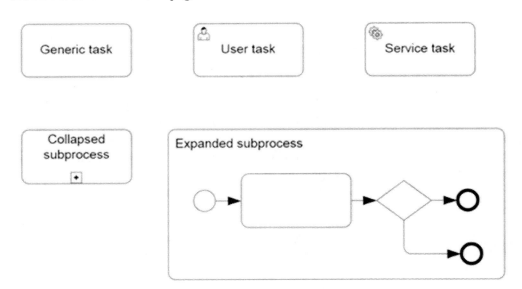

Figure 33. Activities in BPMN

Gateway

Gateway (Figure 34), the diamond shape, represents a branch point in the flow. Different gateway types are denoted by markers inside the diamond. A gateway with no marker, the

---

Swimlane Mapping for Non-Swimmers

most common, is called an *exclusive data-based gateway* or an *XOR gateway*. (You sometimes also see it with an X inside, which means exactly the same thing.) An XOR gateway means an instance will follow one of the outgoing paths, based on the result of some data condition. Unlike flowcharting, a gateway in BPMN does not make a decision, such as approving a request or determining that form data is complete. Making the decision requires a task. The gateway then follows the decision task to branch one way or another based on the result of the decision.

An XOR gateway may have two or more outgoing paths, called *gates*. If only two, it is common to label the gateway as a question and label the gates yes and no. With XOR gateways, any process instance just follows one of the gates.

The *parallel gateway*, also called *AND gateway*, has a + marker inside. It means that the instance is split into two (or more) paths that are all followed in parallel, that is, at the same time. The parallel split is unconditional, meaning it happens in every process instance. For that reason, do not label the outgoing sequence flows from an AND gateway, as a sequence flow label implies a condition.

Flows split from an XOR gateway can be merged directly, since any instance follows one or the other, not both at the same time, but the same is not true for AND gateways. Directly merging parallel paths would trigger activities following the merge multiple times, which is never what you mean. You must insert another parallel gateway called a *join* – with multiple incoming sequence flows and one outgoing sequence flow – to merge parallel flows.

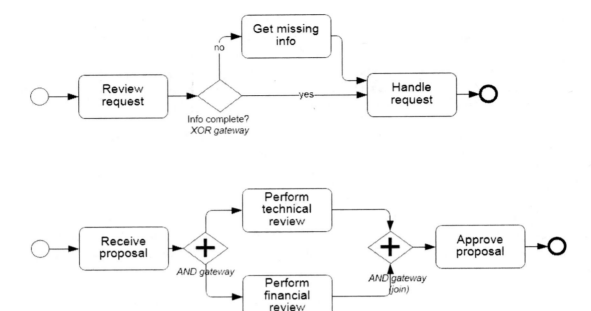

Figure 34. Gateways in BPMN

As with activity, there are additional gateway types, but the Level 1 working set incudes just these two.

Event

Events (Figure 35), the circle shapes, denote the start and end of a process or subprocess. The Level 1 working set includes *start events*, with a thin border, and *end events*, with a thick border. You may also see intermediate events with a double-ring border, but these are outside the Level 1 set.

An optional icon inside the circle indicates the *trigger*. A *Message start event*, with an envelope icon, means the process is started upon receipt of an external request, such as from the Customer. The request is shown as a message flow from the Customer pool to the start event. This is the most common situation. A *None start event*, with no trigger icon, means the process is started manually by a task performer inside the organization providing the process. A *Timer start event*, with a clock icon, signifies a recurring process.

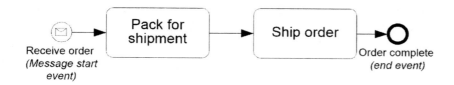

Receive order
(Message start
event)

Order complete
(end event)

Figure 35. Events in BPMN

Pool and Lane

A *pool* (Figure 36) is a rectangle enclosing the process. Essentially, it separates things inside the process from things outside. Drawing the process pool is optional, but it's a good place to put the process name in the diagram (as the pool label).

In addition to the process pool, which contains activities, gateways, and events, external entities such as the Customer (and other processes inside your organization) may be shown as *black-box pools*. Black-box pools are completely empty – no activities, no lanes, nothing at all inside them.

Lanes are subdivisions of a process pool, corresponding to the swimlanes of traditional flowcharts. They represent the performers of the activities inside them. Since gateways and events have no performer, lanes really apply only to activities.

Sequence flows, the solid arrows, connect activities, gateways, and events inside a process. Every activity, gateway, and event must lie on a continuous chain of sequence flows leading from start event to end event. A sequence flow may not connect outside the process, for example, to another pool.

Message flows, the dashed arrows, represent communications between the process and entities outside the process. They are drawn to the boundary of a black box pool and to a Message event or activity inside the process. They may not connect two elements within the process, for example, in different lanes.

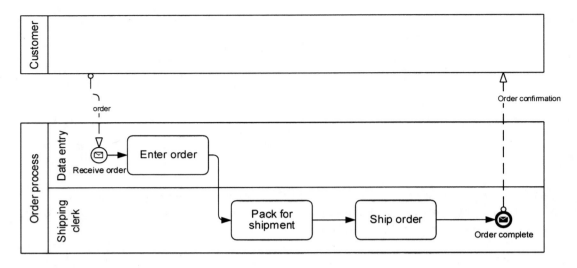

Figure 36. Pools and Lanes in BPMN

Data Flow

Data flow is not a principal focus of BPMN, but the notation allows some representation of data in the diagram (Figure 37). Representing data in BPMN diagrams is *completely optional* and not frequently done.

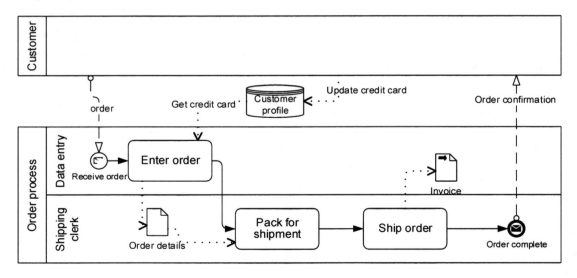

Figure 37. Data Flow in BPMN

A *data store* (the "can" shape) represents any information stored in a file, database, or application. It should be labeled with the name of the information, such as *Job Openings*, not the name of the system or database that holds it. A data store should be connected to a process activity or black-box pool with a dotted line arrow connector called an *association*. If the arrow points into the data store, it represents creating, updating, or deleting the information. If the arrow points out of the data store, it represents querying and retrieving the information.

A *data object* (dog-eared page shape) represents temporary data accessible only inside an active process. When an output of one activity is passed to another downstream activity, draw one association from the first activity to the data object and a second association from the data object to the downstream activity. In diagrams used in BPI Projects, you probably should be using data store, not data object.

Arrow symbols inside the data object shape turn it into a data input or data output of an activity. A *data input* (white arrow) represents information required by the activity, and a *data output* (black arrow) represents data output by the activity. Use associations to link the data input or data output to the activity shape.

CHAPTER 6

WHAT TO MEASURE AND WHY?

The purpose of tracking process metrics is to make decisions and take action. These measures provide the quantitative data to make decisions objectively. Organizations are used to tracking certain measures, such as monthly and quarterly financials, head count and personnel cost, and weekly production data, but most companies do not have measures for their processes and subprocesses. The reason for this is that companies tend to measure at the functional or system level. They don't often think cross-functionally, and their organizations are not managed from an end-to-end process perspective.

Measuring processes is critical, but you want to have a clear understanding of what will be done with the metric once it is gathered. For the process improvement project, it will be some combination of the following:

- Understand the current situation
- Improve the process
- Monitor the process against history, a competitor, or a benchmark
- Determine the size of a gap from the target goal and prioritize projects

This chapter will explain key categories of measures, needed measures at different points in the process, and methods for selecting and gathering data in each phase of a BPI Project and beyond in the Continuous Monitoring and Sustaining stage.

TYPES OF MEASURES

Metric Categories

Customer satisfaction metrics are data from the customer: what they want or require from the process, and how it is currently performing from the customer's point of view. In the Hiring process, the internal customer is the Hiring Manager, and an example of a customer satisfaction metric would be the degree to which the qualifications of the candidates provided match the Hiring Manager's requirements.

Waste-directed metrics describe sources of inefficiency in the process. They include items like waiting, defects, inaccurate data, and rework. They are explained in detail in Chapter 8, but many of them will have been listed under Issues in the I-4 Lists. One example of waste-directed metrics from the Hiring process is multiple signatures. The detailed categories for wastes discussed in Chapter 8 overlap with time and quality metrics below. In fact, wastes are the most comprehensive category for data gathering and metrics, but it is still helpful to consider time and quality metrics specifically, especially if they are included in the Improvement Targets.

Time metrics include *cycle time,* the total duration of a process or subprocess; *process time,* how long each activity takes with no interruptions; *wait time* between steps or within steps, etc. Examples of time metrics in the Hiring Process include how long it takes for the Hiring manager to prequalify the prospective candidates and how long it takes the recruiter to prepare a recruiting plan.

Cost metrics provide cost data for personnel, equipment, facilities, process segments, wastes, etc. They put a dollar value on direct costs and indirect costs of an individual process element and for the process as a whole. In the Hiring Process, a cost metric might be the cost to hire an employee for a single instance, and variations in values between instances and between job classifications.

Quality metrics reveal how well some process output is meeting customer requirements or output specification. In the Hiring Process, a quality measure could be the percentage of prospective candidates that meet the minimum job requirements agreed by the Recruiter and Hiring Manager.

Volume metrics show the quantity of items at a certain point in the process or produced as output. This count is critical for many processes because the total quantity tells of the size of the item or occurrence, which often indicates its importance. For example, in banking, the number of transactions of a certain type is a volume metric.

In addition to the categories listed above, additional process metrics include profitability, repeat business, market share, throughput, resource utilization, and productivity, to name a few. The choice of metrics employed depends on the project objectives and what decisions and actions will be taken from the measure. The six categories of measures above are enough to keep it simple and be successful.

Properties of Metrics

Metrics can also be classified as quantitative or qualitative, and leading vs. lagging indicators.

Quantitative measures capture a specific number, count, or physical magnitude. If possible, it is always best to get quantitative data because it is objective. It represents what is happening in the process now, or designates a specific goal value desired in the future. Quantitative process data can be gathered in many ways, including real time instances captured in BPMS, from reports summarizing data, from data mining, from surveys, and from observation.

Qualitative data is usually more ambiguous. It uses more general terms (such as satisfactory, large, infrequent) and comes from informal sources, such as personal stories. It does not have an objective quantifiable count, but can be useful to provide ideas and context for items that could later be quantified. In composing the I-4 Lists with the process diagrams, the process participants provide anecdotal qualitative information from their own experience.

Leading Indicators are measures at an early step in the process that identify the health of the process. The leading indicator gives a signal as to whether the process is on track or not toward the necessary output. A leading indicator enables the employee or manager to monitor the process before completion and intervene to make adjustments as needed. For example, if the output is accurate invoices, then a leading indicator might be the completeness and accuracy of the buyer's information at the time of product request.

Lagging Indicators also provide information on the health of the output, but they happen late in the process. A lagging indicator example would be the number of warranty claims for a washing machine. Clearly, if warranty claims increase, there are some problems with the washing machines or their installation. Lagging indicators are used to monitor trends overall.

Where Metrics Occur in a Process

Measures are also classified based on where they occur in a process.

Input metrics capture data about inputs to the process from outside suppliers or customers, either before the process begins or at steps within the process. For the Hiring Process, an input metric would be how much of the hiring request is incomplete. The number or percentage of incomplete fields on the hiring request is a quantity metric; it is also an input metric because the information comes into the process as an input.

Output metrics measure some aspect of the product or service that is produced by the process. This is the most general measure of the health of the process. This encompasses many types of measures, including throughput, customer satisfaction, profitability, productivity rate, and quality rate. Which output metrics are selected for use depends on how the Process Owner decides to measure the product or service outcome.

Metric Values

Measures typically have numerical values.

Baseline values show the starting reference point for the BPI Project – what the data is at present. I use the term specifically in the Chartering and Staffing phase, but a team could collect baseline values for any number of items at the beginning of their BPI Project or during the Process Analysis phase. They are baseline values because they represent the current state.

A *Goal value* is a target quantity that the Process Owner provides to indicate how the process should be performing after the improvements are implemented.

Key Performance Indicators (KPIs) are performance measures that companies use to evaluate the success of a particular operation or the progress toward a strategic goal. They have goal values. In finance, a KPI might be maintaining a margin of 45%; in operations, it might be keeping inventory levels at 10%. In a BPI Project, the Process Owner or Executive Sponsor would select a KPI for the process, and the Process Owner would continue to monitor the KPI and maintain the goal value at a certain value or improve on it. The KPI might be the same metric associated with the BPI Improvement Target or something else.

METRICS AT EACH PHASE OF A BPI PROJECT

Each of the phases uses metrics to provide understanding of the current situation, identification of the gap between today and the goal, and clarification of the size of the problem. All the phases will be using some form of the metrics.

Chartering and Staffing Metrics

The Chartering and Staffing phase uses metrics based on the relevant *Improvement Targets*. The baseline and goal values compare the process today to where the Process Owner wants it to be in the future.

At the beginning of a process improvement project, the Project Charter identifies general Improvement Targets and then identifies measures for each Improvement Target

In the Recruiting and Hiring example, the Executive Sponsor was the Chief Human Resources Officer for the Hiring Process. She stated the current hiring challenges: "We have four different divisions with business units under them. And right now, we have 15 different recruiting processes." Then she articulated two Improvement Targets:

Improvement Target #1: Standardize the recruiting and hiring process for our organization

Improvement Target #2: Make the process more efficient

The first target says the Executive Sponsor wants *one* standard process – not 15 – for doing recruiting in the organization. We can easily identify the measure category for this Improvement Target:

Improvement Target #1: Standardize the recruiting and hiring process for our organization

   Measure: Count of recruiting and hiring processes

The Executive Sponsor kept the second Improvement Target more general by using the term "efficient." So it's necessary to figure out what she meant by efficient, and then to identify a relevant metric with available baseline data that quantifies how the process is currently functioning. The Process Owner and Project Lead decided to use, for one aspect of efficiency, "Time to job fill," meaning the elapsed time from the initial request until when a candidate is hired. The sponsor also wanted to reduce the amount of paperwork in the system, so, as a second aspect of efficiency, the team noted each place where there paper was used or data re-entered from paper into the system. The following two metrics were selected.

Improvement Target #2: Make the process more efficient

   Measure 1: Time to fill jobs

   Measure 2: Count of paper checklists and places where information is re-entered

Baseline Values

For each measure, actual quantitative data must be gathered. Baseline values for the metric tell the story of the current state process. The Executive Sponsor stated in the challenges section of the Project Charter that there were 15 different recruiting processes, so she gave the baseline data for the current situation, namely:

Improvement Target #1: Standardize the recruiting and hiring process for our organization

   Measure: Count of recruiting and hiring methods

Baseline Value: There are currently 15 recruiting and hiring processes.

The team might want to check the validity of this data value; maybe there are 18 methods or only 14. In this case, the team did check and found that there were 15 methods.

For the current time to fill jobs, the team had to find and review emails from hiring managers requesting new hires and then get the start dates of the selected employees as well. (If the Human Resource system had recorded these dates, it would have been easier, but that was not the case here.) As they discussed this measure further, they realized that they needed to clarify the exact meaning of the start and end time to fill jobs and possibly modify the metric. For the start, the date of request by the hiring manager seemed right. For the end, they considered the date the employee accepted the offer vs. the employee's first day at work. For many employees, the first day at work might be weeks or months after the offer is accepted, making that date less useful for the metric. In this case they decided to revise the end for the metric to the date of acceptance of the offer. The Executive Sponsor agreed.

For counting the checklists and re-entering information, the team found there were 22 different checklists and three places where re-entry of information from paper occurred. The final quantified values for baselines for Improvement Target #2 are given below.

Improvement Target #2: Make the process more efficient

Measure 1: Time to fill jobs

Baseline Value: Current time to fill jobs from request to candidate acceptance ranges from 4 to 18 months.

Measure 2: Count of paper checklists and places where information is re-entered

Baseline Value: We have 22 inconsistent checklists and 3 places where we re-enter information from paper into the system.

Process metric data is often hard to collect because it is not readily available in existing reports. It may need to be gathered manually or compiled from information in several reports. For example, for Improvement Target #2, you would need to find emails that tell when the request came into HR and when the candidate accepted the offer; and it would also be helpful to do that for different types of candidates in different divisions, probably for 10-20 candidates.

Checklists probably exist at various steps in the process. Start by collecting samples from the four divisions and see how many there are. This baseline information does not have to be exact. Since it may be hard to gather, pick a reasonable period of time to look at or a reasonable number of data points, and use that number. A range is often better than just the mean. It is likely that the quantitative data gathering will go on in parallel with other teamwork in the Process Discovery phase, and then be inserted into a revised Project Charter.

Goal Values for the Improvement Targets

The Process Owner sets the goal value for each Improvement Target metric. This value shows what quantitative value the Process Owner wants to achieve after implementation of the improvements in the new process. These goal values are part of the Project Charter, but are not articulated until after the values for the baseline are gathered. If the goal values for the metrics are established too early, the Process Owner may just give a thumb-in-the-wind guess of what he wants, not even knowing what the current numbers are.

At least one goal value is needed to show the gap from the current baseline value. Once the baseline values have been quantified for the measures of each Improvement Target, ask the Process Owner to articulate the level of improvement they want, and use that number for the value for the goal. For example, in the hiring project:

Improvement Target #1: Standardize the recruiting and hiring process for our organization.

> **Measure:** Count of recruiting and hiring processes

> **Baseline Value:** There are currently 15 recruiting and hiring processes.

> **Goal Value:** There is one standard recruiting process for the organization.

In this simple situation, the Executive Sponsor wanted a single recruiting process. She might also have selected another value for the goal, such as Reduce the number of recruiting processes to no more than three, but she did not.

Improvement Target #2: Make the process more efficient.

> **Measure 1:** Time to fill jobs

> **Baseline value:** Current time to fill jobs from request to candidate acceptance ranges from 4 to 18 months.

> **Goal value:** Time to fill jobs from request from hiring manager to candidate acceptance is 6 weeks to 9 months.

> **Measure 2:** Count of paper checklists and places where information is re-entered

> **Baseline value:** We have 22 inconsistent checklists and 3 places where we re-enter information from paper into the system.

> **Goal value:** Standardized formats are accessible and readable in one system. No re-entry of data is needed.

Goal values for the metric set the size of the Improvement Target. Smaller increases over baseline values are expected for processes with a narrower scope. Larger goal values imply a larger stretch, and are expected in larger cross-functional projects or enterprise projects.

Process Modeling Phase Metrics

Metrics are implicitly articulated and gathered in the Process Modeling phase when the team identifies *Indicative Data* as part of the I-4 Lists. This is an informal way of identifying data the team might like to collect in the Process Analysis phase.

Process Analysis Phase Metrics

During the Process Analysis phase, the team identifies *wastes* in the process, inefficiencies such as defects, wait time, or excess work related to inventory. (See Chapter 8 for the details on how to do Process Analysis.) The team investigates these wastes and gathers data on them to determine how to eliminate them and close the gap between the current baseline value and the goal value.

One technique is to add data indicators to the swimlane As-Is diagram. The team already gathered some information while compiling the I-4 Lists, namely on the Indicative Data list. Begin by noting the appropriate indicators on the current state process diagram at the step where they happen, or along the bottom if they go with the whole process. They will not yet have measurement values. Then ask the team to notate on their As-Is Swimlane Model other places they would like to gather data because they know it will be useful—in three or four places only. With the team as a whole, look at all the data that the team might collect and decide which three or four make the most sense to gather. Choose data that will inform your progress toward your Improvement Targets, emphasizing places where there are many issues or wastes. Then gather the data and put the actual values up on the current state process diagram as well.

The data gathered during the Process Analysis phase will show the size and range of problems and indicate the greatest gaps from the expected target. Use the data to decide if additional analytical techniques, such as root cause, need to be applied. The size of the gap helps the team and Process Owner determine where to put their effort.

Teams may be tempted to skip data gathering because they think they already know what the problem is. However, such anecdotal data is often erroneous. In one of my client engagements, the team initially announced that the biggest problem was a particularly complex situation that took a lot of time and frustrated both customers and the employees helping them. But when they actually measured the types and frequency of problems in this process, they found that this situation only occurred 2-5% of the time, while two other items made up 80% of the problems. Hard data is critical: to make sure the team is focusing on the right problems, to ensure accuracy in comparing today's "before numbers" against later "after numbers" when the improvements are implemented, and to ensure objectivity vs. pooling the team's suspicions and impressions.

For example, in the Hiring case, the BPI team also looked at productivity data for each recruiter, including how long it took each recruiter to close a candidate and how many candidates each recruiter could manage at one period. The head of human resources had little idea about what the range of capacity was for each recruiter. This data was used to identify the current best practices in the organization, and then to step back and figure out how best practices might be shared.

Collecting data for each recruiter can be risky if it is construed as studying the performance of individual employees and using it for performance evaluation. The team is trying to get process performance data to establish metrics around how many candidates any recruiter can handle at one time. So if these are shared, you need to remove any reference to specific employees and just show the range across the organization. Also, employees as a whole could discuss best practices required to move toward the two Improvement Targets. Do not forget that variation in recruiter workload might be based on other elements of the process, such as how many candidates were needed at a certain time, or how much of a recruiter's available hours were spent on recruiting vs. other Human Resource activities. The point here is that the team is trying to gather baseline data for the process, not for individuals.

Process Design Metrics

Process simulation can provide estimated output metrics for the redesigned process under a variety of scenarios, measuring costs, cycle time, queue time, items sitting in inventory, staff utilization, and others. Simulation scenarios are discussed more in Chapter 13. The purpose of simulation analysis is to compare the improvement expected under a variety of redesigns and configurations. If the redesign involves automation in a BPMS, that system can provide real data to identify the level of improvement. Real data is always the most accurate.

Data can also come from estimates gathered manually by the team in the workflow, from a variety of reports, or from team members' estimates of mean values. It is important to have some estimated data for the new design to see how close it comes to the Process Owner's goal values, or if it exceeds the goal values. So the team needs to identify the anticipated metrics for the new design and be able to explain how the metrics were gathered or estimated for the new design, what assumptions were used as a basis, and how they were calculated.

Implementation Plan and Implementation and Check Metrics

Implementation metrics are mostly not BPI process metrics. They are project management metrics that show whether the implementation team is meeting or not meeting the milestone dates and costs of the Implementation Plan, and any other indicators that the project is getting off track, so that adjustments can be made. Project management metrics should be identified in the Implementation Plan and reported out to the Process Owner and other relevant executives on a regular basis, according to the schedule designated in the Implementation Plan. Since pilots and prototypes could be part of Implementation and Check, these would include some process measures to see how the improvement is meeting the pilot's Improvement Target goal values.

Monitoring and Sustaining Metrics

Once implementation is complete, the BPI Project is finished, but the process continues in the Monitoring and Sustaining stage. The first data to be gathered here are measures to see if the new process has met the goal values associated with the Improvement Targets. Additional data should be gathered to see how the new process is flowing and working. For example, are employees well trained and able to perform their jobs? Are there any bottlenecks in the process? Have the improvements implemented created the expected changes? In addition, it is often useful to measure some of the items that the team previously measured during the Process Analysis phase, such as wastes that were to be eliminated or time that was to be reduced.

During the Monitoring and Sustaining stage, metrics track how the process is performing in an ongoing fashion. At the operational level, employees doing the process use data to make real-time decisions about the process, such as getting additional resources or stopping the process if needed. On a more strategic level, the Process Owner uses metrics to say if the organization needs to investigate an activity or subprocess, or find out what is happening and take corrective action. The Process Owner also evaluates the process for the longer term, comparing metrics to other industry data to determine if additional improvement is needed, possibly as part of a larger enterprise effort.

Figure 38 summarizes the metrics used in each phase of a BPI Project, with some examples of quantitative values. The Implementation and Check metrics are not included, as they are project management metrics. Instead, possible metrics are suggested for the ongoing Continuous Improvement and Sustaining stage, which begins at the conclusion of the BPI Project.

	Chartering and Staffing	Process Discovery	Process Analysis	Process Design	Monitoring and Sustaining
	Measures are based on Improvement Targets, with a baseline and goal value for each metric.	Measurement ideas occur while diagramming current state models in the Indicative Data lists.	Data is based on challenges and opportunities in the current state model, and how it impacts the Improvement Targets.	Data is used to estimate the impact from improvements in the new design. Data from simulations can also be used to test different design scenarios.	Data is used to see how the process is continuing to perform.
Customer Satisfaction	Baseline value: 80% of customers are satisfied with the delivered product. Goal value: 95% of customers are satisfied with the delivered product.	Find out how often customers don't get the product they ordered.	Customer complaints fall into 6 areas, with 2 areas accounting for 75% of the complaints.	Test reducing defects in simulation and monitor change in customer acceptance of product.	Ongoing tracking of satisfaction with goods, services, order process, and customer service
Wastes	Baseline value: Data to complete the data load for the web portal is complete 65% of the time. Goal value: Information for the data load comes in 98% complete and accurate.	Identify defects in the process instance that is being modeled.	There are three places where the process uses homegrown spreadsheets since data does not currently integrate automatically.	Estimate with simulation how much data integration will increase accuracy and reduce time to completion.	Ongoing tracking of completeness and accuracy of inputs, and time for full process
Time	Baseline value: It takes 9-18 months currently to hire a scientist. Goal value: It takes 4.5-9 months to hire a scientist.	Find out how long it takes to schedule the scientist candidate meetings and presentations.	Find out how long each step takes in the process and how long the wait is between steps for hiring.	Test out reducing time between steps expected from new automation using simulation.	Identify 2 or 3 metrics collected in Process Analysis phase and monitor them during this phase.
Quality	Baseline value: There were 139 logged technical issues this month. Goal value: There are no more than 50 logged technical issues each month.	What steps have the greatest technical issues? How do handoffs affect technical resolutions?	Number of technical issues by error type	Simulate how fewer technical issues will reduce time and cost.	Monitor volume and type of technical issues.
Cost	Baseline value: There are 475 items, and 80% or more of items were built at standard cost or lower, Goal value: There are X items, and 90% or more of the items are built at standard cost or lower.	Note where big cost items are in the process.	Trend of cost per product over the last four quarters	Test how changing the big cost steps impacts overall costs.	Monitor standard costs and costs of three biggest inputs.
Volume	Baseline value: 60% of patients in the hospital leave in 3 days or less. Goal value: 75% of patients leave in 3 days or less.	Note steps that delay patient stay in hospital.	Determine top three root causes for increasing patient stay in hospital.	Measure time to needed procedure and impact on length of hospital stay.	Monitor number and percent of patients in hospital for 3 days or less and reasons for extended stay.

Figure 38 Values and Measure Category Examples for the BPI Project Phases and Monitoring and Sustaining Stage

SUMMARY

Metrics serve many purposes:

- They provide data to measure and quantify the change from the process improvement effort. Baseline values articulate the "before" situation. After the improvements are implemented, the actual value measured should be compared to the goal value to see if the improvements met, exceeded, or fell short of the goal value documented in the Project Charter.
- They help the organization see the problem objectively through quantitative data. This is the beginning of developing a data-driven organization.
- They can catalyze action. For example, the team can take the organization's current data and benchmark it against competitors or best-practice organizations and use this data to communicate the size of the gap between the company's current numbers and those of other organizations. There is more on this element of benchmarking in Chapter 13.
- Data measures show the variation in time or processes, identify the range in number of defects or wastes, and clarify what is big and small, often implying important or not important issues. Measures therefore help a team prioritize and focus.

THINGS TO THINK ABOUT...

HOW THE DATA MADE ALL THE DIFFERENCE

Some executives call it performance measures, others call it metrics; I prefer to call it *quantitative data* because much of the negative personal accountability is gone from this term. But there is no doubt – whatever you name it, quantitative data is powerful in understanding your business processes.

Here's why. Quantitative data...

- Is objective
- Is a language that communicates clearly across the organizational hierarchy
- Tells a powerful story
- Visually highlights the critical gaps in your process diagram

Let's take each bullet in turn.

Quantitative data is objective. When you gather quantitative data about your current process, the data shows the size of the problem, the range of the scores (variation), and the categories of problems, etc. No longer are you hearing, "That's a big problem," or "It takes too long," or "We have lots of different errors." Now you have actual values to explain those ambiguous descriptive terms accurately, and you can see what actions you will take for improvements since you know their real size.

In one example, when discussing the role of the help desk, the sponsor said that the help desk staff handled the hardware issues well, but he wanted to train the staff more on applications so they all were able to consistently help the customer. The data showed that there were currently 347 applications grouped into eight categories. He further elaborated to say he wanted to identify the top ten applications in each category and then train the team to handle these basic applications.

It is a language that communicates clearly across the organizational hierarchy. Do you ever wonder why it is difficult for executives to talk with employees who do the work? It's because they speak different languages; in fact it is difficult to speak to others who are more than two levels above you or below you on the organizational hierarchy – unless of course you have quantitative data. Quantitative data provides the common standard language that enables organizations to communicate across multiple levels. If an executive asks about cost, employees can translate the operational data into cost; if the employees wonder about priorities, the executive has the data and can comment on priorities in relationship to the strategy.

One Project Lead of a business process improvement team said, "Having the data made all the difference, and having the data from the sponsor's own department as an example was illustrative of the problem. My sponsor suggested another piece of data I had not known, and it helped in our improvements for consolidation."

It tells a powerful story. Quantitative data demonstrates the urgency of the situation. Data moves from nebulous words like "large," "too many," and "frequent" to numbers that shout out their size and impact. I was working with a client on payment systems and the team said, "We have a lot of payroll systems." I asked what they meant by "a lot" and since I knew very few organizations that had more than one payroll system, I assumed they meant that they have three to five payroll systems. Well, when they went and found out, they had 23 payroll systems. Now that number cries out for dramatic improvement!

It visually highlights the critical gaps in your process diagram. I find it very hard to get executives excited about process diagrams, although I think they are the foundational visual blueprints for process improvement. So I have given up evangelizing about reviewing swimlane process models with executives. (Don't do it! It's a snoozer!) But they are fascinated by what I call a Visual Analysis Map. Here you take your swimlane As-Is map and put icons and data on it to visualize the key problem areas. Voila – you have a graphic to engage the executive. You explain it briefly and the executives add their comments: value from both sides. This conversation deepens the improvement effort – maybe new root causes to consider, new questions to ponder about roles and approvals, or improvement ideas to add to the possible solutions list.

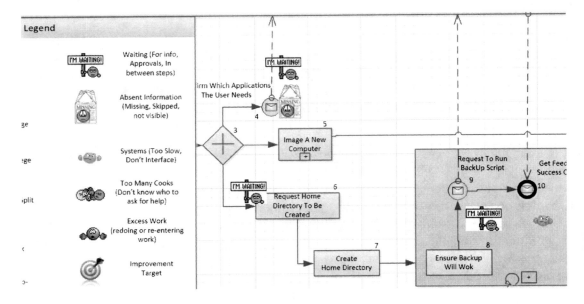

Figure 39. Partial Visual Analysis Map. Source: Kenny Low

One Executive Sponsor from a municipal utility district commented on the impact of the visual diagram to clearly illustrate how many complicated variables had to come into focus to be able to complete a "routine" excavation and repair cycle. She commented that greater granularity of data was needed on both travel time, time to dump and haul, and specifics about the responding worker classifications in order to reduce timelines and the resources supplied.

You may know of more ways that data really helps. We explored four. The good news is that quantitative data is a conversation starter, collaboration enabler, and an idea generator.

PROCESS MINING

In some cases, the data you need to provide baseline values and to map the flow of the current steps already exists in the log files of key business systems like ERP, HR, or CRM. In those cases, new *process mining* technology can scan the log file data to reconstruct the flow of steps, the branch points in the flow, the percentage of instances following each branch, and the time metrics associated with the process. In fact, the results from process maps generated by process mining give a more quantitatively objective picture of how the process really works, as opposed to how the process improvement team recalls it works today.

Dr. Anne Rozinat of Fluxicon developed a process mining tool called DISCO that does this. In addition to generating a process map, DISCO provides actual data on times, bottlenecks, and other issues, allowing the team to see the gaps and problem areas, and decide what to do next. With DISCO, the team can look at the "'real process," discover what happened, and start analyzing from there. Process mining enables the team to gather raw data easily and create a process map directly from real data. Below are some examples of these diagrams.

In Figure 40, the Refund flow is shown for two entry points, via the Call Center and via the Internet. The numbers, coloring, and size of the arrows show the frequency of events. It's obvious from the differences that Missing documents are much more frequent via the Internet, and this causes extra time, because of (1) the needed additional contact with the service provider and (2) the need to notify the customer.

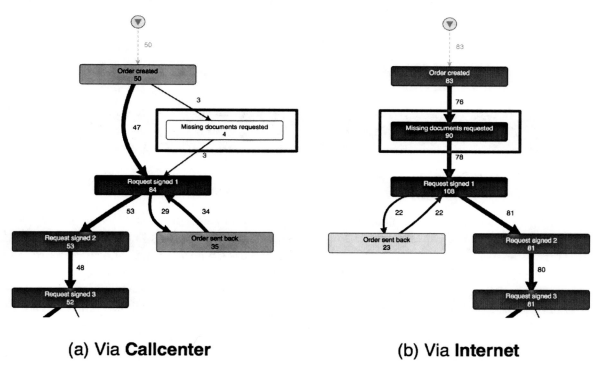

(a) Via **Callcenter**   (b) Via **Internet**

Figure 40. Frequency of flows in current Refund Process.
Source: http://www.fluxicon.com/disco/files/Fluxicon-Disco-Case-Study-Refund-Process.pdf

The Fluxicon DISCO tool can depict several kinds of analysis, including time, bottlenecks, variations, single case performance, process animation, and others. In Figure 41, DISCO shows time between steps. The average shipment from the forwarding company of 16.2 days causes a big delay in the process.

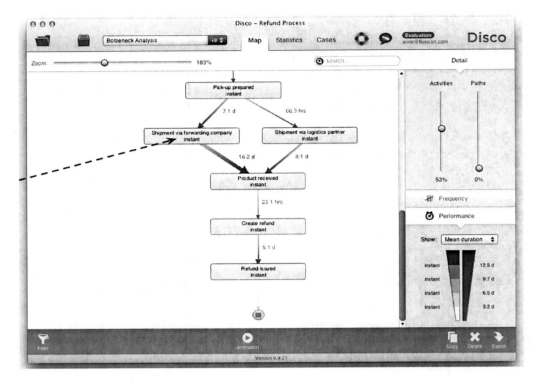

Figure 41. Time Delays in the Current Process.
Source: http://www.fluxicon.com/disco/files/Fluxicon-Disco-Case-Study-Refund-Process.pdf

Another way to get real data is to model and execute the process using a BPM Suite. A BPMS not only automates the workflow but also monitors the actual process and provides real data for further analysis. This data is not the original baseline data, but rather data after the first round of improvements. BPM Suites have been known to let clients develop and deploy their first process in three to six weeks, focusing on basic improvements like automating manual entries, developing simple electronic formats, and building approvals into the workflow. Then when the process executes, it figures the first-round metrics, and the team can work with quantitative data from then on to see what the next level of improvements should be.

Chapter 7

HOW DO WE LEARN TO DO ALL THIS?

TRAINING WITH ACTION LEARNING AND THE BPI STRUCTURED ROADMAP

A BPI Project is a big undertaking. To be successful, leaders and employees need to be trained, and there needs to be a roadmap for all the elements: training, workshops, BPI team meetings, meetings with the Process Owner and Executive Sponsor, orientation, creating the Project Charter, and implementation. The training and roadmap run throughout the five stages of the BPI Project in Figure 42, and this chapter explains how to make that happen.

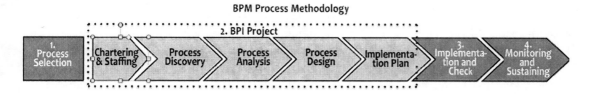

Figure 42. BPM Process Methodology Stages and BPI Project Phases

BPM TRAINING

Which BPM training is best? Well, the proof is in the pudding – in the operational results for the organization and the capability growth for the human resources. For the organization it's important to see process improvements implemented and success metrics achieved. For the human resources – leaders, managers, and employees – the organization expects understanding and advocacy of the business process management principles, development of new skills, and continued usage of those skills. So the answer to the question, *Which BPM training is best?*, lies in the *approach* to training, not the specific vendor, instructor, or content.

There are all kinds of training methods. The basic ones are:

1. **Presentation.** In college it was the lecture; today it is death by PowerPoint. An individual signs up and attends; there is instruction and some question and answer with the instructor.

2. **Self-study,** be it a booklet (traffic school still has them) or on-demand online courses.

3. **Workshop.** Small groups come together to learn something in their group. (My definition distinguishes it from presentation, which entails people coming individually to learn from the presenter.)

4. **Apprentice.** A master teacher instructs one-on-one from his experience through coaching and sometimes on-the-job at the site.

Training can be conducted using different media: online formats, videoconferencing, teleconferencing, or face-to-face. And methods might include interactive exercises that include questions and answers, case studies, skill practice exercises, group discussions, and tests.

So which of these gets the best results? Results need to be measured. Where did the professional capabilities of the staff resources start, and where did they end up? Did the company achieve what it wanted to accomplish? I think the **Presentation** and **Self-study** styles are fine if you simply want to increase the knowledge of individual employees, but without managerial support and behavioral practice the employee's education does not get applied back to the organization. To achieve measurable impact with these methods, you need to send a team of three to six people to the course or self-study, along with a real project they have to complete when they attend the training.

The **Apprentice** method has several advantages. It's learning one-on-one with a real expert. Assuming the Master is a good teacher – he demonstrates first, does it with the learner, coaches and watches the learner do it, and then sets the learner off on his own with a review later – this "see and do" method gives the learner lots of time to practice with immediate feedback. The major drawbacks to this method are (1) it's not scalable to large numbers and (2) it can produce a lot of variation in the process, as different Masters may use quite different methods (i.e., there is no standard process).

For BPI Project training, I think the workshop approach works best. The **Workshop** method brings people together in groups, and these should be particular groups. You might have one to four *cross-functional teams* carefully selected, each one working on a different BPI Project. For the best success with a BPI Project, start with some pre-work before the workshop begins: writing a Project Charter ahead of time with the Executive Sponsor and Process Owner, and as part of that Project Charter, identifying the people on the team. Then send the team to the workshop together. This structure is explained in more detail later in the chapter, but the concept could apply to any workshop approach.

You will increase the results exponentially by having the workshop focus on real work – having each team work on their actual project during the workshop. This method is called *Action Learning*. Action Learning is an educational **process** where people work and learn together by tackling real issues and reflecting on their **actions**. I think the ultimate action learning process is captured with a great basketball team, who start playing the opponents and adjust their game as they play and learn in real time, and with quick team coaching sessions on the sideline for feedback and adjustment.

What this means is that in a workshop offered by my own company i4Process, the team learns skills and uses them right away, applying them to the next steps in their own process. During the workshops, they complete most of the Process Discovery, Process Analysis, Process Design, and Implementation Plan phases of the BPI Project. In addition, they actually apply the skills in the workplace, gathering additional information, gaining more insights (for future improvements to the work process), and reflecting on what is working or not working in their group and organization.

Here's how Action Learning works with the unique *3-PEAT process* from i4Process. I call this the 3-PEAT process because it has business process improvement learning happening for three different teams at once, all in one workshop. If you don't have the bandwidth to handle three teams, put up one or two. That's fine, but there is synergy and efficiency with more than one team.

Quality Indicators: How Will You Know the Training Is Successful?

- The training introduces and builds skills that are needed for the BPI Project phases and members; those skills are different by phase and by role (leaders vs. team members).
- Skills for techniques and tools are applied immediately to the real project of the BPI team.
- The training is iterative and builds, so that skills get reused and new skills are built as the project progresses.
- Training uses instructors for workshop sessions and as coaches for ongoing individual leader-advising or team needs.
- Leaders and team members become more process focused over time, asking more data-driven questions, seeing how different themes come up when analyzing the process, looking across the process for problems and solutions vs. staying in their own silo.
- IT and business team members inquire about challenges and improvements cross-functionally based on the Improvement Targets.

Core Training - Workshops

Figure 43 shows the workshops for the core training process:

Figure 43. Four Core Training Workshops in the BPI Roadmap

Identifying the Project Charter and work team occurs before any workshops. It is the structure that completes the Chartering and Staffing phase of the BPI Project (Figure 43). With the 3-Peat method, the organization decides on one to three projects, and selects Executive Sponsors, Process Owners, Project Leads, and Team Facilitators for each project. Often the organization selects a BPM Program Manager as well who manages the training process and BPI roadmap across the teams for the organization.

In my client work, I act as the outside consultant. I work with each team's Process Owner, Project Lead, and internal Team Facilitator to create the Project Charter, which was explained in Chapter 2. It only takes 90 minutes. This is an essential document, and the Project Lead revises it and maintains it as the process moves along.

After Chartering and Staffing there is a Team Orientation meeting (Figure 43, small triangle) following the first leadership session; it is led by the Project Lead and internal Team Facilitator, and covers the Project Charter (except for the High-Level Map), roles and responsibilities for leaders and team members, why they were selected for the BPI team and what is expected of them, the BPI Roadmap, and a schedule of workshops and meetings. It helps to get everyone on the same page with an understanding of the purpose and goal of the BPI sessions and how they can contribute. It is helpful if the Process Owner comes to introduce the project, explain his Improvement Targets and vision, and thank the team members in advance for their help. The orientation is a one-hour meeting, and it is critical. Without it, the first workshop loses momentum as employees from the teams ask, "Why are we here? Who is behind this? What are we doing?"

After the orientation, there are the four workshops. Other elements of the roadmap and training will be explained in the rest of the chapter.

Each team comes to the same workshop with their Project Lead and Facilitator. At a workshop, they learn skills and techniques and apply them to their process improvement project.

Each of the four workshops covers different terrain:

1. Workshop 1: High-Level Map, team ground rules, current swimlane process diagram, Customer Scorecard, and baseline data
2. Workshop 2: I am WASTED pain points, analytical data, root cause analysis, Notched Timeline, optional analytical techniques customized to the client, and identification of Quick Wins
3. Workshop 3: Benchmarking, value-added steps, rules for redesign, innovative redesign, optimized process, risks, and roles and responsibilities
4. Workshop 4: Second cut at optimized process; Implementation Plan, and presentation to management and guests

In each workshop, the instructor models these different techniques, and the teams apply them to their own process under the direction of the internal Team Facilitator. In Workshop 1, for example, each team builds an instance of their current state map in a swimlane format. In Workshop 2, they identify the I am WASTED pain points and notate them on the current state map. When the teams are applying the techniques with the internal Team Facilitator, the instructor moves around the room and coaches each team. The Project Lead provides subject matter expertise to his team and keeps the team focused on the Process Owner's goals; the internal Team Facilitator guides the team in using the process improvement techniques to model, analyze, and improve the process.

The process takes about three months for the core workshops; additional time is needed prior to the workshops for the Chartering and Staffing phase. Implementation and Check and Monitoring and Sustaining occur after the core workshops. Chartering and Staffing is a critical phase. It can take two weeks to two months, depending on how "ready" the executives are and how fast the schedule can be established. The core workshops can be completed in less than three months. In fact, I have done them in six days to six weeks, but I suggest that you leave some time between the workshops for data gathering, customer interviews, and just soak time.

Core Training – Leadership Sessions

In Figure 44, another element of the BPI Roadmap is added: the four leadership sessions. These are half-day sessions for the Process Owners, Project Leads, and Team Facilitators of each team all together. (So if there were three process improvement projects there would be nine people attending.) The Executive Sponsors come for one hour of each session. The leadership sessions are the ovals at the top of the graphic; one leadership session comes before each workshop.

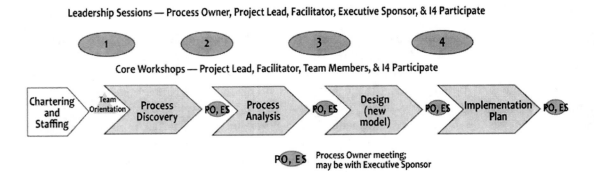

Figure 44. Four Leadership Sessions in the BPI Roadmap

In the leadership sessions, the Process Owners, Project Leads, and Team Facilitators are engaged and trained. They preview what will happen in the next workshop and prepare examples of the techniques they will be using with their teams. (This is an action learning piece for them.) They all need to know the BPM content as well as their role in the project. The Executive Sponsor comes for a portion of the Leadership meeting, so he sees the content tangibles and adds his perspective. In the first session, for example, the Executive Sponsor adds comments on the Project Charter Improvement Targets and vision, and suggests customers that would be good for the team to talk with. In the second session, the Executive Sponsor and Process Owner comment on the baseline metric values collected, and identify goal values.

THE BPI ROADMAP

The BPI Roadmap in its entirety is complicated, so it is best to reveal it piece by piece, as we are doing here. So far we have discussed the Chartering and Staffing phase, the Team Orientation, the four core workshops, and the four leadership sessions. In addition, there are (1) meetings with the Process Owner, and (2) Team Meetings.

Meetings with the Process Owner

There are several hour-long meetings between the Process Owner (and Executive Sponsor if desired) and the Project Lead and Team Facilitator, shown as small ovals in Figure 44. The purpose of these meetings is to discuss with the Process Owner what the team is learning, get his input on data collected about problems and customers, ask for his support for resources and his influence across the organization, hear his perspective on how the BPI team is doing in moving toward his Improvement Targets, and get his ideas for recommended improvements. I recommend the external consultant attend these sessions, too. It is good to have the Project Lead run the meeting, but the external consultant can provide value by coaching the Project Lead or interjecting key questions or suggestions for the Process Owner.

The four leadership training sessions (Figure 44, large ovals) also prepare the Process Owner and Executive Sponsor (if possible) for the meetings they will have between workshops (small ovals) with the Project Lead and Team Facilitator. We suggest these meetings be scheduled in between each pair of workshops and run for 30-60 minutes. They are noted on the graphic with the smaller oval between the chevrons. I provide the Executive Sponsor and Process Owner with a cheat sheet of questions they might ask at these scheduled meetings, and suggest specific actions for them at each stage to support their teams.

The Team Meetings

Figure 45 adds the team meetings, shown as large vertical arrows.

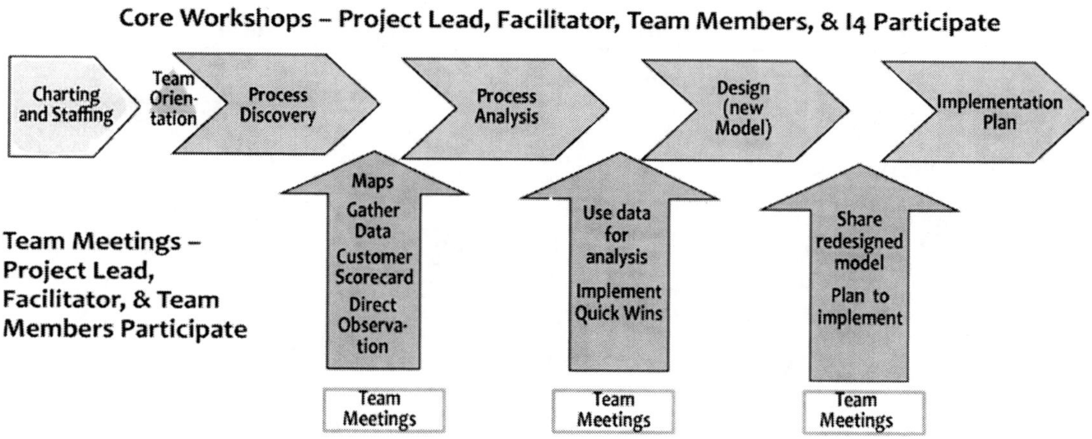

Core Workshops – Project Lead, Facilitator, Team Members, & I4 Participate

Figure 45. Team Meetings (up arrows) in the BPI Roadmap

The team meetings should occur each week. Since core workshops are usually scheduled 3-4 weeks apart, each team will have 2-3 team meetings between each pair of workshops. The team meetings include the Project Lead, internal Team Facilitator, and team members. I suggest they be 90 minutes to 2 hours. One hour is just too short to get real work accomplished. In the team meetings, the team completes the tasks that come out of the former workshop. For example, after Workshop 1 the team could complete other instances of their current state process diagrams, compile the Customer Scorecard, and gather baseline data. It is helpful to have a list of the assignments for the teams at the end of each workshop day.

Team meetings ensure that the team does the needed work and discusses it in a structured way. The Project Lead and Team Facilitator decide on the agenda for each team meeting, and the Team Facilitator runs this meeting. I do not recommend that the Project Lead run the meeting, for two reasons: (1) The Project Lead is needed to provide input as a key subject matter expert; and (2) the Project Lead may not be neutral and could push the team one way or another. In addition, the Project Lead is often the boss of some people on the team and can tend to silence the voice of others. Instead, the Project Lead provides critical SME input at each team meeting and helps to keep the team on track toward the Process Owner's goals and the meeting goals.

I do not attend these team meetings as the instructor from i4Process. It is critical to have the team engage among themselves and build their own BPM skills. Teams really coalesce as a whole in these team meetings and begin to formulate their own ideas – another aspect of action learning. The team meetings iterate the techniques learned in the workshops but enable employees to apply them and reflect on them in new ways. Employees are building their own professional capability here.

Figure 46 shows the complete BPI Roadmap with all the elements combined.

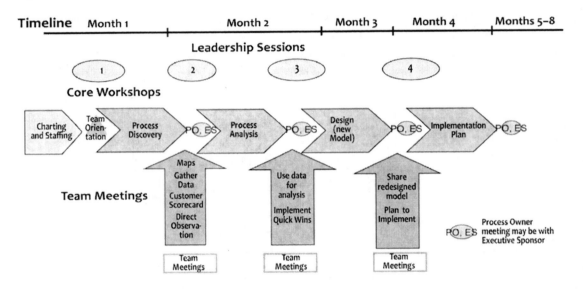

Figure 46. The BPI Roadmap

There is one more element of the BPI Roadmap deserving of mention:

The timeline at the top is an indication of the approximate elapsed time for the whole BPI Project. This timeline assumes part-time teams; in other words, while the BPI Project is important, team members still have regular day jobs. Three to four months for a BPI Project before Implementation and Check maintains an accelerated pace, and allows regular operational work to continue. In my experience, successful projects can be completed in less than 2 weeks, or may take as long as 6 weeks. The point is not to let it drag. Projects that take as long as 10 months are not unheard of, but at that length, it is hard to keep up the momentum.

> ## Quality Indicators: How Will You Know the BPI Roadmap Is Successful?
>
> - The leadership and team members are engaged; they show up at all meetings and fully participate.
> - The team members become empowered; they feel like they are learning from the work and their ideas will be implemented.
> - The timetable seems a bit tight. The team does not have all the answers, but they have enough data to keep moving.
> - Leadership is addressing data-driven and policy questions to the team.
> - Leadership is helping the team with problems and challenging them to wider and deeper thinking.
> - Quick Wins provide early team success and business results, and test the culture's response to change.
> - The Project Leads are ready to take on their role to operationalize the team's improvement.

A VARIATION FOR SMALLER SITUATIONS

Two situations could suggest variations in the recommended Roadmap:

1. If the organization is small and cannot make a team of 6-8 people

2. If the process is simple and the steps and time frame are more comprehensive than needed

In those cases, make the team smaller by combining roles. Don't neglect the charter, but you can shorten some of the workshops by identifying which techniques to use and which to leave out. In my view, four specific techniques are required, and we will discuss them in detail in the next chapter. The organization can also choose to use an outside consultant for the Team Facilitator; that reduces number of people needed from the company but adds some cost. Some of my clients have chosen to use an outside facilitator because that brings additional credibility and expertise to the workshop, and shows that the company is committed to the project.

SUMMARY

Action Learning training is woven into the BPI Roadmap. Leaders and team members have clear roles and responsibilities and have or develop the skills to perform them. Quick Wins (not pictured on the BPI Roadmap, and would occur between workshop sessions 2 and 4) help motivate the team and prototype results. The Roadmap is structured with several different components, and a calendar schedule is laid out from the start, with dates, times, and locations for all the parts. With these guidelines, the project will move along steadily. Watch out for red flags, and pay attention if they materialize, but I have only seen them in 5% or fewer cases.

Chapter 8

WHAT ANALYTICAL TECHNIQUES
DO WE NEED?

There are said to be over 100 analytical techniques and methods provided by three well-respected process improvement methodologies (Six Sigma, Lean, and Rummler Brache). No one expects to use all of them, or they'd be analyzing until the cows come home, but which ones should be used? I4Process works from a set of 19 analytical techniques (not including the additional techniques for chartering, transformation, and redesign). Many are generic and well known in the field, and some are customized by i4Process.

BPM Process Methodology

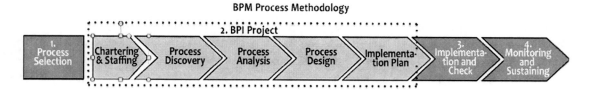

Figure 47. BPM Process Methodology Stages and BPI Project Phases

As Figure 47 shows, Process Analysis begins after the process diagrams have been developed in the Process Discovery phase, although capturing the I-4 Lists while constructing the As-Is process models is actually an informal way of beginning analysis. The I-4 Lists capture issues, indicative data, and instance differences in real time as the team is documenting instances of the current state process. These lists will contribute to the overall analysis.

The purpose of Process Analysis is to look beyond conversation, anecdotal stories, and initial symptoms to understand what is really happening in the current process. It requires objective information from customers and employees, using quantitative data to study the process and find big gaps. It requires listening to customer needs and desires, and categorizing problems so that improvement recommendations are based on a broader perspective. The outcome of this analysis is identification of root causes, articulation of wastes, identification of waste patterns in the process diagram, determination of the size of problems, understanding of customer needs, and realization of the gaps from the target in the current process. By taking time to analyze the process, more improvement ideas surface, Quick Wins are identified, impacts of early problems on later steps are noticed, and relationships among wastes, steps and decisions, and roles become apparent.

WHAT ANALYSIS IS REQUIRED?

First of all, whatever analysis and redesign the team does should be based on the Improvement Targets set by your Process Owner and Executive Sponsor, together with the voice of the customer, and objective data. I call these three elements the *three guiding lights*. These are the guideposts for the later design. If one of the Improvement Targets is to reduce time in the process by 30%, the team had better be analyzing areas that lead to time reduction in the process. If an Improvement Target is to reduce variations in the process across different regions, look at what causes variation and consider standardization. If customers say they need to know where their request or transaction is in the process, consider how to make that information available to them, making the process more transparent. If the data identifies the biggest defects and how much they cost, the team needs to discover the root cause of the defects and figure out how to eliminate them.

I like to say that there are required techniques and optional techniques.

Clients often ask which analytical techniques they should use. The answer is they should use the ones that will help them get to their goals. But in the beginning, teams don't know which of the many techniques (over 100) are best and which to start with. That's how I came up with the concept of the required analytical techniques.

The four required techniques are:

1. Swimlane Analysis
2. I am WASTED Pain Points
3. Customer Scorecard
4. Quantitative Data

If a team uses these four techniques, it gets at most of the problems in a reasonable time, especially if they are working with a simpler process or if they want to find mostly Quick Wins. After doing the required four, then it is important to ask, do we need to use others? In many situations, it will be important to use other techniques to meet the goals of the Improvement Targets. (These other techniques are discussed in Chapters 9-11.)

Quality Indicators – Here's How to Know if the Required Analysis Is a Success

- The team is using quantitative data to prioritize next steps and make recommendations.
- Customer comments have articulated focused needs, which provide new information or confirm what the team already knew.
- A few Quick Wins have been suggested
- The team can tell a compelling story, often using the Visual Analysis diagram it constructs.

Process Diagram/ Swimlane Analysis

Swimlane As-Is models depict what is currently happening. They are the foundation for the team's analysis. Swimlane models enable team members to codify the steps and decisions in the process; the model displays the steps and decisions visually as opposed to a verbal conversation. Often in a conversation people do not realize they are making decisions unconsciously, and they may not articulate them. Process diagrams show the Executive Sponsor and Process Owner the complexity of current practices. They often suggest Quick Wins that can be implemented in 30 days or less.

While diagramming the current state, employees see the whole process and note how their own part impacts other parts of the process. They can identify current problems and suggest improvements. They also learn the basics of diagramming a process and how to use the notations and communicate the flow of steps and decisions.

But the As-Is process diagram provides much more. The picture can be worth a thousand words if you look at it and talk about it *as a team*. Begin with this question first:

What does the current state process diagram show us?

Let team members answer with what they see.

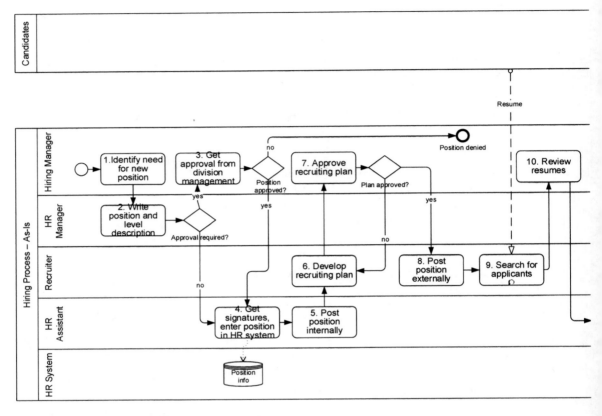

Figure 48. Recruiting and Hiring As-Is Swimlane Map

What Analytical Techniques Do We Need?

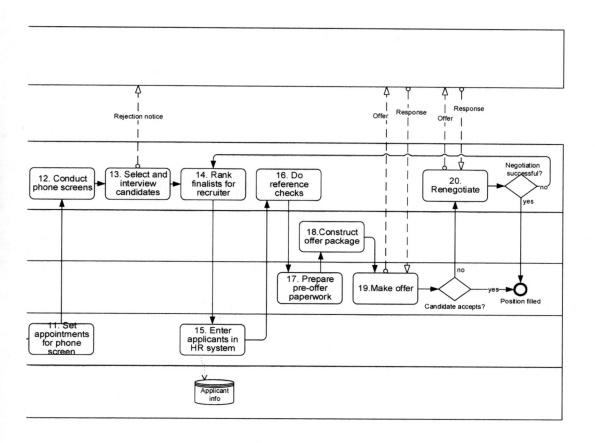

Here are some possible answers from the Recruiting and Hiring As-Is Map in Figure 48:

- It shows us who the players (performers) are and how many there are.
- There are a lot of handoffs.
- We manually re-enter information because systems don't talk with one another.
- We waste a lot of time getting signatures.
- We have some things we could do to improve this process right now.

And so on...

Write this list down for all team members to see, or just let them offer random comments. Keep them contributing by asking "anything else?" Then, for each element that the team raises and a few others you have noticed yourself, ask the next level of question. For example:

Actors

We do have a lot of players. Are any of them duplicative? Could we redistribute the work to reduce the number? Could we train the employees so that multi-skilled employees could do more steps? *Example: I had one manager say, "So much of this work flows through this one role, and yet the role is really just a pass-through. We could eliminate that role in the process and send the information directly."*

Approvals

Which of these approvals do we need? Could we eliminate some of them? Are our policies or practices outmoded, and has that caused us to keep approvals we no longer need? Could performers consult with approvers ahead of time, and then make the decision themselves and eliminate the formal approval process altogether? How could we use electronic signatures to speed the process up? *Example: We were able to eliminate several approvals in one company and drive decision making down to the lowest level – by setting clear criteria for when senior execs needed to review something, eliminating middle manager approval duplication, and reviewing or changing policy or practices.*

Rework

Where is the rework? It is often at gateways with loopbacks to repeat certain steps. Rework often occurs from re-entering data, from systems that don't integrate, or when a department needs to create a shadow system (such as Excel) to get the data to integrate. *Example: I can't tell you how often rework just goes away in a process when you get the right information in at the front of the process and share it widely. One company decreased the process time for the sales compensation by more than 50% by getting personnel information, goals, and incentives right at the beginning of the process.*

Manual Entry and Paper

Where could we automate to reduce the time spent on these tasks? Could we make information available on a system so employees and management could view it there instead? Could we standardize templates to consolidate varied forms of the same task? *Example: In the employee performance management system of one organization, the paper copies of reviews could be kept in any of eight places, and yet sometimes managers did not have last year's review. Was it on a desktop, in a file at HR headquarters?*

Handoffs

When a flow crosses a lane boundary in the diagram, that is a *handoff.* Too many of them slow you down and are sources of error. How many handoffs are there? (Count them and note them on the process diagram at the bottom.) How much time is lost with each handoff? Actually, the swimlane diagram does not show time. Later the team can add a timeline to show time at each step and in between steps. But handoffs increase time, for sure. What else may increase with more handoffs? Answer: misunderstanding, errors. Are there handoffs that are big opportunities for improvement? Here is a place to gather some quantitative data. *Example: The number of handoffs in the current hiring process in an organization was 34. It was reduced to eight in the new process. An additional benefit in the optimized process was that there was a single point of contact, the recruiter, for the hiring manager instead of four different Human Resource roles.*

What to do next?

So there are plenty of ideas above about what can be improved. Don't just talk about them. Gather specific quantitative data to prove the size of the problem. Record them on the Improvement Ideas section of the I-4 List, and discuss which improvement ideas could be implemented now because they are that easy. Often team members leave the process diagramming analysis session saying, "I have that information you need already. I just didn't know it would help you and in what format. I'll start getting that to you this week." An immediate Quick Win!

I am WASTED Pain Points

I am WASTED pain points use the knowledge and experience of the team members to identify different types of waste or frustration in the current swimlane model. Employees who work in the process (the subject matter experts) are a wonderful resource for identifying of pain points because they know the work. And they can't wait to tell you these pain points because they have been experiencing the frustration in their daily life. These pain points are qualitative analysis descriptors.

Prime the pump by giving the team the list below of the I am WASTED pain points, which were rewritten from the Lean wastes to give them a service and information process focus.

W   **Waiting (for information, for approvals, in between steps)**

A   **Absent information (missing, skipped, not visible)**

S   **Systems (don't interface, have different definitions, too slow)**

T   **Too many cooks (need to consult, many approvers, not clear responsibilities, don't know who to ask for help)**

E   **Excess work, materials, inventory, redoing, approvals, re-entering work**

D   **Defects (inaccurate information, change orders, not meeting customer spec.)**

Figure 49. I am WASTED Pain Point Elements

Review the I am WASTED pain points and talk about examples. Note that some of the wastes are not distinct from one another, like Defects and Absent Information, but the point is to bring to mind wastes in different arenas, and this list creates a useful broad range. It is not important to classify wastes in the "correct" category; rather identify wastes across a wide spectrum.

Next, ask employees to identify their top three wastes, categorize each with one of the I am WASTED letters, and write a short phrase to describe the waste, each on a different small green sticky. Employees then put each of their wastes on the current swimlane diagram at the step, decision diamond or gateway where it belongs. If it goes with a subprocess, put it there, or at the bottom of the map if the waste applies to the whole process.

Putting the wastes on the model creates a *Visual Analysis Map*. This visual is a big discussion generator and helps in prioritization. Have someone read all the pain points. Then ask, "What do the I am WASTED pain points tell you?" The team looks for patterns or clusters of waste. The wastes may occur at the beginning of the process, at specific steps, or in one subprocess. Or they may have themes, such as we have a lot of waiting, we are missing information and that causes rework. I ask them to summarize the findings with three bullet points and put the summary on the bottom right of the model. If you use an electronic model, you can use green dots and letters for the waste category as text callouts, with a supporting sheet for the actual wastes behind it. In Chapter 14, we depict the I am WASTED pain points in IBM Blueworks Live using a custom attribute that can be viewed in the tool's Analysis Mode.

Figure 50 is an example of a Visual Analysis Map. The ovals are I am WASTED pain points. The size of the oval represents the number of wastes of each type at the step.

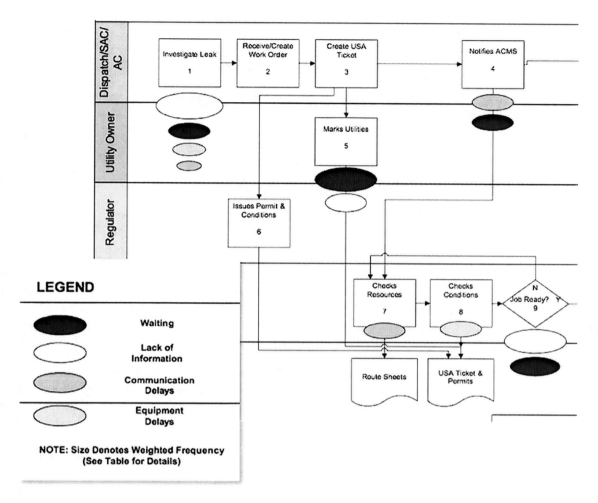

Figure 50. Visual Analysis Map with Wastes. Source: Leann Gustafson

Executives love the Visual Analysis model because it gives a focus for their discussion and generates comments as well. It's a much more powerful visual than just the swimlane diagram.

I am WASTED pain points are likely to represent 80% of the problems in the process, so they provide a pretty comprehensive overall view. The Visual Analysis Map then enhances the pain points by locating them, clustering them, and summarizing them. In continuing their analysis, teams may choose to gather quantitative data or find the root cause of certain wastes.

Customer Feedback

Every BPM methodology includes getting input from your customer, often called *Voice of the Customer*, and there are many methods for gathering this critical input. But I have three methods that are easy for the team's BPI Project and will really help the team learn.

They are:

1. Customer Scorecard

2. Quantitative Data (from or about the customer)

3. Go and See

1. Customer Scorecards

Customer Scorecards provide a method to identify what customers require from the process and indicate the process's performance against the customer's needs today. They help to focus the team. Customer feedback is the second guiding light for the new improved process. It is a critical piece of data that provides a common focus that all team members, the Process Owner and the Executive Sponsor will rally around.

I learned the Customer Scorecard from Dan Madison, and he has a section on it in his book, *Process Mapping, Process Improvement, and Process Management*[23]. I have altered it slightly. Here are the highlights:

First, determine who your customers are. *Customers* –they could be internal or external—are the people who receive and use the output of your process. The customer of the Patient Intake process in a clinic is the patient. The customer of the Printer Manufacturing process is the distributor or end customer. The customer of the Tech Support process is the end user with a problem.

Stakeholders are not recipients of the process product, but their voice cannot be ignored. They are typically significant players who contribute to the definition of quality for the process. For example:

- Regulators are stakeholders; they define constraints the process must meet.
- Senior executives are often stakeholders who constrain the budget, schedule, and scope of the process.

---

[23] Madison, Dan. *Process Mapping, Process Improvement, and Process Management*, Chico, CA: Palton Press, 2005, pp. 129-133.

What Analytical Techniques Do We Need?

- In the public sector, citizen advocates may be stakeholders, since they can disrupt the process if they are unhappy with its operation.
- The IT department could be a stakeholder if they have constraints that limit the availability of IT infrastructure. For example, IT may mandate the operating system or the definition of variables for any software supports to ensure they will blend well with other IT systems in the company.

Stakeholders are sometimes mistaken for customers because they insist on copies of the product, or periodic reports on process operation. But their concern is oversight or compliance. They don't actually "use" the process product to do work; they just check on the operation of the process. Here is an example of the difference between the customer and a stakeholder: in the Environmental Safety Resolution process, the customer is the department head where the accident occurred; a key stakeholder is the Department of Energy, which provides funding to the organization overall. The Department of Energy acts as a regulator that only continues to provide funding if certain safety criteria are met.

Once the customer has been determined, the team identifies the names of 6-12 actual customers they will interview. I recommend that each person on the process improvement team do one interview, and if the team is small, each member should do two interviews.

Now script the introduction to the interview call. It should go something like this: *"Hi, I am Susie Chang, and we are studying our [XXX] process, in order to be able to improve it. You are one of our customers. I would like to get your comments on the process, so we can hear what our customers' needs are. This will take about 15 minutes of your time."* (You probably should schedule the time ahead, but don't send the customer the questions by email. You learn much more by talking to them.)

Now follow the questions below. Think of them as though you are following a recipe for the first time. Don't change them. Just ask them, and you will get great and specific results.

What do you need/require from the [XXX] process? (Get a short list. Ask them to rank the list.)	How are we doing today? (A-F)	What does an A look like?	How have you seen this done at a similar organization?

Figure 51. Customer Scorecard Template

The Interview Questions and Sequence

What do you need, want and require from our XXX process? Give me the top three items. (If they give you two items, ask for a third. If they try to give you five, ask them which are the most important.)

Now ask them to rank these top three items. Since you are doing this on the phone, and you are taking the notes, read them all the items and then ask them to rank them.

Now take the first ranked item and ask: For this need (read it), *how are we doing today?* Give us a grade of A, B, C, D, or F. (If they start to tell you specifics about the grade, take notes, but don't let them elaborate for too long.)

Next ask: *What would an "A" look like?* You want to hear the specifics. They should tell you, for this need exactly, what an A would mean. They are spelling out their requirements in detail.

Ask if they have ever worked with another company or one of their competitors. If they have, ask, "*What was your experience like with this other provider in relation to the first need?*" They could give you another grade and elaborate on why. In this question, you are trying to find out if the competition is perceived more highly by the customer. Often the comment can suggest some simple improvements the customer would highly value.

Now take the second item of the two to three ranked needs, wants, and requirements in the first column and work across that row, asking the questions in columns B, C, and D. Then ask the same questions for the third ranked requirement.

Thank the customer for the interview and tell him what you are going to do with the information provided. Say something like, *"Our team is going to interview Y customers, analyze and summarize what they all say, and use this input as the customer's perspective on how the process is working today and what could be improved about it."*

Analyzing and Summarizing the Customer Scorecard

Once all the team members have completed and documented their interviews, the team (or one to two members of the team) needs to read them all.

- Look for how answers might be categorized to determine what the top three needs, wants, and requirements are for your customers.
- Determine from the grades where the process is performing well, and where the big gaps are.
- Determine whether there are any themes across all the comments, in addition to within each requirement. These might be themes around defects, time, manual efforts, re-entry of information, or poor systems performance.

Summarize all the Customer Scorecards into a single scorecard and display it in a table or chart. Talk with the full team about it, and tell the Executive Sponsor and Process Owner what you have learned from the customers.

The examples below in Figure 52 and Figure 53 illustrate two different ways that teams can summarize their Customer Scorecards, one with qualitative data and one with a bar chart to show the quantitative ranges.

Customer Need	# of Comments, Range of grades	What makes an A performance
Finding qualified candidates	15 A, B, C, D, F	Candidates that match my criteria at least 80% of time; I have tools to filter resumes, I can see cover letter as well as resume, I can see new resumes daily online; want candidates for my particular job not just candidates for company;
Recruitment process	9 A, B, C	Database and history of recruitment plans, sourcing results for job types; specific recommendations from recruiter on top candidates per week; use my ideas for recruiting when sourcing
The offer	6 A, B	Process the offer in 2-3 days; provide guidance on the offer package
Position Description and Posting language	4 A, C	Good leveling of the job; Web posting language represents our company well and differentiates if from competitors
Understanding the process	3 A, B-,D	Clearly understand my role and what to do to get best results

Figure 52. Example of Customer Scorecard Summary for Hiring Process

In Figure 52, the top five customer needs from the 15 interviews are listed in column one. The second column shows how the customers graded this need today, as well as how many people commented on this need. The letters represent the range of grades for each need. The last column represents specific examples of what the customers (the hiring managers) said they wanted in an A performance. These responses do not represent a statistically significant sampling, but this method is an easy way to gain an understanding of the customer needs. If the process is very complex, the team may want to put together a more detailed Voice of the Customer, dividing customers into important segments and using interviews, focus groups, and written surveys to gather data from a much wider range of customers, and with more specifics and greater depth. But this method is a sufficient start!

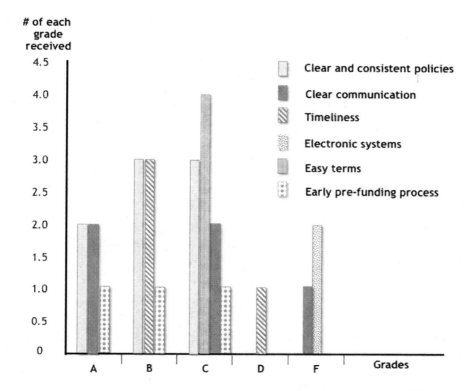

Figure 53. Example of Graphical representation of Customer Scorecard results.

The bar chart in Figure 53 shows the number of responses from the customer interviews for each grade within a particular category. There are six categories:

- Clear and consistent policies – two A's, three B's and three C's
- Clear communication – two A's, two C's, one F
- Timeliness – three B's, one D
- Electronic systems – two F's
- Easy terms and conditions – four C's
- Early pre-funding process – one A, one B, one C

Summary statements the team could make from this chart:

- All four who spoke about Easy terms and conditions gave it a C.
- Only two people spoke about Electronic systems, and they both gave it an F.
- Eight people mentioned the need for clear and consistent policies, and the grades ranged from A to C.

The bar chart makes an easy numerical summary, but the qualitative text comments are important also.

Some Don'ts for the Customer Scorecard

Don't ask the customer, "How are things going in working with our department?" This is not about the department. It is about a specific process the team is trying to improve.

Don't ask, "What's working and not working in our process?" The structured Customer Scorecard gets at that in a better way. And, you don't want a long list of things that are or are not working. You want to know their requirements, how the process is doing currently, and what it would look like if the process were worthy of an A.

Don't worry about getting a lot of F's on the Customer Scorecard. It hardly ever happens. Customers are fair-minded most of the time. If the customer gives you an F, it is likely that the process just doesn't contain that capability right now.

2. Customer Quantitative Data

Customers vote with their feet, so gather and analyze key data about your customers. After you have done the As-Is swimlane models of the process, look at the customer touchpoints in the process. Identify where there are pain points and what you would like to learn about each interaction. I like to take the key themes from the Customer Scorecard and notate them on the As-Is swimlane model at the activity where they occur. This adds more to your visual analysis model.

Here are some simple examples:

Entry Point. One web group I was working with said, "Our requests come in through all kinds of media – system tickets, emails, in-person drop-bys and phone calls." So find out how many of each entry point occur over a month, and see if there are any patterns to indicate what kind of customer prefers which method, and if there are any differences in the complexity of requests by entry point type.

Same Call Resolution. Our customers told us they wanted to get an answer in one call when they called customer service. So track what actually occurs. It's usually easy to do in a call center, where a lot of items are measured automatically. Find out how many get resolved in one call, and pick up some other data while you are at it, like how often a caller's issue gets escalated to another level, and how long the total customer contact is.

Accurate Sales Compensation. In another situation, the company and the sales people wanted to reduce sales compensation check corrections by 50%. Sales people were the customers of this process. When the company studied the process, they asked what the reasons were for mistakes in the process, and used a fishbone diagram (a quality technique described in Chapter 12) to identify the major areas. One of mistakes was having incorrect sales rep goals in the goal tool. Quantitative data gathering across the three global regions showed that the largest area of errors (36%) was from goal sheets not being signed and approved. The team used the fishbone and quantitative data gathering techniques to determine possible root causes. Then they were able to implement simple Quick Win fixes and recommend some longer-term automated improvements.

3. Go and See the Customer

By going to the customer's site and seeing how customers do the process in their own environment, a team member can see much more than from attending a meeting "discussion." Why? Two main reasons:

- Customers (users) are often unconscious competents! They know how to do their work, but they may not be able to explain it to someone else since they have done it so long. Or if they do explain it, they leave out key parts, such as decisions they make automatically without even realizing they've done so.
- The customer's environment influences how they perform the process and what they need from it. How far do they need to go to find information? It could be physical distance or multiple screens on the computer. How often do they get interrupted and how does that interruption impact their work? Who else do they rely on in the process? How well do their tools perform and integrate with other systems and databases?

When organizations do usability testing, they watch users perform specific operations, search, enter information, etc., for a particular application in the workplace. Most organizations do this usability testing with users in test areas in their own company. But Intuit goes out to customers' locations to see what they are doing when they want to design the next version of one of its accounting or tax products.

So go visit the customer's workplace, watch what they are doing, and ask questions to find out more. Whenever I ask business process improvement teams to do this, they always come back wowed. Remember, the customer can be external or internal. It is pretty easy to go observe the internal customer. BPI team members gain real respect for the worker, see the process from a human-centric and more holistic perspective, and often come up with some Quick Wins.

Use all three methods to learn from the customer. Don't ever assume what the customer will say or do. Find out! They will tell you and show you what is important, and you can count the quantitative data to verify the learning or gain new insights as well.

Quantitative Data

Quantitative data is the third guiding light and one of the required analytical techniques. Quantitative data enables you to be objective and prioritize what is important. Later it will prove the level of success after implementing your improvements.

The first data the team gathers is metrics about the current state of the process, which becomes quantitative baseline data. Then the Process Owner designates the goal data, the level he wants the metrics to achieve once the improvements are made. The team needs one to two pieces of baseline data for each Improvement Target in the Project Charter, and each of these needs a goal value as well. As the team continues in the Analysis phase, it identifies other places where quantitative data is needed – from the Indicative Data on the I-4 Lists, from I am WASTED pain points, from the Notched Timeline see Chapter 11), from stipulating activities within the process where qualitative data would be helpful. All of these types of data have been included in Chapter 6 so they will not be repeated here.

In order to make this methodology simple, structured, and successful, I have focused on the four required analysis techniques. Additional techniques follow in the next four chapters, and the team should use these additional ones if the Improvement Targets suggest it. But the four required techniques of this chapter are where the team should start. They may be sufficient for the level of improvement required.

THINGS TO THINK ABOUT

THREE GUIDING LIGHTS: FOCUSING BPM PROCESS IMPROVEMENT

Dear i4Process,

How do I know where to focus?

Here's my problem: every three years our contracts are renegotiated with our customers, which means changes to customer information, contract elements, terms, and pricing. We need to get the right information and then update the contract in two systems, one for the system of record for all contracts and a second time in our ERP system that generates the billing.

Currently there are several problems with the contract data management process:
- *The contract number creation process is quite manual and error prone.*
- *There are costly work redundancies when duplicate contract numbers are assigned to different contracts.*

- *Reporting from the contract system of record is not user friendly and always requires a specialist.*
- *A new initiative requires that contracts be available in SalesForce.com and be accessible to sales people all the time and in real time.*

My boss says we need to (1) improve workflow around contract management, (2) get accurate data for contract management, and (3) utilize Salesforce.com for contract management and transparency.

I work in the Policy, Process and Technology Office of the organization. How should we prioritize where to put our focus in this improvement effort?

Yours,
Overtaxed

Dear Overtaxed,

You are off to a great start. In essence, you've identified the key issues today, and you have some goals from your sponsor. When deciding where to focus, follow the three guiding lights. Keep those at the forefront when modeling, analyzing, and redesigning your process, as you probably can't do everything.

The Three Guiding Lights are:
1. The Process Owner's Improvement Targets
2. What the customer needs, wants, and requires
3. Quantitative data

Since you told me your boss was the Process Owner, you already have the three Improvement Targets listed above in what your boss said.

These Improvement Targets don't have any metrics or values associated with them yet, so there is the first piece of quantitative data you have to gather: baseline data – or how does the process perform today. Find out either how long the current workflow takes or how many handoffs there are. Find out the accuracy level of the current contract data information. Find out what the key capabilities of the current contract management system are as far as reporting and transparency for sales people. Once you have this baseline data, ask your boss (the Process Owner) what success goals and their data values he wants in the improvement process. Now rewrite the Improvement Targets to include the baseline data and the Process Owner's quantitative targets. They might look something like this:

- Improve workflow around contract management by reducing the number of roles and handoffs – currently there are 10 roles and 15 handoffs – by 50%
- Get accurate data for contract management, reducing current defects and changes from 5-20 per contract to 0-5 per contract.
- Utilize Salesforce.com for contract management and transparency. Provide 100% visibility to sales people, standard reporting, and user-friendly ad hoc reporting or searching. The current system has no visibility to sales people, and only specialist-assisted reporting.

Now go and talk to your customer – in this case the sales people – and find out what they need, want, and require of the Contract Data Management Process and what they need in Salesforce.com.

Here you told me the sales people and sales managers wanted:

- Real-time availability of the contract in Salesforce.com. This will make the contract visible and will automatically calculate the margin for the company, which the sales rep currently calculates manually.
- The ability to attach specific contract information when sending out automated quotes to the customer, which they currently do manually as well.
- Further automation of the cumbersome discount approval process and inclusion of this feature with Salesforce.com data.

The customer's needs are different from some of the issues first mentioned by the Process Owner, but they dovetail nicely.

You have some basics, but the Business Process Improvement team is not finished. You need to finish the Project Charter (it is started here), model the current process, see what additional analytical data you might want to gather, determine the root cause of critical data problems, redesign the process, and recommend improvements. But don't make this work encyclopedic. Instead, keep focusing on the three guiding lights to see how to select what techniques to use and what depth to go to.

WHAT IF WE CAN'T INTERVIEW THE CUSTOMER?

Yes, there are certain tools that are required when analyzing a work or service process, and one of them is Customer feedback. Specifically, what does the customer need, want, and require from your process and how are you currently doing? But what if you can't get input from the customer? What should you do then?

What stands in the way of getting input from the customer? In my experience "on the front lines," there are three reasons teams give for not being able to interview the customer:

1. Their boss doesn't want them to. The boss thinks the customers will be really negative and "we don't need to hear this stuff."

What should you do? The best thing to do here is to wait. First collect all the problems that employees can identify, then collect some quantitative data that shows challenges, and maybe use some other analytical tools. Then go back to the boss and explain that you must hear from the customer. The customer is one of the three guiding lights for process improvement. Start slowly and explain the simple method to your boss; then test it with a few customers (internal or external) and show your boss the results. No disaster will occur! In my experience, I have had a few bosses be hesitant, but each one has come around.

2. The team doesn't want to. They don't feel customers will be honest with them, either because they are too "friendly" now or because they don't know them. I have also had team members who don't speak English well who are fearful of doing the interviews because they are not confident in the language.

What should you do? Pair up to do the interviews. Pairs can support one another, and one person can introduce the other if they already have a relationship, while the second person can ask more of the questions. With pairs, non-English speakers can be there and hear what the customer says, but do not have to drive the interview by themselves.

3. The sales force controls the external customer and only Sales can speak to the external customer. Since this BPI team is not Sales, they cannot talk to the customer.

What should you do? If the company has a policy specifying that only Sales can interact directly with the customer, you need to honor that. This if often true in companies where sales people have very large customers with multiple buying centers. Some alternatives are: You can ask Sales to do the interviews while you listen in so you can hear it from the customer's mouth. You can use the customer interview process with each sales person and ask the sales person to speak for the customer. If the customer is a retail customer, you can go out in the field and interview the direct customers in the retail store. But this is risky. It might offend Sales, although this is less likely in B2C situations.

So be patient but don't give up. The customer's input is vital and unique. Make sure you incorporate it into your process improvement effort.

Chapter 9

ARE WE DONE YET?
WHEN IS ENOUGH ENOUGH?

After applying the four required analytical techniques, what's next?

It's time to go back to the three guiding lights: Where do the Improvement Targets direct the team? Does the customer input suggest additional work? Does the quantitative data call out for specific analysis? Let me give you several different examples. The Project Lead and Team Facilitator usually start with reviewing the Improvement Targets. If the targets are about time, such as reducing time to market or minimizing production time or delivery time, the team better look at Time analytical techniques. If the Improvement Target states the team needs to standardize the hiring process, the team better look at standardization techniques. If the Customer Scorecard notes that the customer has concerns with defects, the team should find the root cause of the defects. If quantitative data tells the team that information coming into the process is incomplete and inaccurate 35% of the time, it's helpful to do an input evaluation.

After reviewing the three guiding lights, the Project Lead and Team Facilitator decide if the team should use additional techniques. The team won't know because they are not familiar with the range of techniques they might consider. The Team Facilitator, who knows the BPM methodology the best, should discuss what techniques might be helpful. (The instructor in the Core Workshops is a good coach as well in selecting which techniques to use.) The Project Lead helps with the decision based on his knowledge of challenges in the current process and the Process Owner's goals. Although it is not necessary, the Project Lead and Team Facilitator could also review their suggestions with the Process Owner and/or team.

It is also possible that the BPI Project has a limited scope and minimal complexity; then, it could be time to stop analyzing and move to designing the new process, as described in Chapter 13. I find it useful to review the three guiding lights here as a gateway to see where the team should go next, whether to one of the additional analytical techniques or on to designing the new process. It is also possible that the team has discovered so many Quick Wins while doing process diagramming and using the I-4 Lists that they want to pause and implement these. I highly suggest implementing some Quick Wins (see Chapter 15), but don't neglect to check against the three guiding lights to see if there is more to uncover in this process improvement effort.

Figure 54 summarizes several analytical techniques and their purpose. Teams can use this table to evaluate what other analytical techniques are needed beyond the original four required techniques.

At this point, the Team Facilitator and Project Lead

1. Review and decide which additional analytical techniques the team should use (and what guiding light led them to make that decision)

2. Introduce the technique to the team and apply it to their process

3. Step back and see what the team learned from the technique

Standardization will be discussed in Chapter 10, Time in Chapter 11, and Errors in Chapter 12. Shorter explanations are provided for the other techniques at the conclusion of Chapter 12.

Category	Technique	Purpose of Technique	Relevant Improvement Targets
Standardization	Assess and draft consistent forms or templates Assess and build consistent subprocesses Assess several instances of As-Is process diagrams, then build one consolidated process	Reduce process variation; stabilize steps, sequence, and roles in a process	Increase scalability of the process so it handles more volume Reduce complexity of the process Automate the process once we have it stabilized Combine processes to write requirements to software vendor selection
Time	Notched Timeline	Determine bottlenecks and major areas of wait between steps or within steps; enable major improvements in process cycle time	Reduce cycle time for this process Decrease time to market for this process Streamline this process Increase throughput
Errors	Fishbone diagram; Check sheet; Pareto chart 5 Whys Input Evaluation	Qualitative and quantitative methods to determine root cause and identify which are the critical few to work on first Method to go beyond initial symptomatic causes and identify root cause, including political and cultural ones Determine what you need from each key input, in order to identify information and service needs from suppliers to improve your process	Reduce rework in this process Increase efficiency of the process Reduce defects Integrate information better with our suppliers Increase employee productivity
Costs	Cost of quality	Find large costs in process activities because of errors and rework, from scrap work in progress/inventory, or other wastes	Reduce costs Increase worker productivity
Roles and Responsibilities	RACI chart	Identify roles for each step in the process to see who is responsible, where there is overlap, if there are too many approvals, where informing would be better than approving or consulting	Streamline process and reduce approvals Build clear escalation mechanisms
Risk Management	Risk Assessment	Identify risks in the current process and create controls for each	Reduce risk exposure Prevent or control all financial/regulatory risks in the process

Figure 54. More Analytical Techniques Related to Improvement Targets

Chapter 10

STANDARDIZATION

Standardization of work and information processes can take many forms. At the basic level, standardization means that processes have exactly the same steps, in the same sequence, and are completed by the same roles for all units doing the process. At a more stringent level, standardization means all of these things and two more: that the process runs at the same speed and maintains a stated level of inventories. There is no variability between processes across units, and there is no variability in the process on Monday vs. Tuesday vs. Wednesday.

Standardization eliminates variability, reduces cost, provides better quality, and enables consistency across units. In fact, if you don't have standardization you can't make improvements, because people and business units do the process differently to start! The ultimate standardized process means one single method for the process enterprise-wide.

Quality Indicators – How to Know if Standardization Is a Success

- The team has reduced the number of subprocesses or instances to one consolidated process that represents 80% of all the others. Allowable variations outside the consolidated process have been noted.
- Users are willing to test the new standardized forms or processes.
- After implementation, the reduction can be measured and substantiated – fewer forms from the baseline, fewer instances of the same process.

Below, three main areas for standardization (templates, subprocesses, and full processes) are discussed.

STANDARDIZE A FORM YOU ALREADY HAVE

There are several situations when it's beneficial to standardize and improve a form or screen.

1. If the team looks at an electronic format and sees open fields that produce unclear or incomplete information or other fields that are not working, it is time to change the form and make it standard, user friendly, and one that produces clear, accurate output.
2. When the team notices that there are different forms for capturing requests or inputs, it is time to build a standard electronic form/template.
3. When inputs are coming in through multiple channels (phone, self-service online, in person, fax) and different formats are used, it is time for standardization of the form.

How to Standardize and Improve the Template/Form/Screen

One component of standardization involves streamlining and imposing consistency on templates or electronic forms. In revising a template or form, the BPI team wants to remove unnecessary information and capture required information, clarify confusing fields or fields that provide ambiguous data, and make the data consistent across the organization. To do this, you need to assess, simplify, and then test your forms (Figure 55).

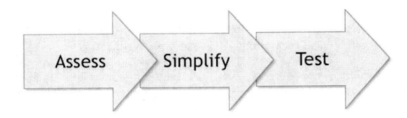

Figure 55. Assess, Simplify, and Test for Standardization

Assess
- Look at examples of the different versions of the template or form.
- Observe how the form is used in the workplace and talk to employees using it. If the form is part of a process, ask what comes before, what comes after, what information is difficult to get, etc. Watch how an inputter completes the form on the screen and ask what works and doesn't work.
- Identify what information is required on the form/screen. Identify what is ambiguous, what is unnecessary, what is missing. Use quantitative data to identify problems with the template and the extent of each.

Simplify
- Create a new format for the form. Simplify as much as possible.

Discuss your ideas with IT to see what is possible electronically. With larger changes, it might be helpful to have a forms designer or usability professional help with the construction as well.

Test

- Test in the workplace – both for information and usability.
- Revise as needed.

Work with IT again to incorporate the revisions and integrate it with needed databases or applications.

Here is an example of a standardized form that was developed by a client.

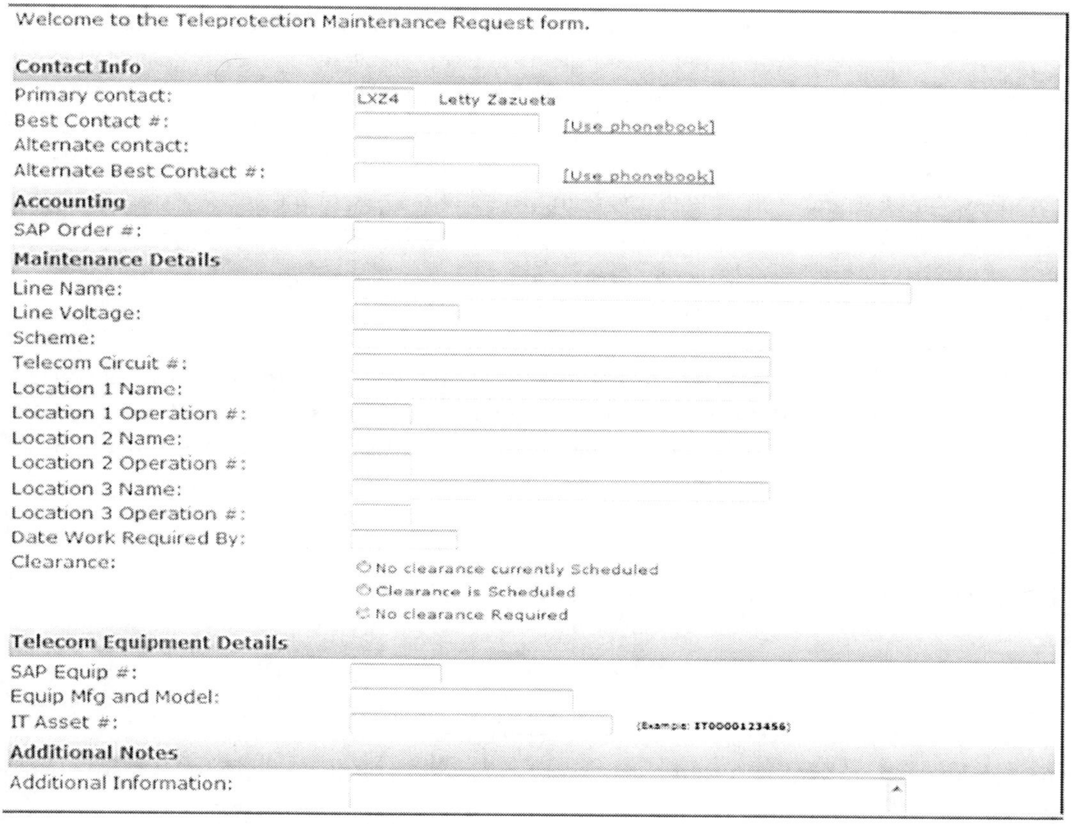

Welcome to the Teleprotection Maintenance Request form.

Contact Info
Primary contact: LXZ4   Letty Zazueta
Best Contact #:   [Use phonebook]
Alternate contact:
Alternate Best Contact #:   [Use phonebook]

Accounting
SAP Order #:

Maintenance Details
Line Name:
Line Voltage:
Scheme:
Telecom Circuit #:
Location 1 Name:
Location 1 Operation #:
Location 2 Name:
Location 2 Operation #:
Location 3 Name:
Location 3 Operation #:
Date Work Required By:
Clearance:
    ○ No clearance currently Scheduled
    ○ Clearance is Scheduled
    ○ No clearance Required

Telecom Equipment Details
SAP Equip #:
Equip Mfg and Model:
IT Asset #:   (Example: IT0000123456)

Additional Notes
Additional Information:

Figure 56. Standardized Form Example. Source: Pacific Gas and Electric

As this client said, "Standardization is really the low-hanging fruit and the easiest to implement from a quick hit perspective. Prior to implementing this form, there were many inconsistent ways work came into our organization. Also, there was only one order number we could use to track for this work. That meant we needed to create multiple tickets to track different order numbers for test activities happening at different stations. Now we have a single entry point for the different station test activities."

Often organizations have a variety of entry methods for customers or suppliers to submit information, and these different methods use different formats and forms. It is helpful to look at these to see what information is really required and what is optional. The method of entry should not drive the information needed. In fact, it is likely that the different forms just grew up over time, so now is the opportunity to standardize.

STANDARDIZE SUBPROCESSES IN THE AS-IS PROCESS DIAGRAM

There are many reasons a team might want to look further into a subprocess. Often this is because a particular segment of the process diagram is not working, or needs clarification. It may also be because the team wants to take a subprocess and detail it out more, or that the subprocess needs the input of other performers who were not at the initial documentation session. It could be because a subprocess has different steps or performers in different parts of the company. In all of these situations, the team needs to document the subprocess, analyze it, and then create a new view of the process that will be the new "standard."

How to Standardize a Subprocess

Standardizing a subprocess is similar in many ways to standardizing the full process. Since a subprocess is smaller than the full process, standardizing it is simpler. Additionally, the subprocess child level may still need to diagrammed and then assessed to see if there are instance differences for the subprocess.

Assess
- Identify the subprocess you want to stabilize or standardize.
- Write one or two Improvement Targets for this subprocess that will support the overall Improvement Targets of the full process.
- Document a swimlane instance for the subprocess in its current state. Document additional instances. Build an I-4 List for this subprocess.
- Add employee I am WASTED pain points to the subprocess using the method learned previously.
- Now step back and review the current subprocess. Is the team ready to create a new standardized subprocess or does it need some additional information? The team might need to gather some quantitative data or do a root cause analysis. It might be necessary to find out why instances are different today: is it because of regulatory issues, customer segment differences, various systems accessed, or just because different versions grew up over time?

Simplify

- When the team is ready to build a new standard subprocess, take a piece of flipchart paper, butcher paper, or use a modeling application on your laptop and project the image. Put performer roles down the left; the team might choose to reduce the number of roles.
- Develop your new subprocess.
- Once you are finished, step back and review it. This is your first iteration. Does it accomplish what you want? Does it move toward the Improvement Targets?
- Determine whether you need other elements of standardization within the subprocess – new templates, reduced approvals, etc.

Test

- The simplest test is just to review the new template or form with the different groups that use the subprocess and see if it makes sense.
- Do an operational test in the workplace where the employees use the form. Determine baseline values for how the current form works (how many defects it produces, how often there is absent information), and then indicate corresponding values with the new form to determine the change. The test may suggest additional needed revisions.

STANDARDIZE THE WHOLE PROCESS

Probably the reason a team wants to standardize the whole process is because the Process Owner made that an Improvement Target. In the Hiring example, there were 15 processes for hiring (one in each division), and the Executive Sponsor wanted to have one standardized process. In other client examples, the Process Owner knew that there were many different processes for procurement, or paying invoices, or something else, and he wanted to have one consistent way of doing it across the organization before he developed the requirements for vendor selection. In another situation, the organization wanted to move from providing customized web solutions for each client to having a standard product development and release schedule. In this case, the client wanted to build a new process they had not had before – the product development process. This would be a standard that introduced new features and functionality, and then clients could ask for specific customizations on top of that.

After doing the first instance of As-Is process diagramming in a BPI Project, the Project Lead and team have to decide whether to map other instances. The question to answer is: Are there other instances that are different enough from this one that we should diagram as well? The most obvious instances to consider are (1) different customer segments, (2) different regions or units with the same process, and (3) different end states. The examples that came up on the I-4 Lists in the Instance Differences category are another place to look for important instances. This was discussed in more detail in Chapter 5. So go ahead and model a few different instances and see what the team learns. Often the team learns that the second or third instance is 80% the same as the first, but there are one or two subprocesses that are different. In that case, you probably don't need to standardize the whole process, just standardize those subprocesses.

Sometimes a team says, we have several (8-15) different ways of doing this process, and we want to map each one to see how different they are and to begin to understand the process overall. I find this happens most in situations where many different regions or units have the same process but do it differently. I had one team that reviewed 14 different budgeting processes. They actually mapped all 14 processes and then looked at them together. They found different names for the same task, different roles or different job titles that performed the same role, different order of steps, and different approval processes or number of approvals. They also found that the 14 processes were very similar, as most of the differences were minor or really not differences at all. Once they had diagrammed and understood all 14 processes, they very quickly created a *consolidated As-Is process* for the budget process. Then they felt comfortable to do further analysis using the one consolidated process, and have it meaningful to them. They analyzed the consolidated process further and then built the redesigned process off of the consolidated process.

Really, this consolidated process could be called a *stabilized process*, which is the first step in moving toward standardization. It includes documenting the process, having the same steps in one sequence, and having the same defined roles for the process. Organizations can implement a stabilized process as a prototype. The point is to take an intermediate step to get everyone following one process and then iterate again and move to the redesigned process. In this case, everyone would be moving from a consistent stabilized process to the single redesigned process. That makes implementation easier, as groups are moving from a single method to a single new method. In this budget example, the group did not take the intermediate step of implementing the consolidated process; rather, they just used it as a consolidated process to work from as the basis of redesign in the BPI Project. At the end of this chapter, you will see another example of developing a consolidated process for requirements gathering.

How to Standardize the Whole Process

The purpose of standardization is to reduce process variation, and to stabilize steps, sequence, and roles in a process. Here is how to do it.

Assess

- Hang all the As-Is swimlane maps from the different instances of the process with their I-4 Lists, improvement ideas, indicative data, and instance differences next to the maps. If you have done the models in top-down BPMN, it is helpful to print and hang each subprocess so you can easily see them all in one flow. Or change the BPMN model into a flat model and print it like a large blueprint, or view it on several monitors simultaneously. The human eye can more easily see similarities and differences with this method.

- Discuss the maps. One person stands at his map on the wall and walks through it step by step, then quickly reads the issues and improvement ideas. The next person does the same. The rest of the group mostly listens, asking only clarifying questions. No problem solving should happen here, or this will take all day!
- Once everyone has reviewed his map and I-4 Lists, the recorder creates a flip chart with 3 columns: Similarities, Differences, and Musts. First, capture the similarities from the instances in your group. Then discuss the differences and put them on the flip chart. Only list the top three. You may discover, as you discuss differences, that some items you thought were different are really the same. They could be just wording differences, or they could be different levels of detail. Last, make a list of musts – requirements that the process must have to provide information, reporting, etc.

Simplify

- Now create a consolidated map on the blank butcher paper, or model it on a projected computer screen. Put the name of the consolidated map at the top.
- Start with the first step and last step. If you have done these with flowchart notation, continue with it; if you have done it in BPMN, continue that way.
- Fill in all the subprocesses and specific steps that are the same first.
- Now start at the beginning and fill in the others. See if you can create a consolidated map that would represent 80% consistency or more.
  - If steps are the same but have different names, note that under the step saying "naming differences."
  - Where steps are mostly the same but with slight differences, list the differences under the step in bullets, with the heading "Slight differences."
  - If steps are truly different, put a red dot on them, and make a bulleted list called "Bigger Differences.
- Now step back as a group and review the consolidated map out loud. See if it represents what you want. Make revisions as needed. If you have done this with flowchart swimlanes, now is the time to change them to BPMN. Have a BPMN documenter do that after the session and bring it back to the assembled team to review for accuracy

Test

As with the subprocess standardization, the test should have two parts, first a visual and verbal review with key stakeholders of the different use cases, and then an actual test in the workplace.

Other Approaches – Best Practice and Large Groups

If there is one map that you think is a best practice and would be a good basis for the consolidated map, use it as your foundation.   Put it right next to your blank butcher paper and keep referring to it, but create a new consolidated map. Follow the same approach as above, but use the main steps from the best practice map and then revise as needed.

If you have a large group with 10 or more different instances, see the variation explained at the end of this chapter, "A Faster Way to Gather Business Requirements (and Win a Prize)."

STANDARDIZATION PROVIDES MANY BENEFITS

While it may seem like extra work, a standardized process has many benefits:

- Creates a single stabilized base to improve on and implement
- Streamlines work
- Enhances scalability
- Provides cost economies
- Avoids errors from misinterpretation
- Removes duplication
- Prepares for automation

THINGS TO THINK ABOUT

A FASTER WAY TO GATHER BUSINESS REQUIREMENTS (AND WIN A PRIZE)

 *As a prestigious university, we had over 100 varied graduate programs, all of which had their own application process. With a budget crunch we wanted to buy or build a system that would enable us to consolidate the multiple programs and standardize them into one application process. How could we understand the requirements for all these different programs and build the requirements we needed to go out to RFP?*

Dear Graduate Division,

If you look at the workflow of the different graduate programs and determine where subprocesses are similar and where they are different, you can create a standardized process that will represent 80% of what the graduate programs do. If there are critical variances in the 80% process, they can often be included by using gateways that lead to different subprocesses as needed.

Since you want this done quickly, I suggest you use a large group process and bring in employees (in twos and threes) for at least 15 of the graduate programs to plan a new graduate admissions system. On Morning 1, explain the goals, have participants model their own current processes, and then have them work with two or three departments together to create a combined process, noting what parts are similar and what parts are different and critical. Morning 2, use a core group of volunteers from the 15 graduate divisions, consolidate the group process diagrams into one university process, and note important variations. And on the third morning, the whole group can reconvene to make final decisions for the new graduate admissions process.

I did this in a real client situation. It worked like a charm and everyone had a good time. In fact, we had time on Morning 3 to share best practices around common and frequent problems.

And here's what the client, the IT Director of Systems for the Graduate Division, said about the process and project:

"On a more traditional project where a systems analyst interviews a selected group of users to produce a spec, most people have no opportunity to have their views heard. The workshop approach gives everyone who wants a voice a say in the project."

The traditional approach produces a long list of requirements with little sense of their order of importance to the group. The workshop approach produces consensus on the most important requirements, allowing limited resources to be concentrated on top priorities.

The traditional approach requires a lot of time and money. Creating a spec for a campus-wide project like this can take three to six months and require a business analyst who works at least half time for that period. The workshop took three half-days and required two business analysts for a week.

The traditional approach starts with defining the computer system. The new approach starts with defining a new business process and then asks how the computer system can be built to support it. This new approach helped us find inefficiencies that had nothing to do with our computer system. For example, we discovered that we could save the University thousands of dollars each year by handling transcripts differently.

She continued, "There are many other very positive consequences of your work with us, but I think you can see from just the examples above how important you were to the success of our project. We really appreciate all you did and hope to have a chance to work with you in the future."

And they won an award from the university for the project.

STANDARDIZATION OR FLEXIBILITY?

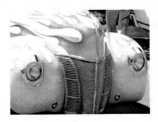

You probably know experts who state that standardization is critical for work and information processes. They dogmatically declare that you get reduced variability, cost reduction, better quality, and consistency across the organization with standardization.

Yet, on the other side there are experts who say that flexibility is critical, the only way to stay current in the marketplace and to satisfy varying customer needs. A flexible process is better able to respond to specific demands, to be agile, and to make adaptive decisions.

Standardization of work and information processes can take many forms. At the basic level, standardization means that processes have exactly the same steps occur in the same sequence and are completed by the same roles for all units doing the process. At a more stringent level, standardization means that the process runs at the same speed and maintains a stated level of inventories.

Flexibility, on the other hand, means that the work process is different under varying conditions, and these conditions are created by the need for differences. The most obvious need is a difference in customer type, which demands a different output from the commoditized standardized process.

So how do you know which is more important for your process – standardization or flexibility?

Many clients have asked me to help them standardize their processes, either because of the recession, mergers, new technology, globalization, or just for streamlining and simplification. In one situation, I was asked to help standardize the way an organization did procurement. This project was part of an enterprise effort to streamline the process, utilize one method across the organization, and apply the new eProcurement software application they had recently acquired. We asked 35 different business units to come together to model how they currently did the procurement process, determine what flow and information they needed, and agree on one way that would work at the 80% level for the organization. After they looked at their maps, a core group was able to create one consolidated As-Is map. And the participants learned best practices in their study along the way. This was a great beginning. Then we analyzed the process further and came up with business requirements.

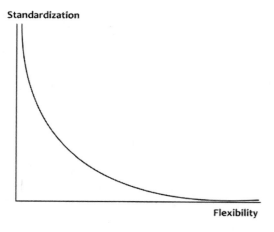

Figure 57. As Standardization Increases, Flexibility Usually Decreases

It is true that the more standardization you have, the less flexibility you have, but there are many places on the curve where you can have a combination of each. And I assert that you need to have both. Standardization and flexibility are both strategies for maximizing return, and they bring different results, but you need to consider both to get the best result for the customer and the organization.

Standardization and flexibility are both important in understanding and improving your processes. Standardization moves the needle toward a single method, process, and outcome. Flexibility provides for variation where the customer situation requests it and it makes sense for the business. Both can differentiate a product in the marketplace, one more for price and consistency and the other more for distinctive customer requirements. In order to get to the best combination:

- Get both sides seeing the common goal.
- Look at several instances of the way the process is done today.
- See what is the same and what is different in the different instances.
- Standardize where you can.

Keep distinctions where different processes/subprocesses and different approaches make sense for special customer requirements.

The sponsor in one client situation said this was her vision: "Customization comes from a modular and predefined set of options, not an infinite set of options that needs to be created from scratch each time." Your redesigned process could be (1) one standard process, (2) two to three processes to address different customer segments and their needs, or (3) one standard process with choice points where you can choose different modules (a method to control the amount of variation).

Chapter 11

TIME AND VISUAL ANALYSIS

TIME

There are all kinds of factors that contribute to the cycle time of a process, the total time from when the process starts to when it produces the final output. Some of the big factors are:

Setup time – How long it takes to set up the process before the work can even begin. In manufacturing, that is how long it takes to get the equipment set up, but in service and information, it entails how long it takes to boot up the computer, open up the needed files and applications, or find the information to begin. This is probably only a small percentage of the total cycle time, but setup time begins to increase when each actor following a handoff has to do the setup, or when a single employee gets interrupted and works on multiple projects during the day, so that he or she does setup multiple times for one process.

Processing time – How much time it takes to complete a single step in the process, from when the performer picks it up and starts to work on it until he is ready to send it to the next step. The amount of time here is a combination of active time doing the work (how long it takes if the performer is not interrupted) and wait time. The performer may start on the work at 8 AM and then be interrupted by meetings, by phone calls, by other tasks not in this process, or by waiting on someone to get something to him. It is useful to know both pieces of time data – how long it takes with no interruptions and how long the elapsed time is.

Moving – The length of time it takes (1) to move information or goods in the process, which would include physical transportation and electronic transfer, and (2) for performers to move in doing the job, such as getting up and going to find a paper file or form, going to the copy machine, etc.

Inspection – The length of time to inspect a part or program. Inspection can happen at several places in a process.

Waiting – Waiting time occurs in two places in the process diagram – in between steps and as a segment of the process steps. Both should be measured, but in between steps is the longer of the two.

Rework – The time it takes when there is a loopback and some task has to be redone or revised because of defects or changes. The process didn't get it right the first time.

Usually setup is a small percentage of the total cycle time. Moving can be small or larger, but is likely to be small in most information processes, since so much of the movement is electronic. What most people don't know is how much of the process time is due to waiting. It can be as high as 70% of the total cycle time. I had one client say to me, "If we could get rid of the waiting, we would make such big improvements we could leave the process as is." That is the point. Addressing long wait times can reduce the cycle time tremendously. However, the percentage of cycle time that is in the process steps is not nearly as large as the waiting time between steps. So reducing time in the steps doesn't have the same bang for the buck. In addition, reducing problems such as rework can reduce time.

The Project Lead and Team Facilitator know that the Time analytical technique is important when Time is part of the Improvement Targets or when the customer says that something takes too long. The Notched Timeline provides quantitative data about process time and wait time and an easy visual to add to your Visual Analysis map.

Category	Technique	Purpose of Technique	Relevant Improvement Targets
Time	Notched Timeline	Determine bottlenecks and major areas of wait between steps or within steps; enable major improvements in process cycle time	Reduce cycle time for this process Decrease time to market for this process Streamline this process Increase throughput

Figure 58. Time-based Analysis Techniques

Notched Timeline

As much as I love the process diagram as a foundational technique, time is not evident on the process diagram. But it can be added by creating a Notched Timeline (Figure 59).

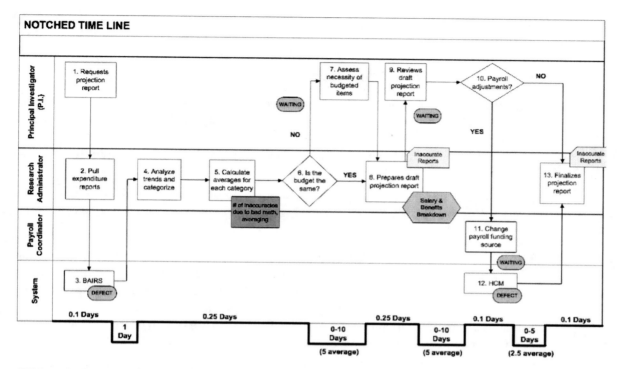

NOTCHED TIME LINE

| | 0.1 Days | 0.25 Days | 0.25 Days | 0.1 Days | 0.1 Days |

1 Day | 0-10 Days (5 average) | 0-10 Days (5 average) | 0-5 Days (2.5 average)

WHAT I LEARNED: This notched time line was a great analysis tool to determine which steps are wasting the most amount of time and draws the eye towards areas of process improvement. A lot of time in this process is spent on waiting which could be a future improvement target.

Total: 14.3 days
Waiting: 13.5 days

Figure 59. Notched Timeline. Source: Donna Lee, University of California, Berkeley

The Notched Timeline is added to the process diagram to show the time for steps and in between steps of the process. Here are two methods to create it.

Method 1 – Get Real Data

The most objective approach to create a Notched Timeline is to gather real data. The team can ask employees to complete a time log for each of their parts in the process, indicating when they picked up the task, how long a step took, and when they sent it on to the next person or activity. It is helpful to log the times for several instances, vs. just for a single instance. The team might also be able to get a good deal of this data by manually reviewing email and system timestamps for the different steps in the process. It does take some legwork to do this manually, so be thoughtful about what data you are gathering. Try to get a representative sampling, but you don't have to get data for 12 months if it needs to be done manually. I find teams can usually gather this time information in 4 hours or less.

Another way to get real data is to get it from instances that are being captured in a BPMS. Of course, this data may not be available until after you implement the new process using a BPM suite, so it would not be available on the first BPI project. But then after implementation, it could be available.

Method 2 – Gather Time Estimates from the Team

1. Start with step 1, asking the team how long it takes to do that step. Write the time on the top of the notch. (Facilitation Tip: Since the team is likely to say, "It depends," ask for a range, as shown in later parts of the Notched Timeline in Figure 59.) Note this process time will include both time doing the work of the activity and any waiting time within the step for interruptions.

2. Then determine the time it takes between the end of Step 1 and the beginning of step 2. This is wait time between steps. This duration goes on the bottom part of the notch in the timeline.

3. Then go to step 2 and determine how long the next step takes. (Tip: If the same person performs several steps in a row, these steps can be combined into one time estimate. In the example in Figure 59, steps 4-6 are all performed by the Research Administrator and they are combined into one time notation of 0.25 days. If the tasks move across performers, it is best to get separate notations. But, in Figure 59, steps 1-3 are combined from three different lanes into one time notation. It makes sense to do that when a few different steps seem to be one activity occurring in several quick parts, which is the case here.

4. Continue until all the steps and the durations between steps are covered.

5. Optional: Go back and separate each activity into two parts: total activity Process Time and activity Process Time without interruptions. This also enables the team to figure the wait time within a step.

Summation for Both Methods

1. Add up the total time for the steps and for the time between steps. Write this on the process diagram as Total Time. Add up the wait time in between steps. Write this on the process diagram as Waiting, as shown in Figure 59. Calculate wait time as a percentage of the total cycle time.

2. Optional: Write the activity Process Time without interruptions on the process diagram as well. Activity Process Time without interruptions is interesting because it tells you how fast the process could move right now if there were no interruptions within the steps and no waiting between steps. So this is really a target time without any automation, any changes to rework, etc.

3. When using process modeling software, the tool often provides methods to enter the time information. This will not produce a Notched Timeline, but it will record the times and enable calculations using this data. The tool may allow calculations of the current state

times, followed by development of scenarios to explore time with different processes to evaluate different improvements for the future state process. Make sure you take advantage of these capabilities. We will see an example of this in Chapter 14.

What Did the Team Learn?

Step back and discuss what the Notched Timeline tells the team and what the time summary suggests. The Team Facilitator can ask these questions:

- In our example, wait time is 94% of total time. What does that suggest for improvements?
- Where could we reduce wait time? And how?

Any improvement ideas should be added to the I-4 List under Improvement Ideas.

Review what the team discussed, and note additional data to gather on the Indicative Data list. The Team Facilitator asks the following:

- How does this information on time help attain our Improvement Targets?
- Does it suggest any Quick Wins?
- Do we have any additional improvement ideas for the long term?

Quality Indicators – Here's How to Know if Time Analysis Is a Success

- The team has identified the steps, subprocesses, or wastes that take the most time.
- The team has calculated what percentage of the total process time stem from these time expenditures.
- The team can verbally and visually relate how reducing or eliminating the time wasters will impact the Improvement Target.
- The team has discussed possible root causes for time expenditures, and noted improvement ideas. The team has discussed which time expenditures they can influence and which will be difficult to influence.
- The Process Owner, Executive Sponsor, and other colleagues can see where high time expenditures are on a Visual Analysis Map. These managers and employees can now tell the story of the impact of time on the current process.

VISUAL ANALYSIS MODELS

Long process models of 30-90 steps can be overwhelming; reading each step to executives (or anyone!) would be boring. But the team can bring the model alive by turning it into a *Visual Analysis Model*, a model which has the swimlane flowchart as the foundational background and

---

uses graphical icons for customer comments, I am WASTED pain points, time, data markers, and risks to point out key analysis elements. It is up to the team what to put on the map.

I use small green stickies on butcher paper to mark the I am WASTED pain points, and I have team members write the waste right on the green sticky and put it at the step or subprocess where it occurs. The team can summarize comments from the Customer Scorecard and use an unhappy face to note them where they occur on the process diagram. Real data for the number of errors, % complete and accurate, process time, wait time, etc. can be entered at key steps. The Notched Timeline can go at the bottom of the diagram. Categories of risks can be shown with red dots.

Figure 60. Visual Analysis Map on Paper

The Visual Analysis Model (Figure 60) provides a picture that enables the team and the Process Owner to see problem areas where further analysis might be helpful. Problem areas are obvious because the icons tend to fall in clusters. Or they may also follow certain categories or topics, such as missing information, delays for approvals, re-entering of data. Every time a Project Lead explains the Visual Analysis Model to the Process Owner or Executive Sponsor, the conversation becomes animated with questions and ideas flowing.

One of the challenges with the Visual Analysis Model is that it can get complicated with all the different icons. Here's where BPM software tools can help. For example, some tools have stencils of icons you can add to the process diagram in different "layers." By selectively enabling the layers, the documenter can show different views of the same process diagram, for example, one showing Wastes, a second one showing the customer comments, and a third view with data on different steps. Or all the views can be combined to show all the various icons together. Each modeling tool has its own methods of highlighting the analysis elements. Visualizing them in the context of the process diagram helps to prioritize areas of focus for the team and provides fodder for further discussion of underlying causes.

IBM Blueworks Live has a similar capability, as we shall see in Chapter 14, with the crucial advantage that the Visual Analysis Model is shared online in the cloud, available to the whole team and external stakeholders as well.

With any software tool, because of the small size of the icons, it's important to have backup sheets linked to the process diagram to explain the specifics of each icon. So number or notate the icon on the overall process diagram, and provide the details for each one in the underlying sheet or document. These views are not hard to do and provide focused and powerful infographics.

Figure 61 shows a portion of a client's Visual Analysis map showing different I am WASTED pain points, data, and customer comments.

Time is critical to most processes, so analytical techniques are often part of the Process Analysis phase. It is important to get actual data – manually, through walking the process, through following timestamping, or through other means such as process mining. Real data provides measures for objective analysis as well as comparisons between the current state and the improved process.

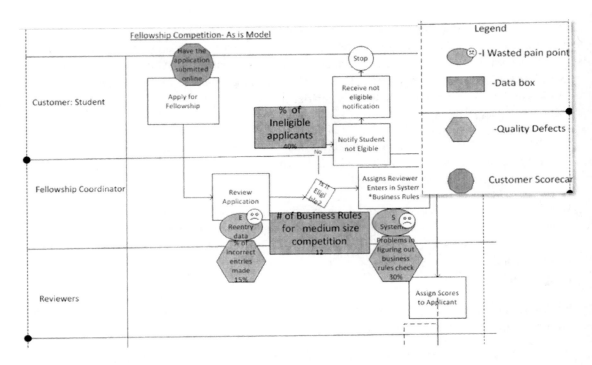

Figure 61. Visual Analysis Map. Source: Kenny Low

Chapter 12

ERRORS AND A FEW MORE

ERRORS

Errors offer a big opportunity for process improvement because they slow the process down, cause rework, increase costs, and can lead to defective outputs and customer dissatisfaction. They can occur all over the process and comprise two areas of the I am WASTED pain points: Absent Information and Defects.

Although there are many methods for finding root causes and reducing or eliminating errors, this chapter focuses on the following analytical techniques:

- Fishbone Diagram, Check Sheet, and Pareto Chart
- The Five Whys

Fishbone Diagram, Check Sheet, and Pareto Chart

The Fishbone Diagram, Check Sheet, and Pareto Chart are related and often used together.

The *Fishbone Diagram* goes by three names: Fishbone Diagram (for how if looks), Cause and Effect Diagram (for its purpose), and Ishikawa Diagram (for its Japanese author). It is a qualitative diagram developed by the team of subject matter experts who understand the issues. Its purpose is to develop and categorize a list of possible causes for the defect or effect shown at the head of the fish.

An example is shown in Figure 62.

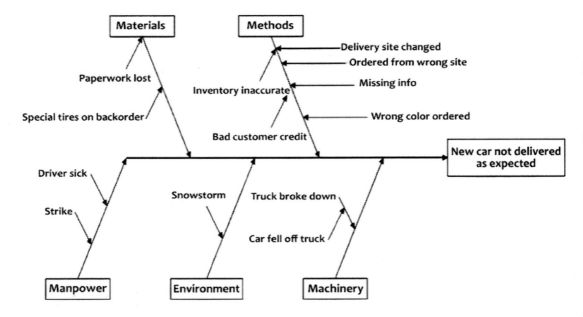

Figure 62. Fishbone Diagram Example

Directions to Complete a Fishbone Diagram

1. Start with the effect, that is, the defect or outcome that the team wants to analyze, and determine its root cause. Choose one from the I am WASTED pain points (good choices are A = Absent Information or a D = Defect), but make sure it is one that will impact the Improvement Targets. In the example in Figure 62, the effect is "new car not delivered as expected." Now the team will develop possible causes for why the new car was not delivered. To do that, the Team Facilitator makes a diagram that looks like the bones of a fish, with the effect in the head position. All of the possible causes go on the bones of the fish in the appropriate category.

2. Label the bones of the fish. The generic method is to label each bone with one of the following categories (Materials, Methods, Manpower, Machinery, and Environment). These are informally called "four M's and an E" for their first letters. Some people use five M's and an E, with the sixth bone labeled Management.
    *   Materials means supplies used in the process.
    *   Methods are steps or procedures currently used.
    *   Manpower is people.
    *   Environment means physical environment and culture.
    *   Machinery means equipment. Many groups rename the category "Systems," meaning software applications and systems.

- Management is management in the organization.

  Alternatively, the team can choose their own categories/bones if they think that is better for their needs in this situation.

3. Brainstorm the possible causes for the effect – in this case, "The car was not delivered on time." The person who suggests the possible cause gets to say where it goes on the diagram, and the Team Facilitator writes it on a whiteboard or captures it on an electronic fishbone diagram. Team members should suggest possible causes that have happened at least once in any instance of the process, not creative ideas that might happen in the future. This is a qualitative data-gathering exercise.

4. Bones can be put on other bones to show more details of that situation as is seen in "The truck broke down and the car fell off the truck" in Figure 62.

5. When the team has run out of possible causes, the Team Facilitator leads a discussion about what the Fishbone diagram tells the team. The Team Facilitator might ask, "Where are most of the possible causes?" (In Figure 62, this is on the Methods bone.) Or does one bone seem to impact another bone?

6. Now use the Check Sheet and Pareto Diagram.

Check Sheet

The Check Sheet is used to assign quantitative values to the possible causes shown on the Fishbone Diagram. In this example, the team decided to get quantitative data about the possible causes in the Methods bone. In another situation, the team could decide to get quantitative data about all the possible causes for the whole Fishbone Diagram. In either case, the task is to gather data that will reveal how often each of the possible causes occurs, for example, occurrences per week over four weeks.

Possible Causes	Week 1	Week 2	Week 3	Week 4	Totals
Delivery site changed	0	1	3	1	5
Ordered from wrong site	1	0	2	0	3
Missing info	4	7	3	6	20
Wrong color ordered	0	2	0	1	3
Bad customer credit	2	0	4	0	6
Inventory inaccurate	4	2	5	3	14
Other	3	2	4	3	12
Totals	14	14	21	14	63

Figure 63. Check Sheet Example

Directions to Complete a Check Sheet

1. Make the Check Sheet template. The first column will list the possible causes and the next four columns will list how many times this possible cause occurred in each measured interval, such as a week. The final column totals the count for each cause over the four weeks. The bottom row totals the count of all events for each week. See Figure 63.

2. Gather data. It's possible that the team can compile the data from several currently produced reports. They may have to develop a new report, or sort through logged issues, or they may have to get it manually. Do what is reasonable.

3. Turn the Check Sheet into a Pareto Chart.

The Pareto Chart

The Pareto Chart is a bar chart showing the causes in descending order from left to right. Superimposed over the bars is a line showing the cumulative percentage caused by this bar plus all bars to its left. For example, in Figure 64 the first bar for Missing Information occurred 20 times and represents 32% of the total errors. The second bar for Inventory Inaccurate occurred 14 times, and the two causes Missing Info and Inventory Inaccurate together represent 54% of the total errors. Similarly, the first 3 items represent 73% of the total, and so these are the important ones to concentrate on. The team uses the Pareto Chart to figure out which few items, often called the "critical few," produce about 80% of the total. This is where the expression the *80/20 rule* comes from.

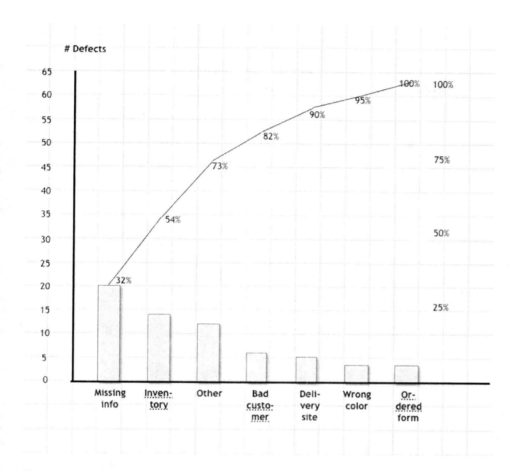

Figure 64. Pareto Chart

Next, the team discusses what the Pareto Chart reveals. Here are some possible answers.

- The big items are Missing Info, Inventory Inaccurate, and Other.
- But Missing Info could be many things. Maybe the team needs to dive deeper to find out what is in Missing Info – which would mean doing another Check Sheet.
- Also, the Other category is too large. Looking deeper into it might provide some further understanding.
- From this discussion, the team might suggest some Quick Wins they want to follow up on. Or they might list some more ideas in their Improvement Ideas list.

These three techniques – Fishbone, Check Sheet, and Pareto Chart – are basic tools from the seven basic tools of quality,[24] and they are still good ones. I like to use the Fishbone Diagram to quickly generate qualitative ideas as a team, but getting some quantitative data in a Check Sheet or other format really adds the data to show the most significant causes. Often managers say, "What is the root cause?" But usually there is not a single root cause. Instead there are several possible causes and a few big ones. So process improvement should determine how to minimize or eliminate the main root causes, and then test to see if those reductions really impact the effect.

The Five Whys

The *Five Whys* is a tool commonly used in Lean and Six Sigma for getting at root causes. I encourage teams to use it when they feel they have cultural issues or a political problem. I find that the Five Whys helps teams think outside their function and their current perspectives when trying to determine possible root causes.

Directions for the Five Whys

It's easier to explain how to do the Five Whys by looking at an example, so review the example below completed for the Hiring process in a research lab.

Why 1

Ask: What is the problem?

Answer: We have so much variability in the Hiring Process.

Ask: Which value added step(s) does the problem impact? A *value-added step* is an activity in the process model that provides functions, features, or services that the customer is willing to pay for. (We will discuss value added more in Chapter 13.) You have to think back to the High-Level Map, Improvement Targets, and vision to determine what value-added step in the process this problem impacts.

Answer: The value-added step is providing quality candidates, in our Hiring process example, the step called *Search for Candidates*. The first Why question actually takes the problem up to the value-added step before beginning to explore more details in the following Whys.

---

[24] Goal/QPC. *The Memory Jogger, A Pocket Guide for Continuous Improvement.* Methuen, MA: Goal/QPC, 1985.

Why 2

Ask: Why don't we always get quality candidates? This is a bigger question than the original presenting problem asked in Why 1. It will often get to a wider range of root causes. Get the team to list the most important root causes for the Why question, such as:

Answer:

- Candidates have to meet compliance standards as well.
- Overworked recruiters do not provide much added value to the process.
- Hiring managers often have customized requests, not a consistent process.
- There is a lot of variability in the process.

Ask: Which one of these possible causes has the biggest impact? The team may want to collect data to determine how much these causes impact getting quality candidates. It is best to try to use real data to make this Five Why technique quantifiable for each possible cause. For example, the team might determine how many candidates did not meet compliance standards in any hiring instance; or how often overwork delayed quality candidates from being considered; or how many customer requests there were over three months of job openings. But my guess is that this data would not have been tracked and would be hard to find. If the team uses its own experience to answer the question, their choice is more qualitative. Another method is to ask the team which one cause has the most impact on the second Why. Later, if the team wants, they can go back and do other possible causes as well.

Answer: Hiring managers often have customized requests, not following a consistent process.

Why 3

Ask: Why does the culture want customization and not value consistency in the process?

- Senior staff want it but divisional managers do not
- Hiring managers know who they want to hire and feel Recruitment is standing in their way
- Hiring managers want to get around compliance
- Our industry doesn't value Recruitment; they feel they know their own research network better than Recruitment.

Ask: Which one of these has the biggest impact? Again, it is best if the team collects real data, but if that is not possible, use the experience of the team to answer. The team should choose one of the four to explore further now.

Answer: Hiring managers think Recruitment is standing in their way and do not value them. (This is actually a combination of the second and fourth bullet, which the team felt were related.)

Why 4

Ask: Why do hiring managers think Recruitment is standing in their way and do not value them?

- Hiring managers don't like to be bothered with the complexity of the process.
- They don't know the Hiring Process and it may be overwhelming at times.
- They don't know what Equal Employment Opportunity (EEO) guidelines exist or what consequences they can have.
- Hiring managers are not held accountable for recruiting well.

Ask: Which one of these has the biggest impact? The team should choose one of the four to explore further now.

Answer: Hiring managers are overwhelmed by the process and do not understand the EEO guidelines. (Again, the BPI team chose a combination of bullets two and four because they felt they were highly related.)

Why 5

Ask: Why does the process overwhelm hiring managers especially the EEO guidelines?

- Hiring managers haven't had the process explained before.
- The "suitable search process" to meet the EEO guidelines is daunting.
- The current system makes it hard to find candidate and hiring information.
- Hiring managers have never been held accountable for hiring quality candidates *and* ensuring compliance.

Ask: Which one of these has the biggest impact? The team should choose one of the four to explore further now.

Answer: Hiring managers have never been held accountable for hiring quality candidates and ensuring compliance.

Why 6

Ask: Why are hiring managers not held accountable for hiring quality candidates while ensuring compliance?

- Their senior managers are not held accountable so hiring managers don't see the value.
- Their job is research, not management.
- There is not much of a partnership between the hiring manager and Recruitment.
- Hiring managers never have enough time to get what Recruitment asks for.

Ask: Which one of these has the biggest impact? The team should choose one of the four to explore further now.

Answer: There is not much of a partnership between the hiring manager and Recruitment.

The group stopped at this point in the Five Whys. (It does not always take five Whys exactly. It could take 3 or 7, but the team keeps going until they begin to see a root cause. Sometimes the answers also just get repetitive.) In this case, the team saw the following answers repeating: (1) hiring managers did not see much value in the HR recruiting staff; (2) hiring managers didn't understand the EEO considerations; and (3) hiring managers just wanted to be researchers and hire whatever researchers they knew.

The BPI team made a list of what the hiring managers would value in Recruiters and in the Hiring process:

- Simplicity
- Having recruiters get the process done for the hiring managers
- A quick hiring process that doesn't take too much of the hiring manager's time
- Having the recruiter provide a network of candidates to the hiring manager
- Having the recruiter do data analysis on the candidates and present that with recommendations to the hiring manager

These ideas all became part of the input to redesigning the Hiring process.

Further Comments on the Method

The reader will notice that the Five Why method here begins by "going up" a step at the first why, instead of immediately exploring specific answers to the presenting problem. While this technique has become a more frequent practice, some teams still skip this step. I find that it is useful to consider the larger picture first and why the presenting problem is impacting the process's value. The presenting problem is probably one aspect of the overall value. After that, the team may decide that the presenting problem is one of the biggest problems or that others are more important to consider first.

In the example above, the presenting problem was about variability. Although the team in this example did not gather quantitative data, it is preferable to do so in the Five Whys but that does not always happen. By the third, fourth, and fifth Why, the answers become repetitive. And the answers seem to be identifying a combination of root causes.

- Hiring managers (especially researchers) don't see value in recruiters.
- Hiring managers don't understand the compliance issues.
- Hiring managers and Recruitment have not worked in partnership together to get quality candidates that meet the organization's compliance needs.

I find that the Five Whys do not produce black-and-white answers. Instead they bring up several issues to consider and the team needs to decide which are the main root causes. Of course, quantitative data would help, but is not always available.

Quality Indicators – Here's How to Know if Error Analysis Is a Success

- The team has identified the errors by activity, theme, or subprocess and has measured the quantitative impact of the important ones.
- The team has done root cause analysis for key errors; improvement ideas have been suggested to eliminate or mitigate these root causes.
- The team has determined if eliminating errors in some areas could be a Quick Win and where automation or integration with other systems would be a useful longer-term improvement.
- The team knows the difference between errors that stem from challenges in the process and human performance errors, and is ready to suggest different improvement ideas.
- The Process Owner or Executive Sponsor can articulate the major errors in the process and can explain how errors have impacted later activities in the process, caused rework, or slowed the process.

OTHER ANALYTICAL TECHNIQUES

There were three other techniques listed in the table at the beginning of the Chapter 9. An overview of each one is provided below, but the reader should seek other resources to get more detail.

Cost

Cost control or reduction is often an unspoken goal, even if it may not be mentioned as a particular Improvement Target. The team may decide to use Activity-Based Costing or calculate the costs of defects or rework as a means of estimating cost for the process. Employee time (and its cost) is often a major part of costs in information and service processes. Most organizations know the employee costs in their function. Total employee cost for the process is different. To calculate employee costs (pay and benefits) for a process, it is necessary to calculate the amount of time each person works in the process.

ROLES AND RESPONSIBILITIES

I use this technique in analyzing both the As-Is and the To-Be model. It helps to see where there are missing roles, where roles overlap, where there are too many approvals, and where consolidated roles might be needed.

The *RACI Chart* (Figure 65) is a common method for looking at:

- Who is *Responsible* for each step. This is the single owner who is accountable for getting the task down and driving to decision.
- Who makes the *Approvals*. The Approver is the individual who is accountable for approving a proposed decision. (In an automated process it could be designated by decision rules.)
- Who the process needs to *Consult with* (not actually shown on the swimlane diagram).
- And who the process needs to *Inform about the task or decision* (also not shown on the swimlane diagram).

The RACI table shown in Figure 65 is the standard format. For each task in the left column identify what role has the R. If more than one role has responsibility, mark a second R. If there is no one designated with an R, leave the R off that row for the task. Then look again at the same task and see if there is an A. (It would usually be followed with a gateway.) Mark that role with the letter A. If there are others in the roles that consult, mark them with a C. If there are others that are informed later, mark them with an I. There is often more than one C or one I in a row. Each task should have an R, but not necessarily an A, C, or I.

As a team, discuss what the RACI table shows you. Look first at the R's to see that each task has at least one R. If there are no R's or multiple R's associated with a task, then the task has unclear responsibilities – no one is assigned or there are multiple people responsible. There may be multiple A's in one row or over the whole RACI chart, which may indicate too many approvers. Does each approver provide value—or is the approver just a rubber stamp? Too many A's will slow down the process.

Extensive consulting roles (many C's at a step) necessitate a lot of time collecting all those opinions. What does each C think he is providing – input or a solution that will be used? RACI issues in the current state should be added to the cumulative Issues on the I-4 Lists. Discuss possible improvements. Consider how to get rid of too many A's. Could they be switched to C's, so the R talks to the A ahead of time and then the R can make the decision on his own? Or could some A's be informed later and become an I?

Figure 65. Example of RACI chart

Requirements

Task	Client	Project Manager	Business Analyst	Sales	Documentation	DBA	Development	Systems	QA	Finance	Executives
Nancy rebuilt relationship, handed off to PM and BA	C			R							C
Make phone call to client to restart the project	C	R									
Discuss feature matrix, business drivers, roll out strategy with client	C	R	C								
Do you want views phased?	A	R	C								A
Draft Project milestones per # client views; gather team from who's available		R									
Send the client questionnaire	C		R								
Provide project overview to client	C	R									
Kick off data analysis (discuss questionnaire, data sources)	C	I	R			I					
Identify/enhance data mapping requirements		I	R			I					
Client completes questionnaire	R	I	C								
Determine crosswalks to be completed and send to client	C	I	R			C					
Client completes initial pass at crosswalks	R	I	C			I					
Discuss how client back end system is configured	C	I	R			I					
Do we need addt'l development for data integration		I	AR			C			C		
Revise project and resources to reflect addt'l development	I	R	C			C	C				
Define data source (based on feature matrix and questionnaire)		I	R			C					
Send client extract code	I	I	I			R					
Provide full data extraction	R	I	I			C					
Prepare scripts, run client data		I				R					
Send client data use case template	C	R							C		

Risk Management and Risk Assessment

The purpose of the risk assessment is to identify where the risks are in the model, determine the level of risk, and develop a plan to control the risk. Here the BPI team is reviewing the process model to clarify where the risks are, determine their potential impact, and determine if they are properly managed or need more management.

I frequently use a Risk Assessment technique with financial and healthcare organizations, or with processes that have regulatory and financial risks. Briefly, the technique begins with identifying where key risks are in the process (at what task or subprocess), rating the probability of its occurrence on a scale of 1 to 5 (1 being unlikely and 5 being frequent), and the size of impact the risk would cause, again rated on a scale of 1 to 5 (with 1 being negligible and 5 being catastrophic). Then multiply the two risk ratings together (frequency x impact); the total number gives a risk level ranging from 1 to 25. These risk levels can then be categorized into groups from low to extremely high, and specific approaches planned for each level. For example, risks at values of 1-4 are unlikely to happen and would have a minimal impact. They do not need a risk management plan. Risks at the opposite end of the spectrum with values from 20 to 25 are probably unacceptable. It is critical to have risk management strategies, but at this high a value, it may make sense to avoid these risks entirely by eliminating activities in the process that create this level of risk. Risks with values between 5 and 20 are mild or moderate and need different levels of risk mitigation plans.

Here's a simple method that BPI teams can use.

1. The Team Facilitator reviews definitions of common risk categories, concentrating on the ones that would be relevant to the process. Standard risk categories include financial, market, operational, security, product, regulatory, and liability. Team members give examples of risks for each category discussed. Then each member of the team takes three red dots, labels the dot with the category of risk they see, and sticks it on the redesigned process at the step or subprocess where it occurs. This can also be done with icon insertions on an electronic model.
2. The team discusses all the red risk points quickly. Then they identify the three biggest risk areas.
3. Determine if there are any controls in place already for these top three risks. If so, discuss if they mitigate the risk sufficiently. Develop plans to manage the top three areas and document them. The team selects controls to put in place to prevent the risk from happening or methods to manage the risk after it happens. These controls could be data indicators that would cause specific actions in the process, or they could be changes to the process to prevent them from occurring, or to mitigate the risk to an acceptable level. Mark where these controls go on the current state process diagram.
4. The team may find places in the process where risk management activities occur that are no longer needed; these often come from historical situations that are no longer relevant. On

the other hand, there may be risks that require a new risk management strategy to be added to the process. Depending on the complexity of the risk, the controls would be implemented immediately as Quick Wins or incorporated as improvements in the new design.

The team can also use this Risk Management technique when evaluating the To-Be model. Then they look to see if the design of the new process has introduced additional risks; and if it has, what level are they and what risk mitigation activities need to be built into the new process. If I had to choose only one place to apply Risk Management analysis, it would be after the To-Be design, as it gives the team a fresh way to look at the new process, and it is a helpful input into the Implementation Plan.

There are more analytical techniques but I have covered the key ones. *The Lean Six Sigma Pocket Toolbook* by Michael George et al.[25] has over 150 techniques simply explained. But when considering additional analytical techniques, use the Improvement Targets and vision to direct the team. Don't just add techniques to provide more ideas. Always ask yourself, what might the team learn from this technique and what action would they take because of it?

---

[25] George, Michael et al., *The Lean Six Sigma Pocket Toolbook*. New York: McGraw-Hill, 2005.

Chapter 13

HOW DO WE GET TO THE NEW DESIGN?

After modeling the current state process during Process Discovery and using key analytical techniques during Process Analysis, it is time to switch gears and redesign the process. I say switch gears, because the work the team has been doing up until this point is more left-brain activity, documenting the current state and then analyzing various instances of the current state using different techniques. Now it is time to shift to a more creative right-brain approach and build the redesigned or optimized process. (I use these terms "redesigned and optimized" interchangeably, but not all people do. Some authors think of redesigned as a more major transformation, whereas the term optimized is making smaller improvements and automating where possible. Others use "optimized" to mean building a process that is agile and able to make frequent, almost real-time changes.)

The purpose of the Process Design phase is to create a better process than the one currently in use. There are different ways to approach the redesign and different levels of improvements. At the simplest level, the team can make recommendations based on several improvement ideas. On another level, the team can create a high-level redesigned model and offer two to three options, with different costs, time investments, and a range of expected returns. Or the work team may create an ideal model of the transformed process and then step back and do a more detailed swimlane model showing the redesigned process with new flows, systems, and roles and responsibilities. Each of these methods may involve technology enhancements. The goal is to meet the Process Owner's Improvement Targets and the customer needs.

For the team, the Process Design phase is usually exhilarating. For some, it seems like the team has done a lot of work modeling and analyzing and they are eager to get started on redesigning the process. For others, developing the redesign is challenging because it has elements of the unknown: will it work, what do we need, will we be able to figure it out, and can we agree? The process I suggest below is simple and structured and has been successful the first time with my client teams 98% of the time. When the teams have completed it, they are amazed at how much agreement they have, how their disparate perspectives have come together toward the common goal, and how inspiring what they have created is.

Below are (1) activities I recommend to set the stage for the redesign, along with the rules and principles that guide the redesign, (2) a creative method to formulate ideas and find common themes, and (3) a method to diagram their new process.

SETTING THE STAGE FOR REDESIGN

Four activities are useful to get the team ready for building a redesigned model:

1. Identify and mark the value added steps on the As-Is process diagram.
2. Do benchmarking or best practice interviews to learn from others.
3. Review a case, showing the before (As-Is state) and after (To-Be state) process diagram.
4. Discuss the Rules for Redesign .

Value-Added and Non-Value-Added Steps

Value-added and non-value-added steps have particular meaning in the Lean concepts and principles. Using their framework and my words,

Value-added (VA) steps are...

- desired functions, features, or services that the customer values and would be willing to pay for if they knew you were doing it. (For nonprofit organizations, reframe this definition to say that VA steps are outcomes or features the customer would say he needs and sees value in having the organization spend time on.)
- a competitive advantage to the customer (e.g., faster delivery, fewer defects)
- essential to perform in order to meet customer needs

Non-value-added (NVA) steps ...
- provide no value in the customer's eyes, and the customer does not want to pay for them. Examples include all the I am WASTED pain points such as rework, duplicate data entry, systems that don't integrate, multiple signatures, time wasted looking for information, etc.

There is a third category, called *Necessary but non-value-added steps (NNVA)*. These...
- are activities that are not of value to the customer but are required for some other reason, such as financial requirements, legal or regulatory requirements
- often reduce financial risk
- can aid in the completion of value-added tasks

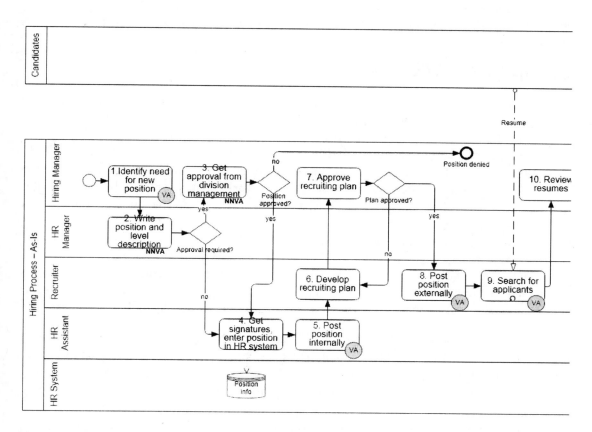

Figure 66. Value-Added Notated on Swimlane Diagram (diagram fragment displayed)

Figure 66 shows some examples of value-added tasks (circles with VA next to them) in a process diagram fragment. The value-added tasks are *Identify need for new position, Post position internally, Post position externally,* and *Search for applicants.* All of these value-added tasks need to be performed in order to meet customer needs. The diagram also indicates some *necessary but non-value-added* (NNVA) tasks: *Write position and level description* and *Get approval from division management.* The NNVA tasks are necessary because of current organization policy and required Human Resources "regulatory" documentation. There are other steps in the process that are clearly non-value-added like *Get signatures for approval* (which means running around and collecting physical signatures from multiple people), and *Develop recruiting plan* (why isn't there one already, at least for most positions?).

After explaining the definitions of VA, NVA, and NNVA, it is a very simple exercise to have the team look at their current state As-Is model and notate the steps that are value-added with a VA or blue dot.

Three explanations are important for the team, before setting them to this task.

1. Many processes have only 5-10% value-added steps. This is not "bad"; the value-added steps are a guideline for the redesign, so the team wants to see where they are, as the VA steps will be ones to pay attention to in the redesign.
2. There are many steps today that are NVA and yet employees have to do them. For example, tasks in a reworked process are not value-added, but they have to be done because the process did not get it right the first time. And the work the employees do in that rework is important today, but it is still NVA. That means the task is not value-added but it does not mean any employee is non-value-added.
3. Talk about how the team will know if the step is VA or not. The first obvious answer is by thinking about what the customers said they needed in the Customer Scorecard. The second is to identify the few critical elements the customer considers valuable in the process – namely, the output (I hope!) and a few tasks along the way to get to that output, or specific features or services connected with the output. Teams do not usually find this too hard.

To make this exercise less time consuming, suggest that the team look at the whole process diagram and pick out the steps that are value-added first, and see if they can agree on those, and then mark them. Lean specialists would probably have the team mark every step in the process, VA, NVA, or NNVA. It takes a long time to use the step-by-step approach, and I find it is better to take a look at the whole process first. It is not critical to get these categories all perfect, but rather to see the VA ones. Often teams are also surprised by the NNVA ones.

The VA steps show which steps provide value to the customer in the process. Like the Customer Scorecard, they give a customer perspective. The Customer Scorecard may have suggested additional VA steps that customers want that are not in the current process, as well. The VA steps and Customer Scorecard provide information for formulating the new design. On the other hand, the NVA steps should be eliminated in the new design. The NNVA steps probably cannot be eliminated, but the time to do them should be minimized in the new design.

Benchmarking or Best Practice Interviews

Benchmarking and Best Practices provide creative or comparative ideas about what other companies are doing in this process. They are not required, but doing one or the other will invigorate the team and suggest some improvement ideas they have not thought about.

First of all, let's distinguish between the two terms.

- **Benchmarking** compares your process with others in your own company or like competitors in the industry.
- **Best Practices** is a method of comparing your process with world-class organizations, often outside your industry.

I have found that most people use the terms as though they are synonyms. That's OK, just as long as you know about the two types of techniques and when and why to use each. It is often easier to get Benchmarking interviews because team members know of other sites in their own company with similar processes, or know of other organizations in their industry that would be willing to share about how they do the work. Discovery of Best Practices requires the team to investigate companies that are known for their excellence. Clearly the Best Practice processes represent the most efficient and effective practices and usually some innovative approaches. They may also provide information that suggests a stretch target. Benchmarking and Best Practices data and summaries inspire out-of-box thinking for the team, encourage the team and executives to make decisions based on their quantitative data, enable the team to mitigate risks in the new process through suggestions they heard, and may help identify relevant software vendors for the new design.

There are two main times to engage in benchmarking and best practices research.

1. Very early in the process improvement project. Often organizations want to compare themselves to how others are doing. They want to know if their work process has the best metrics or where they stand in the pack.

Benchmarked comparative data can be critical for establishing the business case and building the burning platform for the process improvement go ahead. One major university I was working with needed to consolidate staff and reduce costs. The head of Human Resources looked at the current number of people in HR compared with total head count and found that her university had a considerably higher ratio of HR staff to total staff as compared with other universities. She used the comparative numbers in two ways:

- To tell the story of why this project was important now
- To set a success metric for the level of improvement she expected in two to four years.

Why don't organizations do this type of business case benchmarking? Well, if the organization has hired a major consulting firm, they will do it. If it hasn't, the BPI team can do it themselves.

Three good sources of information are:

- The Internet (A few well known sites are: http://www.apqc.org/, http://www.benchmarking.com/, and http://www.globalbenchmarking.org/)
- Professional organizations in your industry or discipline or LinkedIn professional groups

- Current employees who have worked at similar companies or you might reference on LinkedIn colleagues

2. When you are ready to create the redesigned process. The second time to do benchmarking and best practices is after the Process Analysis phase. The team knows what the problems are in the process, has a list of improvement ideas, and probably has lots of questions about how others do it. Begin with benchmarking against other sites in your own company. I worked with a car rental company who got all kinds of great ideas by benchmarking with different retail sites. Additionally, talk to other organizations in your industry and look at best practices around the country or globally. One healthcare organization I was working with, who was studying patient intake, went on a few field trips to see kiosk-like intake centers in large facilities and out in the field.

Asking the Right Questions

Three questions have to be answered to do benchmarking: How do we get started? Who do we benchmark against? What do we ask?

To get started, the team should determine what decisions they want to make or actions they want to take from benchmarking interviews, or what outcomes they want from the study. Then they should identify who to benchmark. When I work with a team, I ask them to use their own resources for comparing themselves with other organizations in their own industry. This is a good place to start, as well as research on the Internet.

Formulate a structured questionnaire that leads to learning what other organizations do that will improve your process in relationship to the Improvement Targets the Process Owner has set. Write down specific ideas and decisions you want to identify for your process.

Then write questions to get to the outcome. They may include items such as:

- How the other organization faced the challenges that your team is not sure how to solve
- What the key steps are in the other organization's process
- Specific technology questions
- How they eliminated wastes
- What policies and practices they changed or didn't
- What they learned when implementing improvements

The Project Lead and one team member could create a list of interview questions as a straw man for team discussion.

The study for your process improvement effort can be simple: talk to five to seven organizations and see what you learn. (Most organizations are not doing four-day onsite visits for benchmarking anymore.) Call up a contact and ask them your structured questions. See what the team learns from the first interviews and iterate the questions to fine-tune what is needed. A team member may ask for the benchmarked unit or organization to send artifacts from their process when examples would be helpful. Don't forget to thank them. Offer them a summary of the findings if they are interested.

The analysis of the data is best completed by a few team members and then discussed with the team in a team meeting. Then the team can decide how to adapt the findings to their organization and apply them in the Process Design phase and Implementation Plan.

Benchmarking is useful in defining what might be possible. But caution the team not to assume that the same process steps from the benchmarked source will have the same outcomes in their situation. These are ideas and springboards, not the answer from a white knight that knows everything.

The Recruiting and Hiring Case: Before and After

The Recruiting and Hiring process that has been used for case examples throughout this book is also a good example for the before and after case. Let's review the Improvement Targets, baseline values, and goal values.

Improvement Target #1: Standardize the Recruiting and Hiring process for our organization.

- **Baseline value:** There are currently 15 recruiting and hiring processes.
- **Goal value:** There is one standard recruiting process for the organization.

Improvement Target #2: Make the process more efficient.

- **Measure 1:** Time to fill jobs
  - **Baseline value:** Current time to fill jobs from request from the hiring manager to acceptance ranges from 4 to 18 months.
  - **Goal value:** Time to fill jobs from request from the hiring manger to candidate acceptance is 6 weeks to 9 months.
- **Measure 2:** Count of paper checklists and places where information is reentered
  - **Baseline value:** We have 22 inconsistent checklists and 3 places where we re-enter information from paper into the system.
  - **Goal value:** Standardized formats are accessible and readable in one system. No re-entry of data is needed.

The As-Is process diagram is shown in Figure 67. There were three different Human Resources roles, 17 handoffs, limited automation, no automated workflow, and no ability to access resumes, recruiting plans, and position descriptions from a database. Customers complained that they could not access resumes and cover letters online, that the recruiting process took too long, that many candidates did not meet their requirements, and that they did not know what the process was or where they were in it.

The redesigned process is shown in Figure 68. The To-Be diagram should not have swimlanes. The team should not be focused on who is performing each step, but simply the best sequence of steps.

The redesigned process moved toward the Process Owner and Executive Sponsor's Improvement Targets although it did not reach all of them. Specifically, the BPI team realized that they did not want to have just one standard process because different job categories required different hiring processes or different tasks within the hiring processes. They identified three job categories: students (hired for summer positions), scientists, and all others (for example, administrative, executive, and operational). Students did not go through much of the hiring process at all. The organization used a list of students from a nearby university, reviewed their resumes, and selected candidates based on their major and letters of recommendation. So this was made an entirely separate process. The scientists and all other categories were similar except that scientists needed to include a presentation task. The rest of the To-Be process was the same.

The BPI team estimated the Time to Hire would be reduced by 25%, which was less than the Process Owner's goal value. They expected this cycle time would get better after employees and managers adjusted to the new process and the new hiring software. The Process Owner was satisfied.

They eliminated all the inconsistent checklists and standardized them in the new software. By purchasing and implementing new software, the process benefited from automated workflow, database access for resumes, recruiting plans, job offers, job descriptions, interview questions, and more, electronic forms for the multiple templates, visibility of candidate folders, and transparency about where a needed hiring request was in the process. There was no need to re-enter information they had in the current state. The Process Owner was very pleased.

There were other improvements in the redesigned process as well. The three Human Resource roles were reduced to one Recruiter role that performed the three HR roles in the As-Is diagram. They added a task for the Recruiter to screen the resumes every two weeks and select the best five and highlight those with summaries for the Hiring Manager. A full set of resumes of candidates who met the job qualifications was still available from the database if the hiring manager wanted to see them. They established a standard recruiting plan for different job categories and began to track the success of different sourcing mechanisms (different job sites, professional organizations, etc.).

Initial Quick Wins included shifting to the one Human Resource role, the Recruiter, and putting two forms into an electronic format. Some divisions were small and did not have a recruiter in their division. For some of these small divisions, a Human Resource Manager in the division performed as the recruiter for the whole process; for other small divisions, recruiters from other divisions took on the Recruiter role for the additional division. They did not need to hire any additional people.

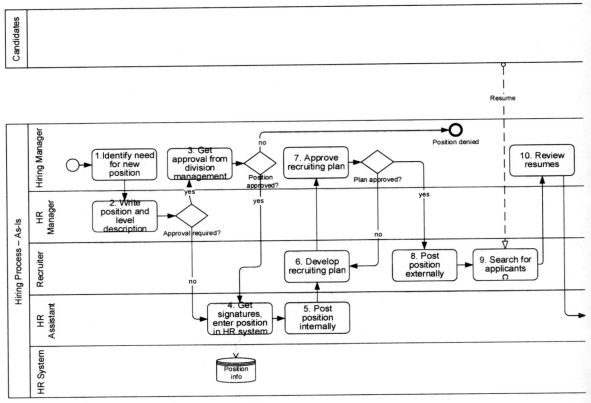

Figure 67. The Recruiting and Hiring Swimlane As-Is Process

How Do We Get to the New Design?

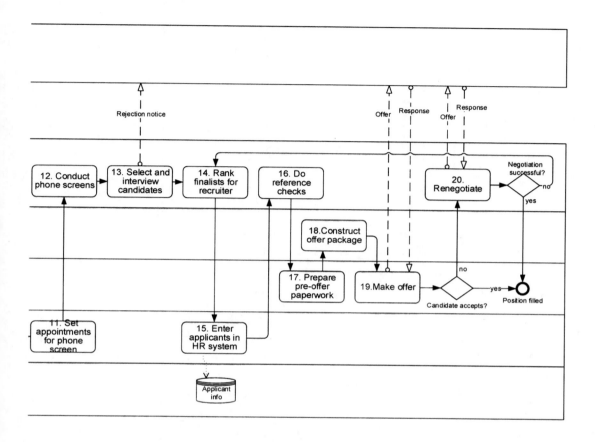

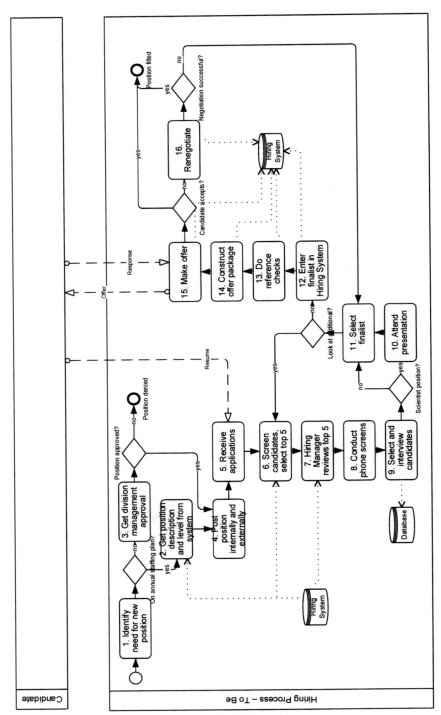

Figure 68. The Recruiting and Hiring Redesigned Process

How Do We Get to the New Design?

Rules for Redesign

Rules for Redesign are principles for the new process design. They are positive statements describing the actions that will be part of the new design. I developed these originally with Dan Madison, and I have continued to revise them since. Although Dan has many more in his book, *Process Mapping, Process Improvement, & Process Management,*[26] I find that this smaller number covers the key rules and the sub bullets give further elaboration.

Below are the Rules for Redesign to explain to the team after the case. It is helpful to provide some examples from client situations for several of the sub bullets, or ask the team for possible examples from their own process.

1. Design the process around value-added activities

- Eliminate wastes, such as waiting, multiple systems that don't interface, multiple approvals, excess work, missing information, etc.
- Add in steps for value where customers told you they wanted it.
- A single point of contact often helps customers and suppliers.

Put the value-added activities front and center when the team does the redesign. Eliminate wastes, insert additional steps where the customer told you they wanted more value, and put the current value-added steps in the direct path to the outcome. The team has already thought about eliminating wastes in the initial improvement ideas captured on the I-4 Lists and during the Process Analysis stage, and noted several on the Visual Analysis Model. So there are plenty of known wastes to eliminate.

The third bullet, a single point of contact, develops the organization-customer relationship, provides confidence in the process, and makes the information exchange easier. A single point of contact is a frequent customer request, but it may not always be possible. When I was working with a client on new and ongoing customer issues, the client decided to offer the customer a choice. If the customer phoned in, he could talk to his regular customer rep directly (if the rep was available), leave a voice mail for that customer rep, or talk to a different customer rep who had access to the information in the database and could take the next steps. Sometimes a client might set up a team to work with the customer with a particular person as the lead. Sometimes a client might have two or even three reps, each with specific expertise, and the client knows whom to contact. Teams take this rule and apply it to their situation if it makes sense.

---

[26] Madison, Dan. *Process Mapping, Process Improvement, and Process Management.* Chico, CA: Paton Press, 2005.

The Recruiting and Hiring case incorporates all three of these bullets. It eliminates all kinds of wastes, adds value that the customer requested (seeing resumes electronically, having recruiters select and summarize five top resumes), and makes the recruiter the single point of contact for the hiring manager.

2. Ensure a continuous flow of the "main sequence."

- Put the value steps in sequence.
- Create flows that enable faster throughput.
- Push decision making down to the lowest reasonable level.

Do what it takes to keep the process moving, such as putting the value-added steps in the critical path, reducing wait time between steps, reducing handoffs, and substituting parallel for sequential processes. Bullet three implies removing unnecessary approval steps that always necessitate a handoff to a new swimlane. Instead, it is best to have the performer who is doing the task be able to make needed decisions. Again, this is not always possible, but additional training or revising approval levels would enable the performer to make the decisions in the redesigned process.

The To-Be Recruiting and Hiring case reduces handoffs and adds automation, which enables faster throughput. It eliminates some approvals at the beginning by using an annual staffing plan to allow many requests without additional manager approval, and that also makes for faster flow.

3. Identify natural clusters in the inputs and build separate flows for each (complex vs. simple, for example).

Sometimes a current process would be more efficient if it were separated into two or three separately flowing paths. For example, in working with the transfer student process, the team realized that instead of taking each application in turn using the First In First Out method, separating the flow into applicants from state community colleges vs. all other applicants would speed up the process. Community college applications were more straightforward because courseware matched the university criteria in most cases. It was just more complicated to determine if applicants from other schools had both the necessary basic courses and courses that met the requirements for the student's selected major. An additional benefit from this triage process was that the Registrar's Office could assign more junior staff to the easier community college applicants. The triage method, leading to alternative process flows, increased throughput because difficult applications did not slow down the whole process.

Another example is the expedited process. Many processes have an ad hoc expedited variant, when the executive says, "I need this done now" and then a number of people run

---

How Do We Get to the New Design?

around with their heads cut off getting it done. Instead, it is helpful to recognize the need for an expedited process and diagram what it would be. Then the organization can know ahead of time how resources could be assigned in the expedited process, and what that will mean for other work. Usually the expedited process means some activities are eliminated from the procedure. The team should look at the expedited process to see if those eliminated activities or approvals are really important in the regular process or if they can be removed from the regular process as well. The actual cycle time for the expedited process could be a goal value for the regular process. Another aspect of the expedited process is defining what requests will be accepted into the expedited process; criteria have to be defined or everyone will want the expedited process.

There are two triage points in the Recruiting and Hiring case. The first is at the gateway where students are separated from all other hires and put on a different path. (This was removed from Figure 68 for simplicity.) The second is at the gateway where scientists are separated from all other jobs. This gateway does not lead to two paths but does show a variation in the scientist-related tasks.

4. Standardize the process.

- Document the process, agree on roles and responsibilities, and implement steps and sequence.
- Agree on standard data definitions and data elements for collection.
- Use standardized modules to allow customization of subprocesses within the whole process.

The Lean methodology has strict criteria for what stabilization and standardization mean. *Stabilization* means that processes have exactly the same steps, occurring in the same sequence, and completed by the same roles for all units doing the process. *Standardization* is more stringent and includes all the attributes of stabilization plus two more: that the process runs at the same speed and that it maintains a stated level of inventories for all the units doing the process. Lean would say the example of building a single process from a combination of instances is really *stabilization*. I prefer to use one the word *standardization* and not worry too much about the differences in definition.

Teams may have looked at many different instances and combined them into one consolidated model. This consolidated instance could be the first level of a new design because it is a combination of the multiple current process diagrams stabilized into one process diagram for all groups to use. If the consolidated model gets implemented as an early prototype, it will represent how standardization starts to work in the organization. (Chapter 10 provides details of how to do this consolidation.)

In one client example, the team first diagrammed a single instance of gathering the data for the budget and analyzed it using the I-4 Lists. The 13 other groups said their process was very different from the initial instance, so the team decided to diagram instances for all 14 different departments. Each group thought their process was different, because it was. Each had different roles, a different order of the steps, different systems or shadow applications, and different levels of approval. Once they had diagrammed the 14 instances, they looked at all 14 process diagrams and saw that they really were similar. After reviewing all 14, they were able to step back and see that several differences were just a matter of semantics, that roles had different names but did basically the same thing, that some roles were combined, that different technology had been created in different silos and had some different functionalities, but mostly performed the same functions for this process. Then they were easily able to consolidate and come up with a standardized As-Is model that represented 80% of what they all did. They used this standardized model from then on and applied the needed analytical techniques. Later they designed the To-Be process as an improvement on the consolidated standardized process model.

The first standardization bullet above is actually the first step. It says, "Document the process, agree on roles and responsibilities, and implement steps and sequence." In other words, in order to be standardized, the process needs to be written down; actors must be clearly delineated and understand their roles in the process; and then the process needs to follow the steps in the order it is documented. The process can't just be in someone's head. It shouldn't be completed by different performers in different ways according to their individual learning or preference. So, in the example above with 14 different budget processes, there are 14 different ways of doing it. But after the team modeled the 14 processes and looked at them, they could see where they were 80% the same. This was an important first step in understanding the consistency of the current process vs. thinking of it as 14 unique processes.

Data definitions that vary across the organization represent a source of waste. If data definitions are different in various applications, rework is needed to transfer them from one application to the next to make them compatible. This is a current band-aid step often performed by departments using Excel spreadsheets or shadow systems.

The last bullet says a team can build standardized modules for subprocesses to accommodate various requirements. That makes the whole end-to-end process one standard, but with variations enabled at certain points. These standard modules would occur after a gateway to show which path and standardized module would be followed.

The 15 initial division processes for Recruiting and Hiring really became two – one for students and the second for scientists and all others, with a slight difference for scientists. Consistent electronic forms replaced the multiple manual checklists and templates. Both of these represented the first two bullets in these rules for redesign.

5. Ensure information is accurate and available.

- Ensure 100% error-free information at the beginning of the process.
- Capture information once, at the source, and share it widely.
- Capture at the beginning what's needed for later steps.

The three bullets under this rule for redesign are important principles about data and information. You want to get 100% error-free information at the start of the process. If the process gets only 65% of the information complete and accurate, the later steps need to include rework to fill in the gaps with that remaining 35% of the information. Often that happens because one department is trying to be "considerate" of another department. They continue to accept the information as it comes in and take it on themselves to fill in the missing information. It may be that the receiving department has never given any feedback to the supplying department about what information is needed, in what detail, and in what format, so the supplying department just goes on providing it the same way. It is important to sit down with the information supplier, be it a person, department, or application, and clarify what is needed.

Then think about the second and third bullets. Gather the information one time from a "single source of truth," and share that consistent information across the process with whoever needs it. Also capture that information early in the process, and share it as needed across later steps. This last rule has an exception. If the process needs information at later steps, it might be burdensome to gather it all at the beginning, as happens when the process begins with a large funnel and keeps narrowing. For example, one client gathered proposals for internal funding. In the As-Is process, they asked for detailed budgets with the initial proposal. When they redesigned the process, they put a step early in the process to determine if the proposal aligned with a strategic objective; if it did not, the proposal was not accepted. Clearly, it is extra work to draw up a detailed budget for a proposal where the need does not meet the strategic objective. But for proposals that meet the criteria, the process continues and the detailed budget can be developed later.

In the Recruiting and Hiring case, the new process collects information about the position and the candidates early and stores them in the hiring software and the associated database. This means that information is captured once, as soon as it enters the process, and is shared across the process.

6. Design the whole process rather than component tasks.

The reason to design the whole process is that the opportunity for improvement is greater. If a team only works on a subprocess, the more limited scope constrains the extent of the improvements. Looking at the whole process end-to-end enables the team to think bigger and design the process backward from the desired output. Ask the question of the team,

"What does our process need to do to get this output the customer wants?" Come up with a few critical items; they are likely be the value-added items already marked.

Then look at changes to get to those items more efficiently and effectively. For example, identify how improvements at the beginning of the process will positively impact tasks later on. Often if a waste is eliminated or reduced early in the process, wastes later on just disappear. Improvements at the beginning of the process have the greatest likelihood of producing a domino effect, to the benefit of later steps in the process.

Visually I think it is easier to look at the whole process on a whiteboard, butcher paper, or in the BPMN flat format (one long diagram) vs. the BPMN hierarchical format (one main diagram and several sub-diagrams). Both are correct, but for analysis and redesign, the flat format enables the team to see all the details in a single view.

By looking at the whole Recruiting and Hiring process, the need for software, a single source of truth, and transparency about the process and each candidate's status in it all becomes evident.

7. *Process flow determines staffing structure.*

- Form work groups for special cases and complex situations.
- Use multifunctional teams and multi-skilled employees.
- Identify the need for generalists vs. specialists.

So many companies reshuffle the org chart when a new executive comes in, and only think about processes later. But it makes more sense to understand and improve the end-to-end processes before new roles and responsibilities are assigned. Jobs should fit the need of the workflow, so don't think about what kind of performers are needed when the team creates the original redesign. That actually constricts the team's creativity because they will tend to fall back into repeating the current roles. It also may not be necessary to change the reporting structure to accommodate a new person's role, but rather to redefine that role in this process. But if the organization has already reorganized, that's OK. Just go ahead with the redesign phase, and consider what roles are needed in the redesign; it may or may not be necessary to make additional organizational changes.

The particulars for recommendations in staffing structure are clarified in the three bullets above. The first one suggests that it is helpful to form small work groups to handle special cases and complex situations. Three examples are: (1) forming a team to do payroll every payroll period; (2) forming a group to expedite a process (as explained earlier in this chapter); (3) forming a finance group to do the quarterly profit and loss or to attend the earnings meeting with external analysts.

The second and third bullets articulate how employees might be used differently and how to expand their roles and responsibilities in the process. Build and use multi-functional teams when the process needs it, instead of just handing off the step to a different function; if the functions work together as a team they will be more efficient. Developing multi-skilled employees means training them to have wider or deeper skills so they understand and can perform more tasks in the process, or fill in for others when needed. Identify when roles should be generalists or specialists. One example would be that generalists might perform many roles (especially sales or customer service) for a particular industry or geographic region. On the other hand, specialists are needed when detailed or complex situations call for a resource that has particular skills. An obvious example is the difference between the doctor that is a general practitioner vs. a specialist in heart surgery. Another role to consider was suggested in the first rule for redesign, namely "A single point of contact often helps customers and suppliers."

In the Recruiting and Hiring case the need for a specialist, the Recruiter, was key for the redesign.

Engaging the Team with the Rules for Redesign

After discussing the Rules for Redesign with the team, it is helpful to give them 5 minutes to identify which rules are relevant for their process improvement effort. It is not possible to apply all the rules, but two or three critical ones provide a good focus.

BUILDING THE NEW DESIGN

Now this is the fun part! The team is ready to be creative and build the first draft of the To-Be model. There are three parts to this section:

1. Reviewing the three guiding lights
2. Getting creative individual ideas and finding common themes in those ideas
3. Making the redesigned model

The Three Guiding Lights

The three guiding lights are the three major inputs into the new process: Process Owner's Improvement Targets, Customer Scorecard Summary, and baseline and analytical data. It is useful to remind the team of them in a simple one-page format. So the Project Lead or Team Facilitator puts them on one page and summarizes them to keep them to this shortened format. Then the team reads them and discusses them for a few minutes at the beginning of this session.

Creative Individual Ideas

Next, follow this innovative method to solicit creative ideas for the new process. The Team Facilitator explains the goals for your ideal state:

Goals for the Ideal State

- Achieve customer delight.
- Dramatically reduce process steps, time, or cost (50% or more).

Don't let money or time worry the team when you are building the Ideal State.

Each individual works in silence for 15-20 minutes.

1. Write a story or draw a picture of how you want the new process to be. The Team Facilitator should ask everyone on the team state whether they want to do a story (3-4 paragraphs) or picture; half the team should do one format and the other half the other. The Team Facilitator should participate as well, along with the Process Owner if he is there. The picture should be like a storyboard but with limited words. It should not be a flowchart; we are not doing a model yet. Of course, it can have pictures, icons, and stick figures.
2. Each individual writes down the rules for redesign he used and how they meet sponsor and customer needs.
3. Each individual shares his story or picture with the team, and states the rules for redesign used. (This should only take 2-3 minutes each.)
4. The Team Facilitator makes a list on a chart of the common themes from the stories and pictures, by eliciting ideas from the group.

TEAM FACILITATOR NOTES

If the participants have less than 15 minutes, the stories will be more generic and not as creative. Make sure this story writing and picture drawing is done in silence so each individual gets to be creative in his own way. In one example, the Team Facilitator did a storyboard using five slide drawings on his iPad.

Developing the Redesigned Model

Now it is time to build the first draft of the To-Be model. I suggest doing it on a whiteboard or large butcher paper so everyone on the team can see it together. Get them all standing up and working in front of the board.

Remind the team that the redesigned model should not use swimlanes to start. At this point, it is best to use BPMN without lanes. As was discussed in the Before and After case study, using

---

swimlanes encourages the team to retain the same roles and responsibilities as the current state, which may not be what the process needs. Instead, as the seventh rule for redesign points out, "Process flow determines staffing structure." If the team wants, you can name the performer in the activity box to point out a new concept or idea (for example, "group manager triages applications") or just leave off any reference to roles.

Build the redesigned model much as you did the current process diagram, but without swimlanes. Here is the method.

1. Put the name of your process at the top of your redesigned map. You can rename your process if you want. In fact, the team should be encouraged to choose a new process name if the new name better reflects what they are trying to do. In one example, the team changed the name from Hiring Temporary Workers to Building an Ongoing Talent Pool when they realized that they wanted to highlight the organization's priority to hire former workers in many temporary project roles.
2. Use a new piece of chart paper and stickies or a new electronic model. Create the redesigned model without swimlanes.
3. Enter the first and last activity on the paper or software tool, and fill in the middle steps and gateways. Constantly apply your common themes and rules for redesign.
4. Some teams build an ideal model thinking five to ten years out; then they create a second model that is a more realistic To-Be model for 6-18 months out to present to the Process Owners. Other teams build a redesigned model that is appropriate for the changes now and in the next six months. Either one is fine. The teams should do what makes sense to them.

TEAM FACILITATOR NOTES

Encourage the team to make a To-Be model that represents the common themes from their discussion. They should make a good first pass at it; everyone does not have to be in agreement with all of it. Sometimes teams like to draw an infographic as a first step, especially if they want to show how different information will come into the process from an overview perspective. Then they go on to draw the process model.

Allow about two hours for the team to draw the model. Since the To-Be process model does not contain swimlanes, it is easier to draw than the current state process diagram. Putting all the ideas together for the To-Be stories and pictures, rules for redesign, and common themes takes an additional two hours as well.

When the team is finished, have them review the model verbally, commenting on what improvements they made and how each will impact the three guiding lights. Have them determine if and how this new design will meet the Process Owner's Improvement Targets, and be ready to articulate that.

Usually the team is quite excited by the new design. They see the process graphically, incorporating many of the improvements they have been talking about and adding other ideas built off the rules for redesign. They see how the process time will be shortened, rework reduced, and complexity removed. Often they see possibilities that they would never have thought were possible as they began the project, and they are excited about telling others about what they have created and then seeing the new process implemented. Instead of having them go through every step in the new process, I suggest a debrief which covers the following:

- What is the team particularly excited about in the new design?
- How will the new design meet the Improvement Targets and address customer needs?

Quality Indicators – Here's How to Know if the New Design Is a Success

- There is a strong consensus among the BPI team to support the new design.
- There is confidence that the new design will be a significant improvement over the former process.
- The team can estimate the quantitative improvements from the baseline values, and they are close or exceed the goal values set by the Process Owner.
- The team can tell a compelling story about the new design which leadership and stakeholders will be excited about.

RACI and Risk Assessment – Two Techniques to Apply to the Redesigned Model

When the team comes down off their "high" from creating the new design, it is helpful to have them apply two analytical techniques against it, namely RACI and Risk. They can use both or choose the one that is more relevant to their process. RACI looks at roles and responsibilities and Risk Assessment simply looks at the risks in the redesign. By using one of these, the redesigned process gets reviewed at a more practical level. Their application will probably not change the redesigned model significantly but may raise questions for discussion and suggest some initial revisions.

RACI Technique for Roles and Responsibilities

The RACI technique was described in Chapter 12. When the team uses RACI on the new process design, the table format cannot be utilized because the diagram is not in swimlanes. Here is another method for the new process design.

How Do We Get to the New Design?

Take each step in the new process design one by one and identify who would be doing it, if there are any approvals needed (probably shown by a gateway following the step), if others need to be consulted, or informed. Make a notation under each step for the R's and A's:

>R – Director of Marketing
>A – None

For the RACI on the To-Be design, I find it best to complete the R's and A's for the whole process. Then step back as a team and ask about the R's. "What new roles have we built in and why? How do these roles improve the process for the customer or move the process toward the Improvement Target? Can we combine roles? Do we have a single point of contact for the customer (or is that not appropriate)?" For the A's, step back and ask, "Do we still need this A? What value-add does each A provide? Does the A performer really know the information needed to make the approval? Is it needed for regulatory purposes? Could the A be consulted earlier or informed later and not have to make a real approval? Could the R be trained to make the decision?" Wait to do the C's and I's until the new design is agreed on at a high level and the team is ready to draft the more detailed swimlane.

It is best not to show the simplified RACI or swimlanes when vetting the new design. If you show employees a swimlane model and their role is not on it, they stop listening. They wonder what is happening to them. Have they been fired? Where are they going?

Risk Assessment

The team can apply the Risk Assessment technique explained in Chapter 12 to the new redesigned model. The method for the technique is the same for both phases of the BPI Project, Process Analysis or Process Design. Applying it to the new design, the team should ask:

- Are there remaining risks from the current state that need mitigation?
- Have any new risks been introduced, and if so how should they be controlled?

RACI or Risk can be applied against the team's redesigned model. The Project Lead and SMEs decide if one or the other, both or neither is best for their process. These techniques are independent of one another, but in keeping the BPI simple and structured, I would not require the team to do both. Applying an analysis technique against the new model is a first step in putting reality against the model; it takes the model from fantasized "ideal" to a more pragmatic state, and enables the team to see how this model might work in operation.

Recommendations for the New Design

While the new design is fresh in the team's mind, it is helpful to articulate some recommendations that align with the new design. These recommendations will identify the rules for redesign or key improvements that were incorporated in the new design. Keep the recommendations to the most important ones, about three to six in number. In the Hiring Case, the recommendations were:

Design the Process around Value-Added Activities.

- Eliminate wastes, such as waiting, multiple systems that don't interface, multiple approvals, excess work, missing information, etc.
  Reduce number of approvals needed. Do this by starting with an Annual Staffing Plan so most positions would already be agreed upon. Take the HR Director out of the approval process.

  Purchase a recruiting and hiring process that will enable workflow and transparency for all in the process.

  Use databases to store and retrieve core documents, such as position descriptions, recruiting plans, and pre- offer letters.

- Add in steps for value where customers told you they wanted it.
  Add in a step that has the Recruiter review the resumes and prioritize the top five, with a summary for the Hiring Manager.

- A single point of contact often helps customers and suppliers.
  Make the Recruiter role the single point of contact for the Hiring Manager. Remove the HR Manager and the HR Assistant.

Standardize the Process.

- Document the process, agree on roles and responsibilities, and implement steps and sequence.
  The redesigned process is a standard process for the organization. All divisions and functions will use it. We know that this will require new tools and training, both of which will be included in the Implementation Plan.

Two to Three Options

It is often helpful to offer the Process Owner two or three options. Option #1 recommendation is the team's priority recommendation; it is the one that covers most of the team's suggestions, but since it could be costly, take a long time to implement, or have political or policy ramifications, that might not fly at this point. Option #2 represents a modified approach (such as less automation, a variation on the #1 method, or no organizational restructuring, etc.). Option #3 could be an even more scaled-down approach. The team is OK with all three of the recommendations; although #1 is preferred, all three will represent significant improvements. Each recommendation would have different Implementation Plans but all three can be successful.

Review of the BPI Team Outcomes Report with the Process Owner

Now that the redesign is done, it is necessary for the Project Lead and Team Facilitator to review it with the Process Owner. I suggest a BPI Team Outcomes Report. It includes these materials:

- The original problems and goals: Use the one-page summary of the Three Guiding Lights (process improvements, data, and Customer Scorecard) that the team used in the Process Design Phase; attach the current version of the Project Charter.
- A visual analysis model of the current state map
- The new design model and specific recommendations necessary for the new design to work
- How the new design meets the Improvement Targets; estimated quantifiable benefits; anticipated costs and challenges in implementation
- The two or three options if you have them
- What you need from the Process Owner to go forward (e.g., his approval, his help with implementation across functions, money, new staffing for the Implementation team)

Here are some tips to make the meeting successful with the Process Owner.

1. Be prepared. Use the one-page summary of the Three Guiding Lights to set the stage.
2. Review the highlights of current process challenges with quantitative data on the visual analysis model.
3. Show the redesigned model and walk through it BRIEFLY, pointing out important changes.
4. Then tell him what the key elements of the new design are that will get to the Improvement Targets, vision, and customer requirements. Go over the specific recommendations that support the new design. Review the two to three options and the benefits of each.
5. Ask what the Process Owner is excited about. Ask what he is concerned about. Ask which option he suggests and why.
6. Talk about any revisions that could be made.
7. Request what you need from him, such as influence with different divisions in implementation, money for technology, new staffing for Implementation, or project status meetings to get implementation completed.
8. Agree on when to get started on the project or next steps.

Some Project Leads prefer to develop a full report for the project with Project Charter, As-Is model, metrics, Wastes, Customer Scorecard, Benchmarking, Redesigned model, specific recommendations with two to three options, anticipated benefits or ROI, and an Implementation Plan. I find it helps to have an informal conversation with the Process Owner as described in the paragraphs above and keep this more formal culmination report for later. All these items should be in the shared repository as well. What is important here is to keep the Process Owner engaged, hear his motivation and concerns, and give him the words to start promoting the redesign.

In addition, the Project Lead and teams members should vet the redesigned process with colleagues, such as other employees or managers in their departments who have not been on the team, other stakeholders who are engaged in the process and will be impacted. Each SME on the BPI team should be keeping his managers and colleagues up to speed throughout the BPI effort, but they need to know the recommendations for improvements. Get their input. The SMEs and other team members can informally use the same conversation as the one described in the meeting with the Process Owner; they should tailor the discussion to the particular audience; at tips #4 and #5, substitute relevant requests for these employees and managers to hear their comments, and request help with testing, participating on an implementation team, or other tasks.

When I work with three BPI teams in parallel as described in Chapter 7, the Project Lead and Team Facilitator discuss the new design with the Process Owner individually. Then a final presentation is planned for the three teams at once, the Process Owner, Executive Sponsor, other employees in the SME departments, and guests. The presentation is a shortened version of the Process Owner meeting. I encourage each team to have large visuals that others can see, such as a model of the new design, and the initial swimlane map turned into a Visual Analysis Model. It is key to review the initial challenges with the Improvement Targets and vision, to have quantitative data to indicate the size of the problems, to share key customer comments, and to show how the new design is different and will get to the Improvement Targets.

SUMMARY

This chapter provides specific techniques to inspire the team to build a redesigned process. Doing the work together and seeing the results is often motivational, unifies the team even more, and builds the momentum to go forward. At the culmination of this phase, Leadership and the BPI team should have a product (the new design) and the Team Outcomes Report, be able to explain how it meets or moves toward the three guiding lights, and be excited about taking it forward.

THINGS TO THINK ABOUT

SIMULATION AND DESIGN

Simulation is a technique that uses a software tool to forecast various time and cost metrics based on a design with estimated values of parameters for average activity durations, branch percentages at gateways, resource costs, and staffing levels. It can be a valuable tool in the Process Design phase. I have been teaching and using simulation with BPM for over seven years, using a variety of simulation tools, including Savvion, Fujitsu, and Process Analytica.

There are two major reasons for doing a simulation during the BPI Project.

1. To test out different workflow designs
2. To evaluate different staffing scenarios

Simulation allows the team to compare metric values generated with As-Is process parameters to metric values in the To-Be process. Knowing the current state metric values helps refine and validate the simulation parameters for the As-Is model. Most simulations concentrate on looking at costs (usually staffing costs) and time (cycle time and bottlenecks at a particular step). Simulation lets you test the effect of rearranging steps, changing the branching percentages at gateways, and adding or reducing staff in various roles. Other variables that can be modified in a simulation scenario are errors, loopbacks, and batches. With each change in scenario, you run the simulation and see how it affects the time and cost metrics.

Often there is a tradeoff between the time and costs or other scenario choices. In processes where work can pile up at one or more steps, obviously you can reduce the cycle time by adding staff to that role, but this also increases the cost. So simulation doesn't magically tell you the "right answer" but gives you estimated data you can use to determine the best design and staffing allocation.

The problem with using simulation is it takes a lot of work both to obtain good values for the parameters and then to enter the numbers in the simulation tool. In order to produce a realistic simulation, it is necessary to have credible data, and that means the team and other subject matter experts need to gather the data manually, find it in different reports, or track against the system in real time to get the data. Here are some of the specific questions that came up while gathering data for simulation of the Hiring process:

- How many new positions come open per day?
- How many full-time equivalent recruiters were there, and what was the range of open positions and candidates that each had at one time?

- What did sourcing mean quantitatively? For example, how many resumes were there and how long were they collected before they were given to the hiring manager?
- How different are the hiring models for different types of positions?
- What are the current percentages and their range for each gateway for different paths out of the gateway?
- What is the variation in wait time and handling time within an activity? Is it worth capturing?

What is interesting to me about setting up a simulation is the team is forced to think about the parts of a process in more detail and the different elements that can impact it. In other words, creating a simulation helps the team ask better questions.

Below are some graphs from a simulation of the Hiring Process that Robert Shapiro of Process Analytica developed with me. They give a good idea of the different analytics and visuals available with simulation.

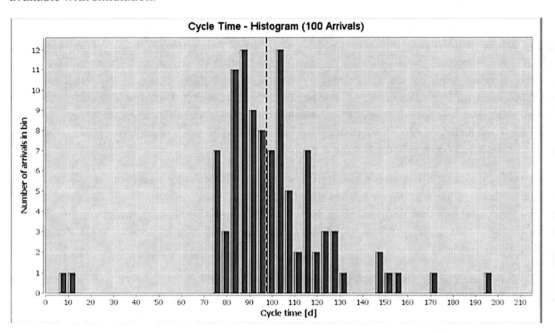

Figure 69. End to End Cycle Time for Current State Hiring Process. Source: Robert Shapiro, Process Analytica

Simulation is a statistical method. Its parameters are typically specified as probabilities. The duration of a task has a mean value and a range. Similarly, each output from a gateway has a probability. Simulation runs many instances using these probabilities, and the results are expressed as histograms. Figure 69 is a histogram of the various cycle times for 100 arrivals in the Hiring process, showing a range of 8 days to 196 days. Figure 70 is a scattergram where the team member can grab any instance and see what is under it.

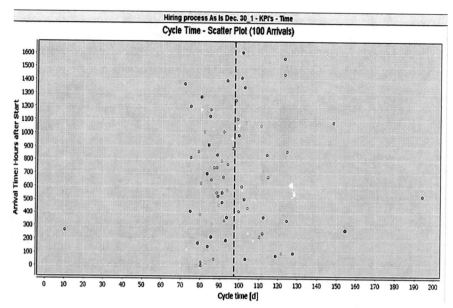

Figure 70. Scatter Plot Showing Individual Instances of Cycle Time for Current State Hiring Process. Source: Robert Shapiro, Process Analytica

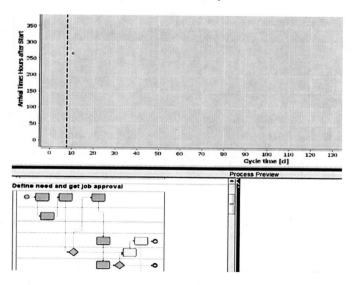

Figure 71. Process Diagram for a Single Instance Showing Where Process Ended. Source: Robert Shapiro, Process Analytica

In Figure 71, the dot to the farthest left is looked at individually; it shows that the process ended early because the process diagram came to an end when the open position was not approved in the very first subprocess.

In Figure 72, the software shows the elapsed time for two of the subprocesses: the interview subprocess and the offer subprocess. Here the team might decide to concentrate on one subprocess vs. another based on the mean and range of elapsed time. In the situation simulated here, there is more opportunity to reduce elapsed time in the Offer subprocess.

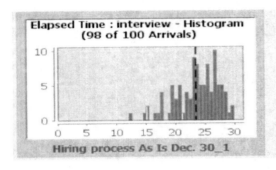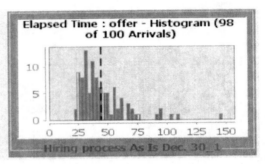

Figure 72. Elapsed Time for Interview Subprocesses and Offer Subprocess. Source: Robert Shapiro, Process Analytica

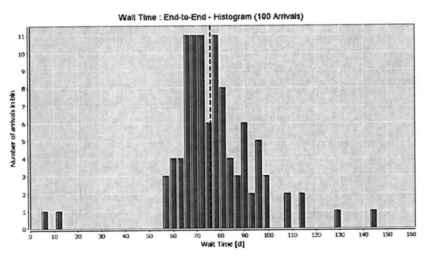

Figure 73. Total Wait Time between Steps for Current State Hiring Process. Source: Robert Shapiro, Process Analytica

Figure 73 shows the number and range of wait times in days for the full end-to-end process, from under 10 to 145. Now the team can look at what causes different wait times (approvals from managers, waiting for the candidate to get back to the hiring manager, setting up interviews, etc.) and see which ones could be reduced or eliminated.

Figure 74 graphs the To-Be (top) and As-Is (bottom) process, comparing overall cycle time. In the To-Be process, cycle time has changed from the current state because workflow automation and accessible databases have been added; the times with these improvements have been estimated. Later the team would want to document the actual cycle times measured after the improvements were implemented.

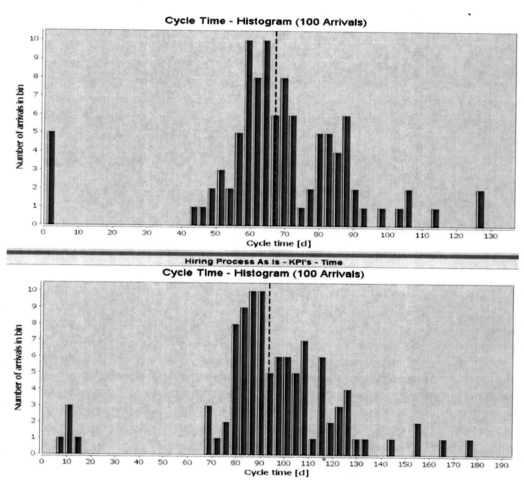

Figure 74. To-Be Hiring Process Cycle Time (top); As-Is Hiring Process Cycle Time (bottom). Source: Robert Shapiro, Process Analytica

Figure 75 shows the elapsed time for the Offer subprocesses with the To-Be subprocess on the top and the As-Is subprocess on the bottom. The improvements included in this To-Be scenario are (1) a draft offer was prepared early in the process, listing compensation ranges and other benefit items and (2) a single human resource person handled the complete offer process. The change reduced the elapsed time for the Offer subprocess from a mean of 43 days to 31 days, decreased the longest and shortest times, and reduced the total range of time variation.

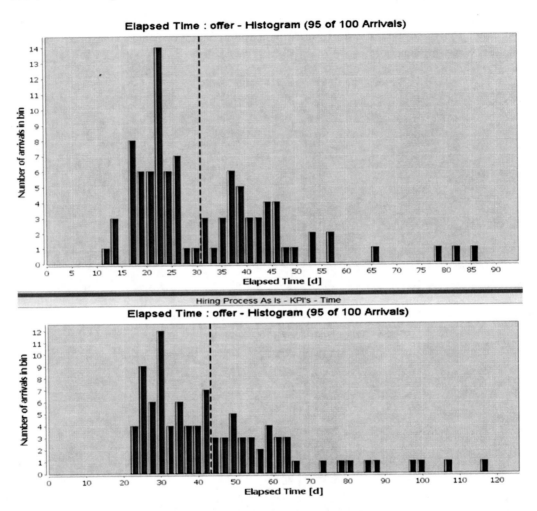

Figure 75. To-Be Elapsed Time for Offer Subprocess (top); As-Is Elapsed Time for Offer subprocess (bottom). Source: Robert Shapiro, Process Analytica

What is obvious from these graphs is that simulations offer a range of data and graphics to help the team understand the possibilities of different scenarios and which changes offer the best opportunities for improvements. The histograms also give the team a framework for considering whether to make further improvements or accept the redesign as good enough for the first round. The redesign should be iteration one, and other iterations could consider other scenarios.

Also, the numbers are just predictive of the future. The transition to the redesign may involve role changes, technology implementation, new forms, and cultural shifts as well as the process changes, and all of these elements will influence the final result.

TOP TEN RULES FOR REDESIGN OF BPM PROCESSES (FROM BPM STUDENTS)

 Well, this is the really fun part! After creating the Project Charter, modeling current state process diagrams, collecting customer and internal quantitative data, and applying the critical analytical techniques, it is time to shift to the right side of the brain and creatively build the new redesigned process.

It's helpful to begin with a one-page document that summarizes the critical elements of the process analysis so far:

1. The Process Owner's Improvement Targets,
2. Customer Scorecard input
3. Data – baseline, goal metrics, and analytical quantitative data

Then move to looking at a case example of the "before and after" for a BPM process and reviewing the rules for redesign. Rules for Redesign are guidelines for concepts or principles that you want to be part of the new process design. They are positive statements describing the actions that will be incorporated into your new design.

Here are two principles that I think are particularly important:

- **Design the process around value-added activities.** Put the value-added activities front and center when you do your redesign. Eliminate wastes, add in extra steps where the customer told you they want value, and put the current value-added steps in the direct path to the outcome.
- **Ensure a continuous flow of the "main sequence."** Do what it takes to keep the process moving, such as putting the value-added steps in the critical path, reducing wait time between steps, and substituting parallel for sequential processes.

In the spirit of creativity, I want to provide some Rules for Redesign that have been developed by students in my classes. Consider adding a few of these to your own Rules for Redesign as you begin the Process Design phase of your BPI Project.

1. **Eliminate redundant and minimally used processes.** Yes, there may be whole subprocesses that can be eliminated.

---

2. **Repurpose and integrate successful existing subprocesses into the redesign.** See if there are subprocesses that are working well in other processes that could be utilized in your process. Also, certain subprocesses may be used more than once in your process.
3. **Use a transition-in plan for new key stakeholders and transition-out plan for old stakeholders.** Clearly, this is part of change management for the employees (stakeholders) involved. It will involve communication, understanding the changes, why they are important, and training.
4. **Put access to information where it is needed the most.** Information is critical to the accuracy and flow of a process. Make it available to people who need it; this could be employees doing the process and others who use the process outputs. Make information accessible and transparent.
5. **Ensure that everybody has the right information from the start.** This rule links with the former rule. Get the information needed from the start so there is not a lot of rework collecting it.
6. **Listen to your data.** Do not use "selective data" to sell your suggestions; listen to the data and follow the trail! The value of data is the objective picture it presents. Use it fairly.
7. **Give resources (people involved in the process) most of the decision making authority.** The correlate of this rule is to remove excess approvals, but this rules says it better. Give the decision-making power to the person doing the job whenever possible.
8. **Minimize the number of departments, groups and persons involved in a business process.** By keeping the roles in the process to a minimum, you enlarge employees' span of work, reduce handoffs, streamline the process, and reduce cycle time.
9. **Collect accurate data required for the proper functioning of the process.** Plan for data integrity and data validation beforehand. This rule is about planning for what data is needed to make the new process work – that is, what data needs to be gathered during the process to identify possible problems early, to produce the right number of quality outputs – all to ensure it is working well.
10. **Think Big, Start Small, and Scale Fast** – Always try to achieve redesign success with simpler processes first before tackling the complex ones. What I love about this one is its vision, realism, and plan. Think Big is the vision, but you can't start there (or you will never get there). Start Small means pick a process that is smaller to start with, or have different phases of improvements as you implement the redesign. Scale Fast is the plan; when you start small for success, be thinking about how the design will scale.

Chapter 14

PUTTING IT ALL TOGETHER IN
IBM BLUEWORKS LIVE

When you are just concerned about a single BPI project, traditional 20th-century tools like butcher paper and stickies often work just fine. But if you want to share your models and project artifacts with other groups across your organization, or if you anticipate additional BPI projects in your organization in the future, you really should be using 21st-century software tools. A really good one for this purpose is Blueworks Live from IBM,[27] and in this chapter you'll see how to use it for a BPI Project.

IBM BLUEWORKS LIVE – A BPI PROJECT TOOL IN THE CLOUD

When business people hear the words "software tool," usually they think of applications like Microsoft Word, PowerPoint, and Visio. You can certainly use those, but you need something more. BPI tools provide features that allow the team to move beyond the confines of butcher paper, stickies, and similar paper artifacts. They allow the team to model in BPMN, and some even validate the model with an explanation of errors. They have collaboration capabilities including shared modeling, cross-referencing, and commenting. They provide a variety of ways to overlay text, data, and graphical annotations on the process diagram to create Visual Analysis models. Many allow the BPMN to be interchanged in a standard format with other tools that provide, for example, simulation analysis or workflow automation. Cloud-based tools, hosted on the Internet, offer an additional benefit. They free you from the constraints of face-to-face meetings, allowing your BPI Project team to be distributed across multiple locations around the world, yet collaborate in real time!

---

[27] www.blueworkslive.com

Blueworks Live from IBM is a good example of a modern BPI tool. It runs in the cloud, so there is nothing to set up and nothing to update as new capabilities are added to the tool. Users access it through a simple web browser. It provides a critical feature for any BPI tool, a *shared team repository*, an organized digital storeroom for all your process models, attachments, and analytical data, accessible by all members of your team and ultimately by other teams in your organization.

Blueworks Live provides features and capabilities you should look for when choosing any BPI Project tool and repository:

- Configurable user permissions to access the team workspace for viewing, editing, and commenting on diagrams and documents in the repository
- Freely configurable organization of the workspace into project areas and sub-areas
- Ability to search for diagrams and documents based on topic, keyword, and other index data
- Ability to instantly save a "snapshot" of any model or artifact as a new version, and restore any previous version on command
- Ability to comment on diagrams, documents, and artifacts, and to be notified of all comments or changes to any specified part of the project
- Ability to create document attachments and associate them with the project
- Ability to create hyperlinks between diagrams, document attachments, and other artifacts, including those stored outside of Blueworks Live
- A BPMN editor oriented to the needs of non-technical business users, supporting both "flat" and hierarchical representations
- A rich set of properties you can populate at the project, process, and individual activity level for use in process analysis.
- Ability to create a Visual Analysis Map based on those properties

In addition, Blueworks Live provides business-oriented modeling of *decisions*, also called business rules, and associates them with policies and other documentation. Decision management is outside the scope of this book, but many business analysts view it as an integral part of their BPM work.

Repository-based tools with features like these are widely available for software developers and enterprise architects, but those tools are usually inappropriate for business users. IBM Blueworks Live, however, is aimed squarely at the nontechnical business user, making it a good choice for BPI project work. It provides an easy way to get started with BPMN, one of the hurdles for many business users.

CREATE A PROJECT SPACE

The first step in using Blueworks Live is to create a dedicated area for your project within your Blueworks Live account, called a *space*. In Figure 76, the space is called *My BPI Project*. Here we add a simple description of the space (i.e., the project) and its goals. The space acts as a shared container for all the process models, annotated with data from the analysis techniques, and document attachments related to the project. In the *My BPI Project* space, there is currently one process model, called *Hiring – High-Level Map*.

The Space Details page also contains an *Activity Stream*, a record of all changes and comments regarding anything in the space, making it easy for any team member to keep up with the latest happenings on the project simply by logging into Blueworks Live.

The space administrator can then invite members of the team to share access to the space (Figure 77). Initially, I suggest either the Documenter or Project Lead as the space administrator, but the Process Owner or Project Lead may want to assign someone else for ongoing administration after the BPI Project is done. The administrator can grant permission to edit process models (Blueworks Live calls this *blueprinting*), manage and edit the space properties, or simply view and comment, on a user-by-user basis. Blueworks Live actually lets you create a whole hierarchy of spaces to hold sub-projects, each with its own set of user permissions.

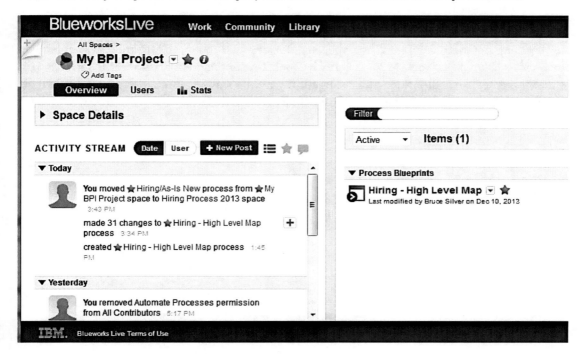

Figure 76. Space Details Page in Blueworks Live.

Figure 77. User Permissions Setup for a Space in Blueworks Live.

HIGH-LEVEL MAP

In the methodology presented in Chapter 5, the leaders created the High-Level Map using flowcharting notation using butcher paper and stickies, and then a BPMN-knowledgeable team member translated that to BPMN in a software tool. One of the great features of Blueworks Live is that it creates basic BPMN for you automatically from a simple outline representation, so this could easily happen in the Project Charter meeting in real time.

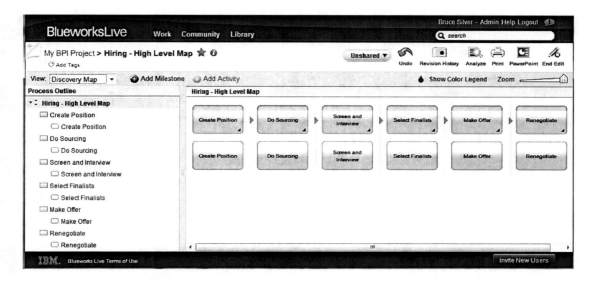

Figure 78. High-Level Map in Outline Form using Blueworks Live Discovery Map

Figure 78 shows the outline view, which Blueworks Live calls the *Discovery Map*. The top level of the outline, called a *milestone*, represents not a High-Level Map activity but just a horizontal region in the generated diagram. The High-Level Map activity is the first activity under each milestone. Upon switching the *View* dropdown at the upper left from Discovery Map to Process Diagram, Blueworks Live automatically converts the outline into BPMN (Figure 79).

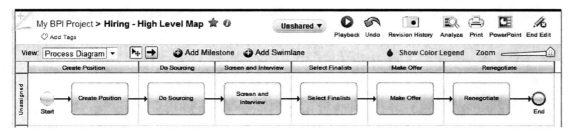

Figure 79. BPMN Generated Automatically from the Discovery Map

The simple BPMN generated in this way is missing a few things we need: the gateways, exception end states, and a black-box pool and message flows representing interaction with the applicants.

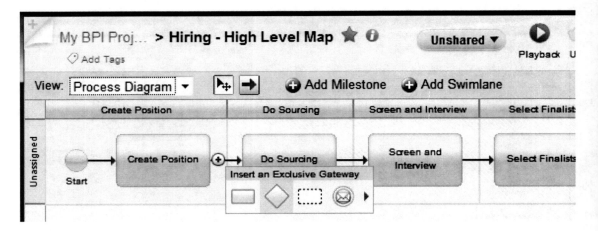

Figure 80. Direct BPMN Editing in the Blueworks Live Process Diagram View

To add the gateways and additional end states, we edit the model directly in the Diagram view. Hovering over the flow out of Create Position, we click on the (+) to insert the gateway. Blueworks Live automatically adds the other path leading to an end event. You can change the other path to go where you want, but in this case the end event is correct. We'll just label the gateway, outgoing paths, and end states (Figure 81).

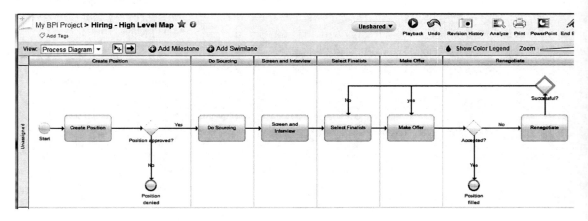

Figure 81. High-Level Map in BPMN, Minus the External Pools and Message Flows

The current version of Blueworks Live does not represent external actors as black-box pools. This is actually not uncommon in tools from BPM Suite vendors, even though Blueworks Live is not part of a BPMS. Since it is important that we represent the external participants in our model, we will use Blueworks Live's *Analysis Mode* for this.

Analysis Mode lets us display selected *properties* of each activity (including custom properties) as colored icons around the activity. We'll use this to create our Visual Analysis Map later on, but for now we'll use a custom *Messages* property to show interactions with external actors. For each activity that interacts with external participants – in this case, the Candidates – we'll attach a Message property labeled *[message], to/from [external actor]*. Figure 82 shows how this looks in Analysis Mode. The text is truncated in the icon, but hovering the mouse over the icon shows the full text in a callout.

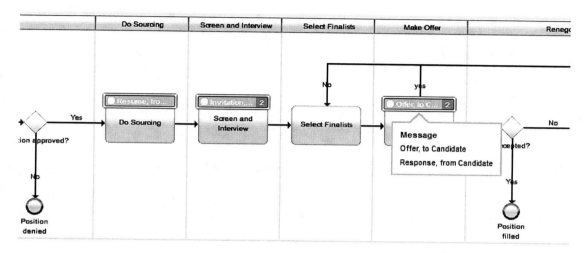

Figure 82. Activity Properties in Blueworks Live Analysis Mode Can Show the External Actors and Messages

THE PROJECT CHARTER

We want to include the Project Charter document in our project space. Blueworks Live gives you two alternative ways to do this, either as an *attachment* or by inclusion of individual Project Charter elements in *Detail fields* at the space (project) or process level.

The attachment is easiest and keeps all the information in one place. We can't attach it at the space level, but we can insert the Project Charter as a document attachment to the High-Level Map (Figure 83). To do that, change the *View* dropdown from *Process Diagram* to *Documentation* (*Show All Details*) and scroll down past the property fields until you come to the *Attachments Add* button. Another way to add this documentation would be to right-click the process background, select *Details* from the pop-up menu, and then select the Documentation tab.

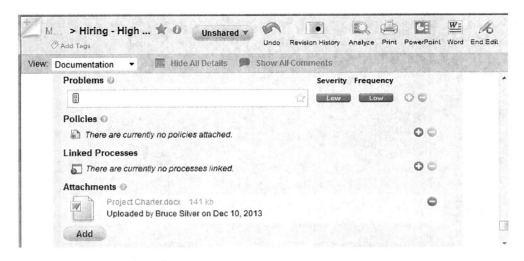

Figure 83. Project Charter Added as Attachment to the Process in Documentation View

Alternatively, you can add individual Project Charter elements directly as project and process details. For example, you can add the Improvement Targets as *Goals* in the Space Details section (Figure 84).

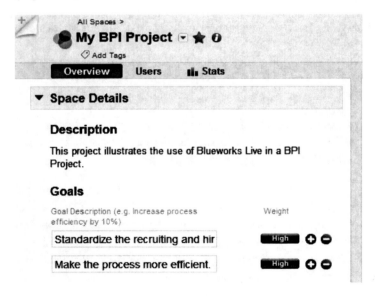

Figure 84. Improvement Targets Added as Blueworks Live Space Details

You can also identify members of the BPI Project team on the Details panel for the High-Level Map (Figure 85).   In the Process Diagram view, either double-click on the process background to bring up the Process Details panel or right-click on the background and select Details from the pop-up menu. Use the Business Owner field to identify the Process Owner (and possibly also the Executive Sponsor), and use the Experts field to identify subject matter experts, Data person, Documenter, etc.

Figure 85. Identify team members in High-Level Map process Details.

That's enough at this point. Since the Details panel does not cover all the elements in the Project Charter, it is best to make the Project Charter a document attachment even if you also use the process Details fields.

THE AS-IS SWIMLANE DIAGRAM

In Blueworks Live, the detailed swimlane diagram starts from the High-Level Map, which is already in BPMN. One of the unique features of Blueworks Live is it lets us toggle easily between a flat model – best for live discussion and analysis with the team – and a hierarchical model, which gives us a bird's eye view of the end-to-end process on a single page. (Most other BPMN tools, such as Visio, require two separate models for that.)

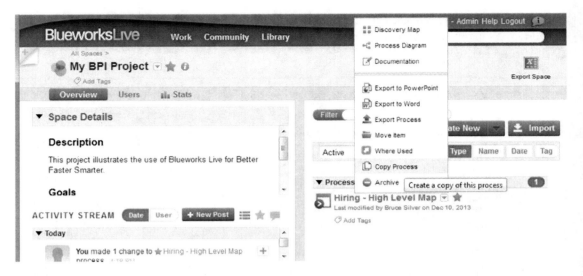

Figure 86. Creating a Copy of the High-Level Map to Begin Building the Swimlane Diagram

Start by making a copy of your High-Level Map diagram, since we want to save that just as it is. Go to your project space, and in the dropdown by the High-Level process diagram, select *Copy process* (Figure 86). Name the copy *Hiring Process – As-Is*. Now you have a copy of the process model in your project space that you will modify to make the swimlane diagram.

Open the copy in Process Diagram view and start by converting each activity into a subprocess as you build it out. Simply right-click the activity, *Convert to Subprocess*, and the tool will open up a mini-process diagram where the activity was (Figure 87). If you click the [-] button at bottom center, the subprocess collapses to a single activity with a [+] button. So it is easy to toggle back and forth between collapsed and expanded views.

This is a unique capability of Blueworks Live. It works because the tool controls the layout; the user has very limited control over it, almost none. That simplifies the modeling to some extent, but the resulting layout does not always use the space in the most efficient way. If you try to look at a big section of the diagram with the team, for instance, the fonts may be small, so you need to pan and zoom. But that is an issue with any flat model.

Rename the first child-level activity and add others using the (+) button on the sequence flow, in accordance with the "what-came-next" dialogue between the Team Facilitator and the team.

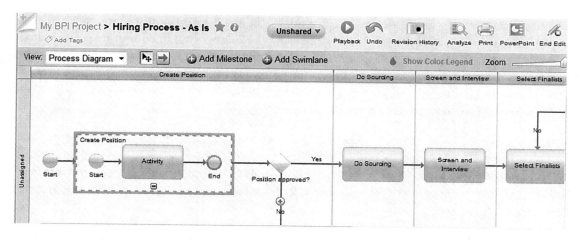

Figure 87. Converting an Activity to a Subprocess

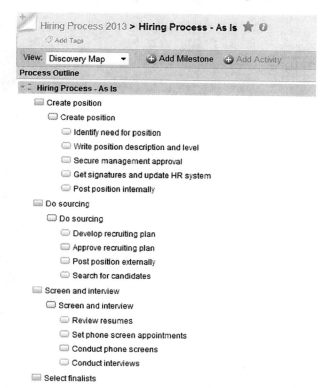

Figure 88. Child-level Activities in Discovery Map Outline View

Since Blueworks Live maintains the Discovery Map outline in sync with the diagram, once the As-Is swimlane diagram has been completed, the child-level steps will show up as indents under each top-level activity in the outline (Figure 88).   The team might find it more convenient to capture the *What-came-next* steps in real time using the Discovery Map outline view rather than directly in the BPMN Process Diagram view. For example, you can rearrange the step order simply by dragging a step in the outline. But gateways can only be inserted in the Process Diagram view, so after rearranging to get the order right, switch back to the Process Diagram view to insert the gateways and exception paths.

The performer for each activity is indicated by the swimlane. In the Process Diagram view, you can either use the *Add Swimlane* button at the top or insert the performer in the Participant field of the *Details* panel for each activity. We will discuss the Details panel later in this chapter. When you have completed the As-Is model, it looks something like Figure 89, showing just the first three milestones.

In Figure 89, I've zoomed out to give a sense of the layout, but at this magnification the text is admittedly too small to read. Blueworks Live lets you pan and zoom to see any part of the diagram.

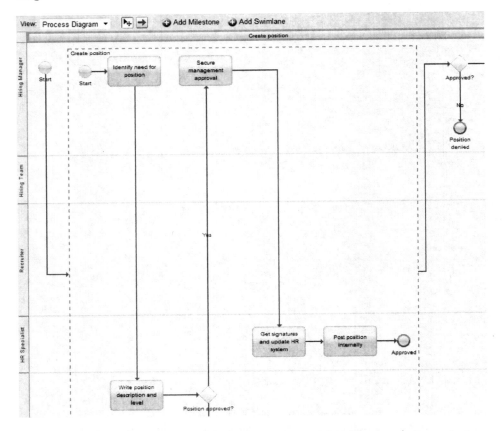

Figure 89. Fragment of Swimlane Diagram in BPMN, with Subprocesses Expanded.

But if you drag the start event in each subprocess into the top lane and then collapse all the subprocesses, you get Figure 90... basically it's still the High-Level Map (Figure 81)! Technically, it's called the *top-level BPMN diagram*, and it may differ a bit from the High-Level Map because of additional details uncovered by the team.

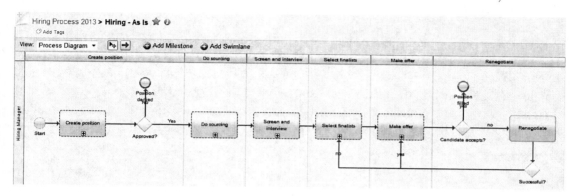

Figure 90. Swimlane Diagram in BPMN with Subprocesses Collapsed

There is also a way to convert this hybrid flat/hierarchical model to a true hierarchical model as we had in Chapter 5 (Figure 28 through Figure 32). Blueworks Live calls it a *linked process*. Right-click the subprocess and select *Save as Linked Process....* Blueworks Live prompts you to name the linked process – usually the subprocess name is appropriate – and assign it to a space, which should be your project space.

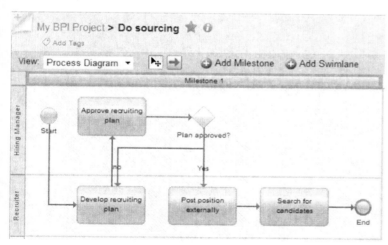

Figure 91. Child-level *Do sourcing* after Conversion to a Linked Process.

The tool then puts the child level in a separate diagram (Figure 91), hyperlinked to the parent-level activity in the normal hierarchical way. Note that it omits any lanes that have no activities, but you can manually add those back in if you like. Linked processes are reusable in the sense that more than one process model can call the same child-level linked process.

THE I-4 LISTS

We saw earlier how to include selected Project Charter elements in the High-Level Map using either the Documentation view or the Process Details panel. We can add the I-4 Lists to the As-Is Swimlane Diagram in a similar way. Open that diagram and select Documentation from the View dropdown. Then click on the pencil icon (Add/Edit Documentation) next to the process name. Alternatively you can go to the Process Details panel and open the Documentation tab. Either way opens up a rich text editor where we can paste or type in our I-4 Lists (Figure 92).

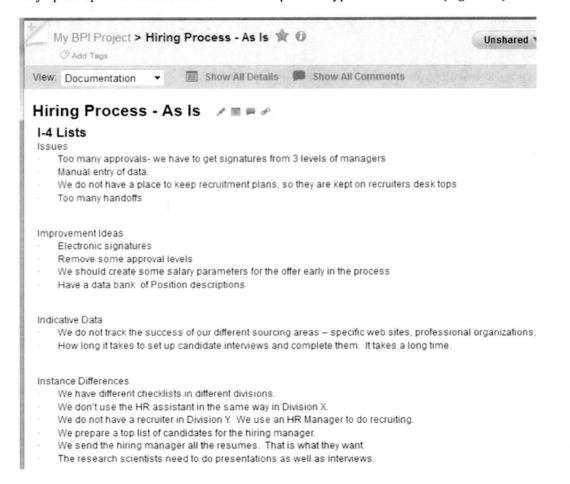

Figure 92. I-4 Lists Added as Embedded Documentation in Blueworks Live

PROCESS PROPERTIES

Blueworks Live defines a number of standard *process properties* you can associate with either a milestone or activity. Administrators can selectively enable or disable them in the Details panel, and also define up to ten custom properties, five text and five numeric (Figure 93).

Visible	Property	Tooltip	Type
Process Properties			
☑	♦ Participants	❷ A role or system responsible for completing this activity. Only one participant can be assigned to an activity in Blueworks Live.	Text
☑	♦ Business Owners	❷ The roles or people accountable for this activity.	Text
☑	♦ Experts	❷ The roles or people consulted about this activity.	Text
☑	ⓖ Systems	❷ Technologies or devices that are utilized by or required to complete this activity.	Text
☑	ⓒ Cycle Time	❷ The total time spent on this activity, the sum of work and wait time.	Number
☑	◆ Cost	❷ The price or value attributed to performing this activity.	Number
☑	ⓖ Suppliers	❷ An individual, group or company that supplies inputs to this activity.	Text
☑	♦ Customers	❷ An individual, group or company that uses the outputs produced by this activity.	Text
☑	◀⊐ Inputs	❷ Business forms or data required to begin this activity.	Text
☑	⊐➔ Outputs	❷ Business forms or data generated by this activity.	Text
☑	⚠ Risk	❷ Commonly used to identify areas of concern or issues that may occur within an activity.	Text
☑	⚇ Value Add	❷ Used to indicate activities a customer would pay for, would not pay for, or are unavoidable for regulatory or other reasons.	Text
☑	🖹 Problems	❷ The common problems or issues that affect or occur in this activity.	Text
Custom Process Properties			
☑	Message	❷ Label "[Message name] To/From [entity/role]"	Text
☑	WASTED	❷ *add tooltip*	Text
☑	Metrics	❷ Measure, baseline and goal values	Text
☑	Customer comments	❷ *add tooltip*	Text

Figure 93. Process Properties Setup in Blueworks Live

In addition, the Details panel has tabs for associated problems, policies, documentation (embedded text), attachments, and user comments. Modelers then define the property values and link them with the process by right-clicking any activity or milestone, selecting *Details*, and entering the values in the appropriate field or tab (Figure 94). Any user with access to the space can then view the attached properties either by accessing the Detail panels themselves, viewing the Details sidebar to the right of the Process Diagram (while not in Edit mode), viewing the Process Diagram in Analysis mode, or through the documentation generated by Blueworks Live.

In Analysis Mode, icons are displayed at each activity indicating attachment of a property, and we'll use that feature for our Visual Analysis Map. In addition, a wider group of users without edit permission can view and comment on the model and properties as a "contributor," a user category without edit permissions.

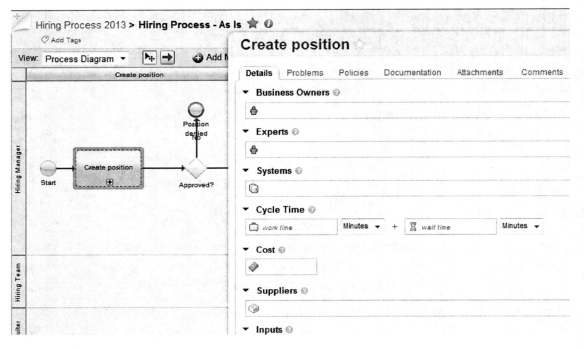

Figure 94. Blueworks Live Details Panel

There are many ways to configure Blueworks Live properties (in combination with embedded documentation and attachments) to capture the details we need for our analytical techniques. Recall that we have already used one of the five custom text properties to model *Messages* to and from external participants. We'll now add four more (Figure 93):

- *WASTED*, to hold the I-am-WASTED pain points
- *Metrics*, to hold various measures and their values
- *Customer comments*, to hold the Customer Scorecard data
- *Instance Differences*, from the I-4 Lists

Instances of each of these four analysis elements can be associated with either an individual activity, milestone, or the process as a whole. To associate one of them with an activity or milestone, right-click the activity or milestone and select *Details.* To associate one of them with the process as a whole, select Documentation from the View dropdown and click the Details icon next to the process name.

Analysis Mode

In addition to the normal Edit Mode, Blueworks Live provides an *Analysis Mode* in which information entered through the Details panel is displayed together with the process diagram (Figure 95). This allows the process diagram to be used for visual analysis.

Figure 95 shows a portion of the As-Is Swimlane Diagram in Analysis Mode. Detail fields attached to an activity or milestone appear as an icon with a bit of truncated text. A number in the icon indicates multiple entries for that property. If you hover the cursor over that icon, the full text appears as a callout. For example, one of the activities has two entries for the WASTED property:

- S1: Systems did not share information, so there was a lot of manual re-entry of candidate data.
- E5: Candidate info from different sources (web site, personnel info, candidate evaluations) has to be manually entered into the HR system.

In addition, all of the properties are listed in the text panel on the left. You can see properties of the process as a whole, such as Customer comments or Instance differences, in Analysis mode, as well as in the Process Details panel or in Documentation View. In this example, you can see the Customer comments listed.

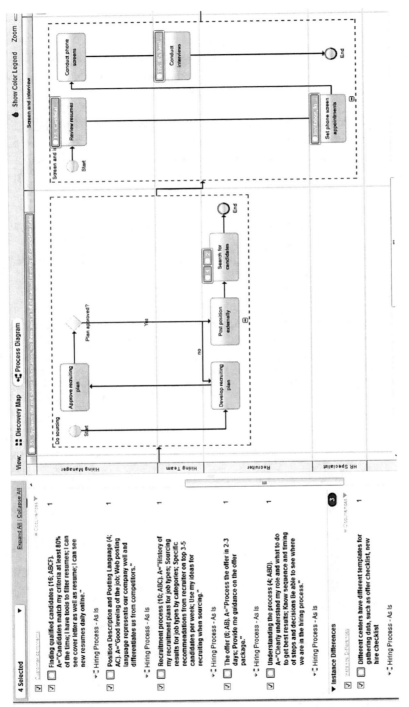

Figure 95. Blueworks Live Analysis Mode Provides a Visual Analysis Map

You can also use Analysis Mode to display time and cost values for each activity. In the Details panel, enter Wait time and Work time for each activity. Use Work Time for an activity to mean the total time from when the activity starts to when it leaves that activity ready to go to the next activity. Wait time means the time between activities; since you are assigning the wait time to each activity, think of it as the wait time before the performer begins work on it. Having both the Work Time and Wait Time at each activity is sufficient, but I would suggest that the team sum the total work time and the total wait time per sub process and also for the whole process. It gives more insight into the opportunities for improvement.

Costs can also be shown over the activity step. They are included per activity (at a salary plus benefits rate for personnel and there may be other direct costs) for the performer for that time period. They aren't totally accurate because within the step the performer may be working on other activities, but they give an estimate.

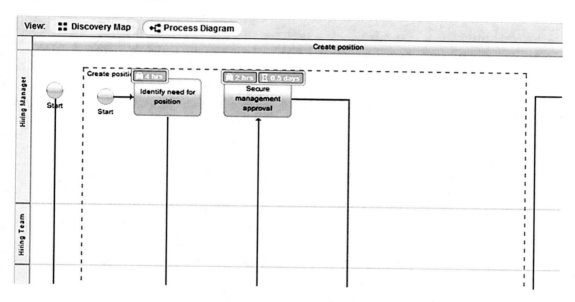

Figure 96. Work Time and Wait Time for Each Activity in Blueworks Live Analysis Mode.

All properties entered in the Details panel, including custom properties, can be displayed as icons above the activity in Analysis Mode (Figure 96). Selection of which properties show their icons is up to the user, so, for example, you can have one view that just shows the WASTED entries and another one that just shows the Customer Comments. The text is often truncated in the icon attached to the activity, but you can see the full text both in a callout that appears when you mouse over the icon and in a list view at the left of the screen.

OTHER PROJECT ARTIFACTS

Blueworks Live provides a convenient repository for all of the BPI Project artifacts discussed in the earlier chapters. In this chapter we have illustrated just a few of them. To review, the basic mechanisms are these:

- **Process models.** BPMN modeling is a Blueworks Live native capability, used for the High-Level Map, As-Is Swimlane diagram, and To-Be Swimlane diagrams.
- **Document attachments.** Documents can be attached at the process, milestone, or activity level. In addition, URL links to externally stored documents can be inserted in the Documentation view. Document attachments are a good way to include the Project Charter, project metrics, including baseline and goal values, the Implementation Plan, and Five Whys, as well as analytic techniques developed using other tools, such as Fishbone, Pareto, and Notched Timeline. The final Team Outcome Report should also be attached here.
- **Documentation view.** Blueworks Live's Documentation view provides a rich text editor, so you can enter text-based artifacts directly in the tool. We saw how to do this with the I-4 Lists.
- **Analysis Mode.** Analysis Mode allows selected properties of a milestone or activity to be displayed as an attached colored icon. We saw how to use this for message flow interactions, processing time, and wait time, and you can do the same thing for costs, problems, and other custom properties. The text of the property is listed at the left side of the screen, and pops up in a callout when you hover the mouse over the icon. In addition, properties at the process level are listed at the left of the screen. You can use those for the Customer Scorecard, Instance Differences, I am WASTED pain points, and others. (Note: All of these elements can be associated with an individual activity as well, in which case they appear as attached icons in Analysis Mode.)
- **Comments** can be attached to any part of the project and displayed with the properties. Even users without permission to edit project artifacts can view and add comments, and all comments appear in the project Activity Stream.

CONTRIBUTOR LICENSE

In addition to fully licensed users, Blueworks Live offers a lower-cost Contributor license that lets you publish your work to a wider audience. Contributors can view models, including the associated properties, and add their comments, but they cannot edit models or properties. This is a good way to expand access beyond the immediate BPI Project team without risking unauthorized edits.

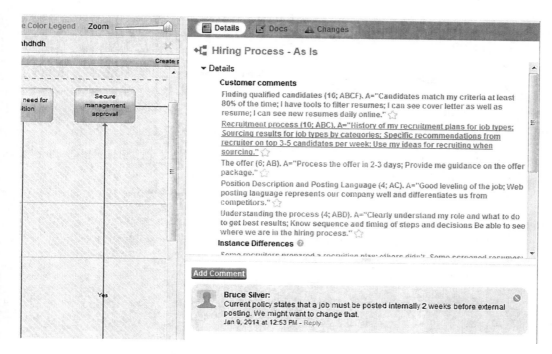

Figure 97. Contributor Interface

Figure 97 illustrates the interface seen by a Contributor, which is very similar to that of a fully licensed user in read-only View mode. For a selected activity in the diagram, or for the process as a whole if no activity is selected, the panel on the right has tabs to display the properties (Figure 97), attached documents, or a list of all changes to the activity or process. Contributors cannot edit the model, but they interact with the modelers and other Contributors through their comments, which are captured not only in the process model but also in the Activity Stream visible to all members of the project space.

In Figure 97, a Contributor has commented on the policy for posting positions internally vs. externally. That would be a clue for the team to attach that policy and review it. In fact, reviewing and revising policies is important. Since teams are sometimes hesitant to tackle policies, the Process Owner should encourage it and help if revisions are needed in the new design.

BENEFITS OF A BPI TOOL

There are benefits of a tool like Blueworks Live at each phase of a BPI Project.

At the Chartering and Staffing phase, the tool documents many elements of the Project Charter, and builds the High-Level Map, first as an outline in the Discovery Map and then in BPMN. It maintains the Charter document as an attachment in the project space for others to see, comment on, and revise.

At the Process Discovery phase, it supports collaborative creation of the BPMN model and allows others to offer their modifications and comments on it afterward. It also stores the I-4 Lists and allows elements of them to be displayed as icons on the diagram, as the beginning of a Visual Analysis Map.

In the Process Analysis phase, all kinds of quantitative and qualitative information can be added through the Details panel, embedded documentation, or attachments. Again, the Details fields, including custom properties, can be displayed as icons in the diagram for Visual Analysis.

In the Process Design phase after the To-Be design is developed, process properties could be used to show anticipated changes and their improvements. In the future, other project teams can go back and review a project, both to learn from it and to lift subprocesses to reuse in their own projects, or possibly directly reference them as linked processes.

These are some specific benefits, but there are many overarching benefits as well. Blueworks Live lets you share models and documents across your whole organization with reliability, security, accuracy, and version control. It lets many people simultaneously work and comment on the process and have all the models and information at their fingertips.

Business-friendly BPMN support gets business and IT people working with in the same language, helping both groups understand one another and clarify any differences. The tool keeps models at different levels in sync, reducing rework and the ongoing chance for misinterpretation. While paper-based modeling artifacts are a time-honored tradition in BPI, tools like Blueworks Live have become a must in today's BPM world.

Chapter 15

What's in an Implementation Plan?

Implementation is the final step in getting results from your process improvement project. Implementation takes the process redesign from a blueprint to reality, putting it in place in the workplace. That means it has to incorporate the new organizational structure, role changes, workflow with steps and decisions, and technology. And employees have to follow the new process. That's what implementation is all about – putting the new process in place and reaping the benefits toward the improvement goals. The new process will be faster, higher quality, have fewer wastes, improve customer satisfaction, reduce risks, increase transparency, and whatever else the team has designed into it. For staff, the process should reduce frustration, increase visibility, and increase productivity.

Before the organization gets the process flowing seamlessly, there will be difficulties in Implementation, and unanticipated challenges; measures will help to identify where these are happening. Then the implementation team or operating staff doing the process will need to consider revisions.

The final phase of the BPI Project is the Implementation Plan. After the Project Lead and Team Facilitator review the new design and Team Outcomes Report with the Process Owner, they need to incorporate any revisions needed into the design model and prepare an Implementation Plan. I recommend that the Project Lead and Team Facilitator put together a first draft and bring it to the BPI team for their input.

They can start by going through the To-Be design itself and the specific recommendations in the Team Outcomes Report that support the new design. For each activity and each recommendation, any issues that occur should be articulated here. Issues could include what employees need to be trained, what system enhancements need to be made, what communication is necessary, what policies need changing, etc. Figure 98 provides an example of the recommendations one client had and the issues that arose with those recommendations. In this example, the client was recommending that the two different funding and accounting systems for grants be consolidated into one system.

Recommendations	Issues
1. Drive gifts to the Silver Fund (not Gold Fund) irrespective of ultimate fund designation.	• Communication with and education of staff units and donors are needed. • A policy change is needed.
2. Assign unique identifier to each transaction and transmit it to Accounting A system and Accounting B system simultaneously.	• Interfaces need to be rewritten.
3. Automate distribution of funds from Silver Fund to Gold Fund and do so daily net of all fees.	• Interfaces need to be rewritten. • This is a significant cultural shift and communication with staff units will be key.
4. Install dual or split-screen monitors at the workstations of those who need to view documents while working in Accounting A system or Accounting B system	• Operating costs of initial installation and ongoing replacement are a concern.
Ensure that staff have appropriate access to both Accounting A system and Accounting B system	• An access guideline is needed.

Figure 98. To-Be Process Recommendations

Although the recommendations have already been given to the Process Owner, this review of activities and issues looks at the process from a holistic point of view and shows what will be necessary from many change management perspectives.

What's in an Implementation Plan?

COMPONENTS OF AN INITIAL IMPLEMENTATION PLAN

A simple Implementation Plan could have the three elements in the Project Milestones table.

Project Milestones

Milestones	Responsibility	Planned Completion

Implementation Team

The Implementation Team needs to include several of the same team members to make the transition from the BPI Project to the Implementation and Check stage. The Process Owner remains the same and continues after Implementation and Check into Monitoring and Sustaining. The Project Lead remains the same for Implementation and Check. The Process Owner drives Implementation and Check, and the Project Lead (and the head subject matter expert) operationalizes the improvements in the workplace. Some of the Subject Matter Experts should remain on the team as well. But others should be added. The new team members should provide the expertise and resources for all aspects of the implementation and could include a Project Manager from the Project Management Office, other SMEs who work on the process (including representative SMEs from different functions and locations), a change management expert, IT developers if technology will be developed internally or Business Analysts and others to select technology vendors and assist in defining needed customization.

Implementation Dependencies and Risks

Dependencies and Risks	Mitigation Approach

It is useful to list dependencies and risks for implementation early on because they make visible the expected challenges. Dependencies could include staff time in functions that have not been involved (or only involved minimally) in the BPI Project, and they may not have time for or interest in what's needed for Implementation and Check. Dependencies can occur at any stage in the critical path, and implementation can be slowed while waiting for the critical path activity – such as technology development moving more slowly than expected, or user testing raising new needs. Risks could arise from limited resources and other priorities that could delay Implementation and Check. Risks could arise from technology that is threatening to employees, from external economic conditions, from additional costs, from changing leadership, and from other reasons. In putting together the initial Implementation Plan, the Project Lead and Team Facilitator have to list any items that are relevant to their implementation.

Basic Ideas for Implementation Planning

Although the specifics of the Implementation Plan are up to the Project Lead, Team Facilitator, and the team members, here are two helpful methods.

1. Iterative Prototype

Use an iterative prototype approach for implementation. This approach, detailed more fully in "How Do You Do Continuous Improvement?" at the end of this chapter, has the team create an Implementation Plan based on time-boxed iterations and prototypes. Each iteration and prototype shows the customer-specific results; they are scoped to get work done and produce a prototype with specific functionality that the team and customer review. They are different from project milestones in that each incremental iteration and prototype has next step deliverables. The emphasis is on producing specific deliverables for the customer that he can see. And, each iteration and prototype deliverable is scoped for the available resourcing and time boxirg. This method is more of an agile approach to project management.

2. Pilot

Or, create a pilot or a few pilots. It is always helpful to implement the new process in a phased approach, and the first phase of implementation is a pilot with a subset of the organization – a geographic region, a particular function, or a friendly group. It is useful to do more than one pilot so that the team sees how the process works in two groups; with only one pilot group, the results could be skewed by an overly positive or negative group of implementers or leadership.

Even before piloting, walk-throughs, user acceptance testing, or simulation can be used to give the team feedback on how employees respond to the process in implementation. This Pilot method is more of a traditional approach to project management.

What's in an Implementation Plan?

CHANGE MANAGEMENT

Change Management is an important piece of any BPI Project. This book does not focus on the topic in sufficient detail to be able to develop a full change management strategy and use it to complement the rest of the BPI Project. Instead the next few pages provide on overview of why change management is needed and some of the critical principles. It explains how change management is already incorporated in the five phases of the BPI Project, and provides further suggestions for incorporating change management into Implementation and Check. I also suggest three resources for further reading: *Organization Change: A Comprehensive Reader* by W. Warner Burke, Dale G. Lake, and Jill Waymire Paine, 2009, "Making It Stick: Embedding Change in Organizational Culture," Dan S. Cohen, Harvard Business Press, 2008, and "The Underlying Structure of Organizational Change," Thomas B. Lawrence, Bruno Dyck, Sally Maitlis, and Michael K. Mauws, *MIT Sloan Management Review*, Summer 2006.

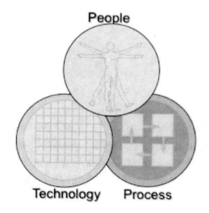

Figure 99. Three Aspects of Any Change. Source: Anna Ewins, "Managing Change and Ambiguity in the Workplace"

Any BPI Project has three aspects to it, pictured in Figure 99 – people, technology, and process. This book has concentrated on the process aspect and has integrated technology through tools and looking at how systems, applications, and data integrate with the process. People are also involved – in doing the work of the process currently, as leaders and team members of the BPI Project, and will be involved in implementing the new design and then operationally doing the work of the new process.

For change management, the challenge is to connect the business value proposition to a personal perspective. Employees and managers need to understand questions such as:

- Where are we going and why do we need to change?
- What is the difference between how we operate now and how we will operate in the future?

- Which of my skills will need to change?
- How will we measure success?
- How will my role/job change to support the future state?
- What's in it for me?

Anna Ewins of Ewins and Winby mentions ten critical success factors in "Managing Change and Ambiguity in the Workplace" in her course at UC Berkeley Extension. They are:

1. Compelling Business Case

2. Aligned Vision and Strategy

3. Securing Sponsorship

4. Committed Stakeholders

5. Change-Specific Communication

6. Aligned Behaviors, Values, and Assumptions

7. Success Metrics

8. Integrated Planning

9. Organizational Change Capability

10. Change Leadership

I comment below on how these elements have been incorporated in the BPI Project phases, but I suggest that the Process Owner and Project Lead contact someone in Human Resources who is a change management expert and use that person as an additional resource throughout the whole project.

Change Management in the BPI Project

The **Compelling Business Case** and **Aligned Vision and Strategy** come from the BPI Project Charter when the Process Owner articulates the challenges today, the Improvement Targets, vision, and how these are related to the organization's strategy. The Process Owner and Project Lead need to be articulating the Compelling Business Case at the beginning of the project, throughout phases 2 to 5 and then during the Implementation and Check stage as well. They should elaborate on how current and anticipated problems and opportunities will impact their business, and how the BPI Project is part of a strategy of moving the organization to higher performance and an inspiring vision.

Securing Sponsorship in the BPI Project means finding the right Executive Sponsor and Process Owner and getting their demonstrable commitment. When initiating the project, their commitment shows up through public advocacy, their ability to get the right resources, and seeing the need for change. During the project, their commitment shows up in removing barriers, handling cross-functional challenges, challenging current policies, and maintaining focus in the face of new priorities. After agreement to the new design, the Process Owner's commitment provides ongoing and new resources for Implementation and Check and influences leaders and stakeholders across the organization. Later, the Process Owner is also responsible for sustaining the change during the ongoing Monitoring and Sustaining stage.

Getting **Committed Stakeholders** starts with having a committed Project Lead and Team Facilitator and committed team members. They are the advocates for the project, and they provide **Change-Specific Communication** to their peers and other stakeholders (employees and leaders internally and customers and suppliers externally). I recommend that the Project Lead, Team Facilitator, and HR Change Management Specialist guide the team to understand who the stakeholders are and determine their level of commitment to the BPI Project. Then they should develop a communication plan that addresses these stakeholders. The plan would engage these stakeholders, using different messages and channels, and be delivered by different individuals and groups.

During the project, the team should observe how stakeholders are responding to the messages to anticipate if they will be aligned with or resistant to the changes they will be facing. Then they can plan how to **Align Behaviors, Values, and Assumptions** during Implementation and Check. As Anna Ewins points out, 20% of behavior is shaped by antecedents such as training, strategic communications, tools, expectations, and modeling (by the leaders and BPI team). These antecedents would occur while the BPI team is doing the project or during early stages of Implementation and Check. About 80% of behavior is shaped by consequences that occur after the change, such as feedback, praise, support, work process consequences, promotions, raises, and others. These would happen during Implementation and Check or soon after in the Monitoring and Sustaining stage.

One excellent way to observe organizational behavior during the BPI Project is to identify and implement Quick Wins (low-hanging fruit). Often the teams start selecting Quick Wins after two full-day working sessions. I suggest they choose one or two Quick Wins and implement them in one month. This seems short to most groups but that's the point. Quick Wins are supposed to be quick. So, if the Quick Win improvement will take longer than that, choose another one or scale it back. What's most important is the early success for the project and having internal or external customers seeing that positive result. The BPI team will be motivated by the Quick Win and will learn a lot from implementing it. They will observe how willing the organization is to try a new approach, how to help employees master the change, and observe if groups are eager or resistant to executing the Quick Win. See more on Quick Wins at the end of this chapter, "Should We Implement Quick Wins? To Do or Not To Do?"

Success Metrics track implementation and progress toward the business results. In the BPI Project, this would include tracking the metrics for each Improvement Target and seeing how they compare to the goal value that was set by the Process Owner. It would include tracking process metrics within the new process to see how improvements are being implemented and are impacting former problem areas. These measures would be at the same points where data was gathered originally during Process Analysis. Measures for these two areas were discussed in Chapter 6. It would also include implementation project metrics to show whether the Implementation and Check portion is on track. In addition to these three, behavior measures could indicate how people are doing things differently as part of implementation.

Integrated Planning has been covered through the roadmap of the BPI Project, and includes having a plan in different stages with clear roles, and input from stakeholders and customers.

Here's a helpful hint for working with the leadership during the BPI Project. Start discussing recommendations and implementation issues with the Process Owner during the Process Analysis. By raising the team's improvement ideas and the challenges of implementing them with the Process Owner, the Project Lead will get a feeling for the Process Owner's and organization's appetite. If the Process Owner has a hard stop "No" about an improvement idea, the Project Lead should share that with the team. Then the team will probably not follow that track anymore or at least will create other options as well.

Assessing **Organizational Change Capability** is part of any change effort. It starts with determining the organization's readiness for this type of change, often assessing the level of this organization against a standard model by rating it on a scale from low to high or 1 to 5. The assessment shows strengths and weaknesses and enables the change management specialist to provide guidance for engaging the organization from the beginning of the project through Implementation. This success factor has not been included in the BPI Project, so get the change management specialist to help in this area.

Guidance needs to be provided to the BPI leadership on **Change Leadership** behaviors. Others in the company see these leaders as models, so they need to take visible actions to support the project. I often provide a cheat sheet to the Executive Sponsor and Process Owner with questions to ask at each process meeting with the Project Lead and Team Facilitator; the cheat sheet also has suggested actions for the Executive Sponsor and Process Owner at each phase of the BPI Project. The change management specialist may have more suggestions.

Implementation of the new process design is the responsibility of the Process Owner, Project Lead, and Implementation Team. The Project Lead is responsible for operationalizing the new process design, and the Process Owner is responsible for driving implementation. These two leaders are constant from the initial team through implementation. I suggest these two and the original BPI team decide who the other members of the Implementation Team should be, but keep some from the original BPI team so that there is continuity; add some new team members for new needs or to refresh the team. Information Technology is a critical Implementation Team member as well.

The BPI Project concludes with an Implementation Plan, but the company follows through by executing against the plan. The BPI method documented in this book incorporates many engagement and change management principles throughout, but the team will be served well to use a change management specialist as an advisor to the BPI Project right from the start.

Implementation and Check is key to the success of executing the new process in the workplace. It probably won't be perfect at first, so plan some data gathering to see where it is working and what adjustments need to be made. Articulate the metrics in the Implementation Plan, and gather them soon and regularly within the Implementation and Check stage. Find out how close the process is to meeting the goal values. Observe if employees are using the new process and if not, why not. Is new technology being adopted or have employees easily reverted to old ways? What are the root causes of these problems? What corrective action can happen quickly, and does it make a difference?

MONITORING AND SUSTAINING

At the monitoring stage of the BPM methodology, the technology aspects begin to come together. Often technology will keep the process running operationally, and will monitor key process indicators like time, defects, loop backs, queuing, bottlenecks, transactions per role, and specific leading indicators and output indicators. And the numbers will come from real operations. So the Project Lead and the Process Owner can look at real data to see where the flow is working as expected and where the problems are.

Metrics are key to Monitoring and Sustaining. Continue watching the Key Performance Indicators from the BPI Project and several in-process measures that have been useful. These metrics are not meant to point fingers at people or groups, but to be used for learning about the process and will point to places where specific adjustments are needed.

A dashboard will be helpful for a visual reminder. Periodic review sessions should be scheduled and adhered to. These would include the Process Owner and a supervisor of the process. If there are problems, employees who work the process should be consulted. Or, even better, the Process Owner and supervisor would directly observe and talk with employees so that both learn what is happening and come up with some countermeasures.

Monitoring and Sustaining has two purposes:

- To make sure the process is continuing to perform well, and when it is not, to identify problem areas quickly, figure out the root cause, and implement countermeasures
- To assess the marketplace to identify new customers' needs, new technology, and new competition so the process can stay ahead of or at least abreast with the market

But Monitoring and Sustaining is not easy. It takes the daily discipline of a strong exercise program. That means regular exercise, measurement, documenting of results, viewing and trying new methods, and evaluating how the program is going. The same is true for the process. Regular exercise means daily (or regularly) running the process, measuring how it is doing, and documenting that. The employees in the process should do all of this tracking and post results for them to see (on a daily or hourly basis) and for others to see and review. Data should be easily visible and accessible to all the relevant leaders and employees – not hidden in the bowels of an individual desktop or in a shared file that no one accesses. Managers should look at the data when employees or supervisors bring up an issue, and on a regular basis as well. Trying new methods and evaluating the process require timetables and people assigned to follow them, just like the maintenance on critical equipment. That's what hard about Monitoring and Sustaining. It can't wait for a problem or an emergency. It has to be regular and proactive.

In addition to monitoring the ongoing operation of a specific process, the BPM effort as a whole needs practices in place for all its processes, and specifically for past BPI projects. Companies soon realize that processes need to be stored for others to see, and updated regularly. Like metrics for today's process, it is no good to have process diagrams and data on a desktop. Shared repositories can be developed in house or purchased. SharePoint is one that is often used, although there are a lot of new applications available on the Internet now. These repositories provide asset storage, accessibility, collaboration, and editing capabilities. Processes on the desktop are just not accessible and often die when the employee moves on.

THINGS TO THINK ABOUT

SHOULD WE IMPLEMENT QUICK WINS: TO DO OR NOT TO DO?

"It seems like Quick Wins will distract us from our overall purpose of improving the process and we are so busy now." Most of my clients over the last 15 years have been really excited about finding Quick Wins and implementing them, but a few have really pushed back and said they didn't think they wanted to do it. So I thought it was worthwhile to tackle the pros and cons here.

I define Quick Wins as improvements that have high value to the customer (internal or external) but are easy and inexpensive to implement. In fact, I use this four-box matrix (Figure 100) to classify improvement ideas; Quick Wins always fall in quadrant #1, the top left quadrant.

What's in an Implementation Plan?

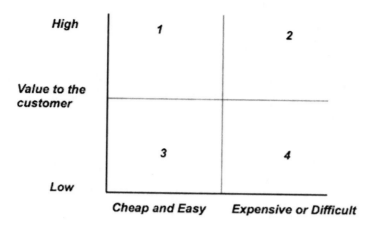

Figure 100. Quick Wins Four-Box Matrix

My time guideline is: can you implement this Quick Win within one month? This is a short period for most teams, as they are not only working on the process improvement project but have their regular work as well. I suggest that teams pick one or two Quick Wins, although they may identify more. The point is not to get sidetracked and only do Quick Wins. Once they have picked one or two Quick Wins, they formulate an action plan with responsible parties and time frames that day. The point is to:

- Show results and success quickly and communicate that
- Motivate the team by doing something early
- Demonstrate to customers that you really are going to make improvements that they care about
- Learn what it is like to execute against an improvement idea

Sometimes the Quick Win doesn't work, but you learn from that too. You learn what the culture is like and how hard it will be to implement any improvement idea; you may learn that taking a different approach with other Quick Win ideas would work better; you find that a small improvement on further investigation turns into more than you want to tackle. (In this case, reduce the scope of the Quick Win or move onto something else.)

Let's look at a few examples of Quick Wins.

- In one situation, the team was studying the leave of absence process. They discovered on their Observation (Waste) Walk that employees had to use four or five different screens to complete the employee's request – slowing the process and frustrating the Employee Benefit employee who was doing the input. Another IT employee on the team was able to combine these screens so the input could be done on one application.

- In another example, the Improvement Targets for providing a customer quote were:
  - o Decrease the time to create a quote from 9 days to 1-3 days.
  - o Increase consistency and efficiency of quote information

The Quick Wins implemented by this organization included (1) creating a case queue scored by priority (customer type, deal size, and close date), which triaged the quotes and reduced times for high priority quotes, and (2) developing three standard global templates and having them accessible in the library, which improved quote information.

SOME DOS AND DON'TS OF QUICK WINS

Do

- Quick Wins should support the overall Improvement Targets. That keeps the team focused on the goals of the project and shows early results. You may have several Quick Wins to choose from in Quadrant 1 above, but pick ones that support the Process Owner's Improvement Targets.
- Choose Quick Wins that will be visible. You want the Quick Wins to motivate the team employees and communicate to other employees and customers about the improvements that are producing results early.
- Look for Quick Wins that can be easily solved with current technology. Often the business identifies an improvement idea and IT says they can do that right away. That means the functionality already exists, and either it has never been turned on or the business just isn't accessing it.

Don't

- Don't do easy Quick Wins that counter your overall goals, just because they are easy. In one example, a team wanted to verify customer mailing addresses for their Quick Win, but their Improvement Target was to move from manual processes to electronic, so this Quick Win was not appropriate.
- Don't do Quick Wins that service one employee group and penalize another. In one example, the team wanted to enforce the credit card expense policy with faculty and thought they would remove cards from faculty who did not follow the policy. Not a good idea! Quick Wins are about small improvements, not punishment.
- Don't give up on the Quick Wins concept. Even if you don't implement them in that one month while you're still analyzing and redesigning your process, put them into your Implementation Plan. If your implementation takes 9-12 months, Quick Wins should occur in the first three months, and that gets everyone excited about early successes.

How Do You Do Continuous Improvement?

So many of the clients I work with say, "We can model and analyze the process and come up with recommendations for improvements but then it doesn't stick. We start implementing the improvements and things get in the way – other priorities come up, the workload is too heavy, whatever..."

I have begun using a new model called Act and Adapt, developed by Stu Winby, Founder of Spring Network, a Silicon Valley design firm. He has used it extensively in large healthcare organizations that are transforming their patient care and medical procedures. You can see his model in Figure 101.

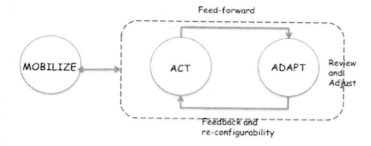

Figure 101. Act and Adapt Implementation Model. Source: Stu Winby, Spring Network

Act and Adapt begins officially after the process has been redesigned/improved. It begins with creating an Implementation Plan. But this Implementation Plan is different from the traditional Implementation Plan. It has

- a different purpose
- shortened time frames
- new participants
- ongoing learning

As Stu Winby says, implementation should not be about making people accountable for deadlines and calling them on the carpet for not getting there. It should be about learning and results.

So let's take each element one at a time.

A Different Purpose. Often an Implementation Plan identifies milestones, outcomes, time frames, and resources. The purpose of an Act and Adapt implementation is to meet specific

---

deliverables in iterations, develop prototypes, and test these prototypes against customer acceptance. So the Implementation Plan is built differently. For each iteration, there is a concise list of deliverables that build functionality or capabilities associated with the product vision and design requirements. Following a number of iterations, a prototype can be constructed and tested. The customers review each iteration and make their comments, telling you what's done (how the iteration met the set of requirements) and where additional changes need to be made. These additional changes become part of the specs for a future iteration and prototype.

Shortened Time Frames. Each iteration is delivered in 2-6 weeks. The scope and functionalities of the iteration are defined and completed in the time frame with the available resources. We know that projects need some urgency, and if you let the time frames extend too long, work just expands to fill up the whole space. Often the iterations are done in a 30-60-90 day build cycle. Sometimes a prototype can be built in the 90-day cycle, and sometimes it takes longer. So think about what functionalities could be done in 2-6 weeks and plan your implementation that way. Each iteration should take approximately the same amount of time, so the momentum keeps going. And of course, you have to consider how much time employees can spend on this project (10%, 25%, 50%) or if you can you add contracted resources.

New Participants. Often during a BPI Project, a strong team is formed, one that really understands the current challenges of the process, sees the process end to end, and is committed to implementing all the recommendations. And they have the approval and go-ahead from their Process Owner and Executive Sponsor. Then implementation begins. Some of the initial team members go on to other work; hopefully a strong core team remains, and some new team members join. Yet, even if the expanded core team is eager, things can get in the way of implementation, such as:

- Employees in other divisions who are needed for implementation (and were not engaged in the initial process improvement) are slow to respond
- Middle managers feel the process improvement work has been done and draw their employees back into other projects.
- Other priorities come up
- Leadership changes
- Or something else (put in your example)

So you have to add new participants to the team, either as part of the core team or as critical subject matter experts and IT employees for implementation. The Executive Sponsor and Process Owner need to make these new people available through influence or direct authority. Part of the Implementation Plan for each time-boxed cycle through prototype defines the resources needed: subject matter experts and customers. You also need customers to help define the requirements for each prototype, consult with the team during the iteration, and be ready to respond to the prototype on completion, based on the agreed specs.

Learning. Each short cycle iteration is a learning phase. At the conclusion of the cycle, there is a meeting where key members convene to...

- review the prototype with the customer
- identify what worked and didn't work in this phase
- incorporate suggestions and detail the next iteration
- get support from Executive Sponsor and Process Owner to overcome any challenges that have been identified from the former phase or anticipated in the next phase

Here we have the whole system in the room. We do not wait for the project to end to do a "project debrief "and learn from it. That's too late. Instead, this meeting is for ongoing project learning and operational improvement. Everyone is learning how to implement and how to do continuous improvement.

Chapter 16

WHAT MAKES THIS METHOD WORK?

A BPI team may choose to use any of the particular concepts, models, techniques, or tools in this book for a process improvement project, and each one will provide value. But to have a successful BPI Project as a whole, there are a few critical elements that need to be combined. Figure 102 represents these elements, which are the basis of the BPI Blueprint.

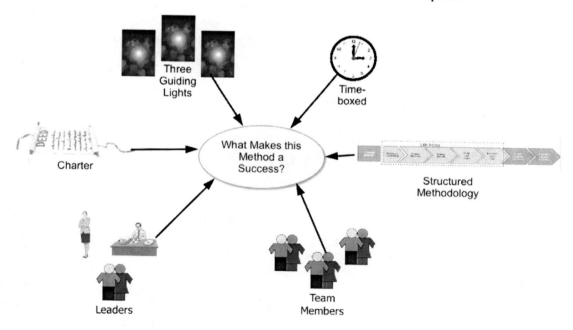

Figure 102. Six Elements that Make This Method a Success

FOCUS: THE THREE GUIDING LIGHTS AND THE PROJECT CHARTER

The Three Guiding Lights (Improvement Targets, Customer Scorecard, and quantitative data) and the Project Charter provide focus for the BPI Project. Focus is critical because it

1. Sets the goal for the project based on the Improvement Targets and the Customer needs, wants and desires.
2. Determines the scope by identifying the start and end points of the process, articulating the geographic scope, the range of instances to be included, and categories of employees, market segments, and use cases that will or will not be included.
3. Sets the metrics for the project both quantitatively and qualitatively. Qualitatively, the Process Owner, Executive Sponsor and Project Lead identify the current challenges and provide a vision for what the process should look like when it is working well. Quantitatively, the Project Charter lists metrics and current values for each Improvement Target and the goal values sought after redesign and Implementation. Data provides quantitative information from the customer during the project regarding how the process is working now.
4. Designates the human resources and explains their roles. The Project Charter lists the leaders – Process Owner, Executive Sponsor, Project Lead, and Facilitator. The Project Charter lists the team members – subject matter experts and others who are needed on the team.

RESOURCES: LEADERS AND TEAM MEMBERS

Getting the right resources is critical for the BPI Project. The right resources include leaders who have authority and influence and are committed to doing the leadership work for the project.

The leaders must include a

- Process Owner, who is responsible for the health of the process, which means setting up the Project Charter, selecting and "conscripting" the best team members, determining the Improvement Targets, selecting and monitoring the metrics, coaching and motivating the team, removing roadblocks, and driving the implementation of the redesigned process.
- Executive Sponsor, who plays more of an enterprise role – advocating for process improvement, keeping a process focus in strategic discussions, seeing the cross-functional implications of processes, and supporting the Process Owner across the enterprise in implementation.
- Project Lead, who keeps the team on track toward the Improvement Targets and follows through by leading the operational implementation.

- Team Facilitator, who knows the BPM Process Methodology and engages the whole team in using the methodology to get to the desired outcomes.

The team members must include subject matter experts who do the work and represent the geography, IT, and a few others who bring special skills to the team.

The team needs to be a team – not just individuals who are called on to add input at various stages. The concept of team means they all contribute their expertise, do work, and work toward the goal of the project together. As a team, they represent their functional area and communicate with peer employees, but they act as one unit in the BPI Project.

STRUCTURED METHODOLOGY

The Structured Methodology uses a BPM roadmap, which shows the elements, where to start, and where to go. The four stages are sequential and have a beginning, middle, and end. If the team skips a stage, the risk for failure goes up substantially.

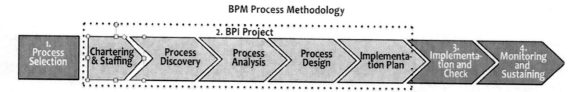

Figure 103. BPM Process Methodology

Process Selection is the first stage in the BPM Process Methodology. Three approaches will help organizations decide where to get started:

- Align with strategy.
- Prioritize candidate processes.
- Identify executive sponsorship.

Chartering and Staffing is the beginning of the BPI Project.

- It provides the goals and names the leaders and the team members.
- It contains the critical charter method, which includes the High-Level Map, the Improvement Targets, vision, scope, and team members.

Process Discovery and **Process Analysis** provide understanding about the current state of the process using process diagrams, data gathering, and a variety of analytical techniques and tools. The critical techniques are

- swimlane As-Is process diagrams
- analysis of the current state process diagram
- I am WASTED pain points
- customer feedback, and
- quantitative data

Process Design means creating the improved process. The new design benefits from two critical techniques:

- the Rules for Redesign, and
- the innovative method for creating a redesigned process.

The work up until this point has been studying data and using techniques to find out what the issues are today. In contrast, the Process Design techniques get the team thinking about the guiding principles that are important in the new process and then shifting their brains to think fancifully about a new process.

Process Design is fun and creative. It could be enticing to have the team and its leaders spend some time early on envisioning a new design. I find, however, that these creative thoughts are likely to be small and arise from siloed perspectives if they occur before the team has understood the current process and analyzed it. Process characterization and data analysis have enormous value, so don't be tempted to jump right into Process Design.

The Implementation Plan creates an initial project plan, including milestone deliverables, dates and people responsible for implementing the new process design, and recommendations from the BPI Project. It should incorporate expected issues, dependencies, and mitigations for risks. A Change Management approach is also critical and could be provided by an internal or external specialist in the field. The preliminary Implementation Plan is not detailed, but connects the project to the next stage, Implementation and Check, which turns the ideas into business results. The Implementation Plan is the last phase of the BPI Project.

Implementation and Check, Monitoring and Sustaining. This book does not cover these stages in detail, although there are comments about what's necessary when the team gets there. Both of these stages are the Process Owner's responsibility. Employees working in the process have responsibilities during these stages, as well. Both the Process Owner and the employees working on the process should provide ideas for improvements on a tactical and strategic level. Critical techniques during these stages of the methodology are

- regularly gathering and monitoring leading and lagging indicators
- attending strategic meetings to determine if the process is continuously improving, and
- identifying if conditions have changed in the company or marketplace and new improvement projects are needed.

What Makes This Method Work?

TIME BOXING

Time boxing for a BPI Project means setting a schedule and sticking to it as much as possible. If this time schedule drags on the air goes out of the balloon, and the team's energy is depleted; the organization begins to wonder what is happening or if anything is happening. The team will never have all the answers; they need to move forward even though there is some ambiguity. Time Boxing is a form of scoping. It articulates priority setting and maintains the focus and momentum.

RESEARCH BASIS

Studies from Edward Lawler III in *High Involvement Management*[28] are foundational to the success of this method for BPM process improvement projects. What Lawler found was that when a work system is designed with the following properties, the work system will almost always show continuous improvement.

1. The producers who do the work **participate in group goal setting** of the improvements. In this book, members of the BPI team are the producers and they review, revise, and challenge the Improvement Targets and vision set by the Process Owner.
2. The producers are given **discretion in problem solving and deciding the actions** needed to reduce the gaps between today's situation and the goals. In addition, the producers have
    *   The **skills they need** to do this work
    *   The **information needed**
    *   The **decision-making authority needed**

    For the BPI team, the members come with knowledge about the process since they perform it; they are taught the skills of the business process management methodology by the Team Facilitator and Project Lead. They have decision authority granted to them from the Process Owner, although they are checking in regularly for the Process Owner's suggestions and inputs during the meetings that the Project Lead and Team Facilitator have with them.
3. There is a **feedback loop** to the producers that shows actual and desired outputs. Here the BPI team uses data to get this input: quantitative and qualitative data come from the customer, the process (time, errors, roles, handoffs, etc.), the inputs to the process, and outputs from the process. After the new process is implemented, a feedback loop continues to measure the success of performing the process as well as the characteristics of the output.

---

[28] Lawler, Edward E., III. *High Involvement Management.* San Francisco: Jossey-Bass Inc. Publishers, 1986.

4. The work team gets **recognition** for the positive gains. In the more than 100 BPI teams I have worked with, the team gets extrinsic recognition, such as praise in sharing with executive leadership and peers about their ideas, recommendations, and success. But they also get intrinsic rewards of personal satisfaction, which seem to have a much greater impact. Teams are very proud of what they learned together, what they accomplished together, how they worked as a team, and how they created something that they never thought was possible.

VARIATIONS THAT WORK AND DON'T WORK

Lawler's research confirms what I have experienced in working with over 100 teams over the last ten years: that certain elements are critical and make the method successful.

- Clear goals are critical and must be co-developed with leaders and workers.
- The right leaders and team members need to be committed.
- A consistent BPM Process Methodology is essential. The methodology keeps people from making natural but unfortunate mistakes, such as diving right in to suggest procedural changes or jumping to easy solutions. If you have a different methodology from the one I suggest, that may be fine, but think about making it simple and structured.
- Time boxing ensures that the BPI effort doesn't die a slow death in the making.

There is a discipline for doing process improvement work, and most attempts to shave the time or skip steps ultimately doom the effort.

Of course, a team and its organization are going to conduct each business process improvement effort slightly differently because every situation is unique. But just like every real estate residential sale transaction is different, there are many elements that must be completed in all real estate deals, and there are elements that make the transaction go more smoothly toward a successful conclusion.

Below are the areas where variations can make sense and other areas where variations can significantly impact the quality and success of the process and the output.

Which Variations?

The Three Guiding Lights

Don't vary here. Gather these three elements, and keep them as the focus of the BPI effort.

The Project Charter

The Project Charter needs specific elements. I recommend all the elements that are included in the Project Charter suggested in this book. But individual organizations may have a Project Charter format of their own and it may make sense to use that format. I offer three caveats in using a different Project Charter format:

1. Make sure it includes these five elements: Improvement Targets, a High-Level Map, baseline and goal values for the metrics, a vision, and the leader and team resources.
2. Don't make it so long that it takes several meetings and over a month to build.
3. Make sure the Project Charter gets used and is revisited throughout the process. Any Project Charter that stays isolated on the desktop or in software is no good!

Don't start without a Project Charter.

The designated leaders and their commitment are prerequisites.

The Leaders

All four of the roles – Executive Sponsor, Process Owner, Project Lead, and Team Facilitator – are needed for a project. Variations that can work are combining some of the roles like Executive Sponsor and Process Owner, or Process Owner and Project Lead, or using an internal vs. an external Team Facilitator.

Don't lead from a staff organization such as a BPM professional group or a BPM Center of Excellence.

The Team Members

Teams benefit from all the roles suggested: Subject Matter Experts, Data person, IT, Documenter and Maverick. The size of the team can vary, though, with smaller numbers for simpler projects. Keep the roles suggested in Chapter 3, but you can have one person take on the responsibility of two roles, such as a Subject Matter Expert and the Data person, or the IT person and the Documenter. It is best to use a team as opposed to just individuals from whom the Business Analyst or Lean Six Sigma Black Belt gets input.

Don't go without both IT and the business on the team.

The BPM Process Methodology

The methodology presented provides a simple, structured path that helps the organization be successful. The four stages are critical. The tools and techniques recommended in those stages provide guidelines for what to do.

Variations in the methodology could entail

- stopping in the second phase of the BPI Project with Quick Wins, and really only implementing the low-hanging fruit.
- automating the process in iterations, such as starting with automating paper forms and manual handoffs, and then doing the larger redesign at a later date.

Training is critical, because the leaders and team members need to have the knowledge and skills to complete the methodology. Action learning is the best method for training, because it enables team members to apply their learning to real work (their project) immediately.

Time Boxing

Don't stray from the concept.

Consider varying the time intervals, but don't let the effort drag. I have completed the team method described in Chapter 7 in six consecutive days, in six weeks, or in three to four months.

Some clients tell me it is hard to get a meeting of more than 90 minutes at a time. I strongly suggest that the leadership sessions and workshops be a minimum of half a day. Shorter sessions just mean more meetings and longer elapsed time.

Now that you've finished the book, you should have everything you need to get started! I hope you've had a particular process in mind as you worked through the material. I encourage you now to STOP READING and START IMPROVING A PROCESS. Put some names to the needed roles and schedule a meeting! Outline a game plan and see if they are ready to start the journey. Let them know you have a blueprint to work from, and you're ready to take the first step.

INDEX

ABOUT THE AUTHOR

Shelley Sweet, the Founder and President of I4 Process, is a respected BPM Practitioner with over 20 years of experience helping organizations improve their business processes. As such, Shelley provides consultation, workshops, and training programs for clients ranging from start-ups to Fortune 500 companies, educational institutions, and government organizations.

Her programs are based on a unique 3-PEAT method of modeling processes and analyzing data that accelerates operational improvements and shows leaders and employees how to sustain operational excellence. Shelley's track record includes over 100 process improvement projects that have successfully eliminated waste, minimized cycle time, and greatly improved customer satisfaction.

Shelley is also a Certified Business Process Management Professional (CBPMP), and teaches BPM courses at UC Berkeley Extension and BPMInstitute.org. Her popular weekly blog at i4process.com/blog provides ideas from her extensive business process improvement experience, including practical guides for process modeling and analysis, recommendations for common obstacles, and discussions about key leadership and team roles.

In addition to writing for her own blog, Shelley is a featured content contributor to BPM.com, an influential news and analysis site dedicated to business process management.

To learn more about Shelley's professional experience, training programs, and consulting services, contact her at:

Shelley Sweet, Founder & President, I4 Process
shelleysweet@i4process.com
+1 650-493-1300
www.i4process.com

CPSIA information can be obtained at www.ICGtesting.com
Printed in the USA
LVOW09s1840290615

444299LV00019B/825/P